D0566998

ASSAULT ON SOCIETY:
Satirical Literature to Film

by
DONALD W. McCAFFREY

The Scarecrow Press, Inc.
Metuchen, N.J., & London
1992

NORTHWEST MISSOURI STATE
UNIVERSITY LIBRARY
MARYVILLE, MO 64468

British Library Cataloguing-in-Publication data available

Library of Congress Cataloging-in-Publication Data

McCaffrey, Donald W.
    Assault on society : satirical literature to film / by Donald W.
McCaffrey.
        p.   cm.
    Includes index.
    ISBN 0-8108-2507-4 (alk. paper)
    1. Comedy films—History and criticism.   2. Motion pictures and
literature.   3.   Satire—History and criticism.   4. Film
adaptations.   I. Title.
PN1995.9.C55M39   1992
791.43'617—dc20   92-4040

Copyright ©1992 by Donald W. McCaffrey
Manufactured in the United States of America

Printed on acid-free paper

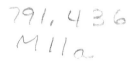

Dedicated to our two daughters, Marcy and Connie, who may disagree with my ranking of *M*A*S*H*, the movie, yet like, as I do, a wide range of comedy films.

FEB 3 1993

CONTENTS

ACKNOWLEDGMENTS

Thanks to Dr. Michael Anderegg and Christopher Jacobs, who suggested films I might have overlooked in the struggle to evaluate the gamut of satirical and dark comedy movies. Also, credit must be given to Ursula Hovet and Christopher Jacobs for their help in the preparation of the manuscript. My New York connection, Dr. Jonathan Levine, has helped me once again with special materials for this work. And, most of all, the perceptive reader, Joann, my wife, who has become my second editor in the preparation of this and other books.

INTRODUCTION

As atomic bombs obliterated the world on the screen and Vera Lynn sang "We'll meet again, don't know where, don't know when, but I know we'll meet again some sunny day" on the sound track, dark comedy film emerged to tower over fluffy, temporal comedies such as the repetitious, polite, predictable Doris Day pictures and the frenetic, bland beach party movies of the sixties. For in 1964 screenwright Terry Southern and director Stanley Kubrick created the irreverent *Dr. Strangelove or: How I Learned to Stop Worrying and Love the Bomb* as an assault on the military-political establishment that seemed to be naively blundering its way into increased Vietnam involvement. Had this work been merely a dark, or as it is often called, black comedy, it might have been as playful as genre spoofs like the take-offs on the serious Western: *Cat Ballou* in 1965 and *Blazing Saddles* in 1974. As a brink of war film comedy, *Dr. Strangelove*, however, seemed to parody war heroics and the intrigue of cold war drama like *Fail-Safe* (1964), which proved to be an abrasive attack on the powers that control our destiny. As a result it created laughter with an undercurrent of grim consequences that made the work satirical.

When I first viewed *Dr. Strangelove*, I realized the indignation it would produce in some audiences. Since our party of four who attended the film in 1965 lived near a Strategic Air Command military base, we witnessed a mixed reaction. Our little group laughed raucously and sometimes painfully as the doomsday blunderers on the screen struggled vainly to prevent holocaust, only to further the annihilation of the planet Earth; others in the audience seemed stunned and finally indignant. It would appear that many of the members of the audience who were attached to the military base felt they were personally being ridiculed.

Obviously, one thing black comedy and satire have in common is the potential to aggravate professional and special interest groups that feel they have been attacked. Critics, in a different way, are irritated by a lack of clear-cut intent in the authors' social criticism and the lack of taste in the assault on society.

Since we are now several decades removed from the most concentrated creation of black comedy films, we can evaluate with more detachment than the journalistic cinema reviewers of the sixties and seventies. However, ambiguity still exists in any evaluator's ability to distinguish black comedy from satire. In fact, the two creative approaches seem to merge, and the intent of the modern author of social criticism, in contrast with some satirists of the past, seems difficult to comprehend. Journalistic film reviewers have faulted black comedy writers for not having the commitment of past masters of satirical writing. Molly Haskell, for example, objects to the efforts of Terry Southern in her review of *The Magic Christian* (*The Village Voice*, February 26, 1970, p. 60, cols. 1–4) because his work did not measure up to Swiftian satire. She called his efforts camp and set forth the view that his approach "lacks the passion or indignation to depict human enterprise as truly repugnant, and the profundity to seek the abiding rather than the fashionable aspects of human folly. Camp is out of place in a politically radicalized world. It supports, so it can parody, the status quo, closed society, sexual repression, snobbery, and gaucherie."

Haskell at least credits Southern with an attempt to gain "Swiftian horror" but questions the modern author's sincerity. The journalistic critic believes she can correctly interpret the intent of Southern—that he does not have the indignation to develop corrective comedy. However, I find it difficult and even questionable to expect the twentieth-century creator of black comedy and satire to adhere to the approach of past masters.

From our historical viewpoint of today, it is easier to detect the social correction universalities of past satirists. Aristophanes, Rabelais, Ben Jonson, Molière, Jonathan Swift, Voltaire were comic writers who attacked the faults of their society with humor that was intended to reform those ills. That is, they hoped their exposure of corruption would resolve some of the problems that existed in their society. Aristophanes, Rabelais, and Swift were adept at lampooning politics, the arts, philosophy, and education. Jonson, Molière, and Voltaire touched on all these matters and were especially skilled in developing tales that exposed greed, pretense, and false moral values.

As readers and viewers of the modern, complex modes of the novel, play, film, television, or cartoon, we cannot expect twentieth-century writers to conform to the classical models of satire. We should also allow these writers lighter moments—buffoonery that makes the comedy palatable to a wider audience. Even the great playwrights of the past—Aristophanes, Jonson, and Molière—filled their satirical works with crowd-pleasing, lighter moments of comedy.

The black comedy and satirical films of the sixties and seventies are part of a modern literary movement—a movement concentrated in the twentieth century with some roots in the nineteenth. American and British novelists Mark Twain, Nathanael West, Aldous Huxley, Evelyn Waugh, and George Orwell have been accepted by critics and the public as significant satirists. Least recognized is West, a writer who now has been acclaimed as the precursor of the nihilistic dark comedy; his short novels, *Miss Lonelyhearts* and *The Day of the Locust*, created in the thirties, have been recognized by critics as a major influence in this movement. Twain's *A Connecticut Yankee in King Arthur's Court*, penned in the late nineteenth century, and Orwell's *Animal Farm*, created in the forties, have a modern slant yet are more traditional satires concentrating on political and social issues. These two authors retain the traditional approaches of fantasy and the fable with these two works. Examining issues of the twentieth-century world with a realistic approach, Evelyn Waugh is best known for his dissecting of education in *Decline and Fall* and the funeral business in *The Loved One*, plus an unusual half satirical/half embrace of the upper class in *Brideshead Revisited*. Huxley, best known for his *Brave New World*, an anti-utopian novel, has concentrated more on the jaded world of the sophisticated in his other novels— which probably accounts for an author who has been almost ignored by the popular media, even though he was a screenwriter who adapted such works as *Pride and Prejudice* and *Jane Eyre* in the forties. He adapted his short story "The Gioconda Smile," which was released under the title *A Woman's Venge-*

ance in 1948. It was not a box-office success, and plans to produce an adaptation of Huxley's famous satire *Point Counter Point* never materialized.

Ironically, both Aldous Huxley and Nathanael West were satirists who wrote in Hollywood with a degree of success, but could never succeed in adapting their own novels to the screen. Their vision of the world was too grim for the Hollywood of the thirties and forties. Both Huxley and West might have been responsible, however, for influencing the nihilistic view of society that evolved into a minor but significant literary movement of the fifties and sixties. Some of the writers of these two decades who became popular among the reading public were J. P. Donleavy (*The Ginger Man*), Joseph Heller (*Catch-22*), Terry Southern (*The Magic Christian*), and Kurt Vonnegut (*Slaughterhouse-Five*). These writers have been identified with a movement that employs dark comedy—a type of irreverent humor that discovers the risible in such serious subjects as death, racial and sexual taboos, and social and mental misfits. While I classify most of the efforts of these writers as satirical pieces, not everyone would agree. Also, I view the handling of such material by these authors as linked to a type of social comment that was the meat of Nathanael West's novels of the thirties. The above mentioned works by Heller, Southern, and Vonnegut have been adapted to the screen with varying degrees of success. They will be explored in the following chapters.

Most comic writers for the popular media engage in some type of comment on our culture, but even when they attack, there is often a spirit of play controlling their thrusts, which mutes their jabs at society. It would appear that they need to hold back the assault to avoid rejection. Such writers contain their lampoons of people's foibles in a way that states, "I didn't really mean it. Just kidding." Woody Allen and Mel Brooks seem to fit into this category. Both were writers for television comedians and eventually became not only writers but producers and actors in their own films. Allen has created many successful movies, such as *What's New Pussycat?* (1965), *Love and Death* (1975), and *Annie Hall* (1977); Brooks has been a popular filmmaker with *The Producers* (1968), *Blazing Saddles* (1974), and *Young Frankenstein* (1974). As time has gone by, many critics have realized that Allen and Brooks may be good entertainers, but they do not have much to say about society. We now realize that such writers burlesque the "hang ups," changing attitudes, and fads of society but are so topical they do not have a universal statement on the faults that exist in our world.

What is amazing to any evaluator of film is the body of satirical films that *did* emerge in the sixties and seventies which does make significant social comment. In most decades satire has limited acceptance. Hope reigns eternally in our optimistic culture. The "just kidding" tone of our popular entertainers tells us that things really aren't as bad as they seem—as if any stinging jab at a social fault is only a playful, temporary reprimand. Psychologically, such playful pokes allow us relief because we have inner feelings that tell us all is not well, but we would rather continue with the status quo in our culture after we have had our therapeutic laugh; we would just as soon ignore and forget the problems that plague us.

A test for the quality of satirical literature, film, or the cartoon might be the rejection such works receive from incurable optimists or conventional moralists. Both seem to view such thrusts as subversive to traditional values. As it will be shown in this examination, many creators of black comedy and satire are indignant social critics. They are not "just kidding."

Dr. Donald W. McCaffrey
Department of English
University of North Dakota
Grand Fork, ND

CHAPTER 1

BIRTH PANGS OF FILM SATIRE

BEFORE THE SIXTIES Hollywood filmmakers had little truck with satirical short stories, novels, or plays unless they could water down the basic material to an intriguing plot for a film drama with popular appeal. The film moguls were obsessed with the box office and the flow of cash, as was stage playwright George S. Kaufman—noted for co-authoring *You Can't Take It with You* (1936) and *The Solid Gold Cadillac* (1953)—who cynically observed that satire closed on Saturday night, meaning that a socially significant comedy would not live long enough to see one more night's performance. Kaufman probably would have liked to have written dramas with more substance, but was, of course, like the Hollywood Studio heads, interested in money.

By reducing the political satire to a children's fairy tale in an animated feature version of Jonathan Swift's *Gulliver's Travels* in 1939, Dave and Max Fleischer were merely applying their cartoon skills to create a movie that would entertain people and bring them the returns Walt Disney was receiving from *Snow White and the Seven Dwarfs* (1937) and *Pinocchio* (1940). By far the most interesting rape of the stories from classic political satires was Hollywood's handling of Nikolai Gogol's play *The Inspector General* and Mark Twain's novel *A Connecticut Yankee in King Arthur's Court*, both released in 1949. These adaptations provided testimony on the filmmakers' creative process.

When first produced as a stage play in 1836, *The Inspector General* reaped considerable consternation from the Russian establishment and even suffered repercussions on the national governmental level. Gogol had dared to attack political corruption in a provincial town and suggested that maybe even regional government inspectors might be easy subjects for bribery. In the plot material of the drama a traveling, ordinary clerk with a little education is mistaken for an official from a high governmental agency arriving to check on the quality of the town's governmental system. This picaresque character—a young man who gambles and drinks away what little money he has—is wined, dined, bribed, and even offered women. He readily accepts the attention of the officials and bilks them thoroughly until his true identity is discovered. The film version of *The Inspector General* would not cause the leaders in the United States to worry about their image in this 1949 movie as they had worried about the portrait of congressmen in Frank Capra's *Mr. Smith Goes to Washington*, a work created ten years earlier. The filmmakers who drained the Gogol classic of much of its substance had lightened the comedy to the point that it was merely a fluffy quasi-musical.

A check of the Warner Bros. file on *The Inspector General*, which is now housed in the Wisconsin Center for Film and Theater Research, reveals the labored creative process that brought the adaptation of this famous play to the screen. First of all, a reader named Hawthorne read the play and developed a plot summary along with a hopeful, brief note that indicated the dialogue was "extremely amusing, could be used as is." Then, a well-developed script by Ben Hecht and Charles Lederer appeared late in 1949, with the locale changed to a mid-European country that was not clearly designated. Since the United States was engaged in the cold war with Russia, it evidently was decided not to use any mention of that country or any character with a Russian name. The movie was designed as a vehicle for the comic talents of Danny Kaye. His wife, Sylvia Fine, became not only the composer of the lyrics and music for his songs, but also the associate producer.*

In her notes to the adaptors, dated December 12, 1947, she complained about the character of the officials of the town losing some dimension that existed in Gogol's original work— meaning, of course, that the satire was diminishing. She later

---

*Sylvia Fine is particularly noted for bright, clever lyrics and the patter songs that were the distinctive feature of so many of Danny Kaye's film comedies.

indicated that the role of the protagonist who had been changed to a cook from the French army of Napoleon had to be altered since comedian Kaye's comic French dialect was not as effective as his lampoon of a mid-European dialect. By February of 1948 the screenplay had a mid-European character named Georgi instead of Fefi, plus the title *The Happy Times*, evidently derived from one of the important songs designed for the picture. This title was dropped and the original title restored several times until the producers settled for the original. Other versions and revisions by Hecht and Lederer followed, but no one seemed satisfied, and other writers were brought into the project.

Five writers in various combinations struggled with the screenplay until the team of Philip Rapp and Harry Kurnitz received the final credits for a screenplay that was ready by August 1948. As late as June of 1949, obviously during the shooting of the film, Rapp added some silly slapstick scenes to provide a broader comedy than can be witnessed in the work conceived by the Russian playwright. Thus, the final adaptation of a satirical classic comedy was more Kaye than Gogol. Film critic Bosley Crowther realized this while recognizing the fact that some of the plot of the original play had been salvaged:

> The whole structure of this picture is carefully and cleverly designed to give unrestrained play and freedom to the talents of Mr. Kaye. And he, being nobody's wall-flower, makes much of everything that's put in his way. As a shill for a medicine-show barker—a harmless and illiterate tramp—who is presumed to be a great inspector general, traveling incognito, by the officials of a town, he brilliantly travesties the terror and then the bravura of this timid lout when he is fawned upon, lavishly feted and slyly bribed by the frightened councilmen. [*New York Times*, December 31, 1949, p. 9]

As this comment by Crowther indicates, the Ivan of the original work suffers a character inversion—he is no longer the rake; he is the innocent who is a fool. Not only is a character change demanded before Georgi can take advantage of the weaknesses of the councilmen, but the satire focusing on the protagonist of the original play is absent. Only the corruption of the councilmen, handled as light comedy, remains as any semblance of satire.

Even less of Mark Twain's intent remained in the Bing Crosby vehicle of 1949, *A Connecticut Yankee in King Arthur's Court*. Part of the emasculation of the original novel evolved from a different creative process than that witnessed in the creation of the filmed version of *The Inspector General*. The Twain classic was already stripped of its political and social comment by two previous screen adaptations. Most of the significance of the original was brushed aside in a silent screen version of 1921 starring Harry C. Myers and released by the Fox Film Corporation. This film displayed even wider variations on the plot of a modern-day man visiting the age of knighthood and chivalry than the sound version of 1931, which was designed to star Will Rogers. The Crosby 1949 restatement of the story deviated even further by turning the film into a quasi-musical providing Rhonda Fleming for the love interest. There is left a sequence drawn from the Will Rogers version showing Crosby battling the knights, using a lasso in the cowboy fashion of comical combat which Rogers had established even in some of his silent screen films. So, the 1949 version strays from the text not only by moving in the direction of the musical but also by drawing from previous versions.

While *The Inspector General* and *A Connecticut Yankee in King Arthur's Court* are two examples of what happened to satire in Hollywood before the movie capital came to a more firm grip with social comment in the sixties, some efforts in the thirties indicated a trend in this direction. The brush with corrective comedy seemed to manifest itself most in the sophisticated comedy of this decade, with some continuation into the forties. The sophisticated comedy had a great deal to say about the battle of the sexes, strained family relationships, plus corruption in some institutions. Among the most important comedies with these tendencies were *Twentieth Century* (1934), *Nothing Sacred* (1937), and *Topper* (1937)—three films that represented the range of the mode.

Twentieth Century, adapted from a New York Stage play called *Napoleon of Broadway*, focuses on the egocentricities of the artist, with John Barrymore playing the role of the flamboyant stage entrepreneur and Carole Lombard enacting

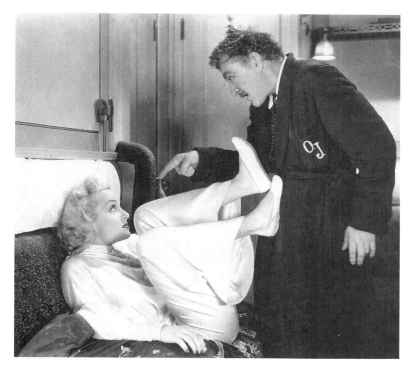

Carole Lombard and John Barrymore engaged in the male-female physical fight in *Twentieth Century* that was to be a common occurrence in the so-called screwball comedy of the early film satires.

the part of a temperamental star of stage and screen. The work comically reveals the hypocrisy of the theater people whose professional skills at depicting emotions become fused with their private lives—so much so that the false and the real emotions merge to the point of comic confusion. This clever film comedy by director Howard Hawks comes very close to being a penetrating satire on the theatrical institution, but is more successful in revealing the game of one person's manipulation of another and a kind of amoral battle of wits between the sexes.

Both *Nothing Sacred* and *Topper* seem to attack specific institutions in our society with even more directness. *Nothing Sacred* (a work to be examined in more detail in the chapter which follows) provides specific social comment on sob sister journalism and the public's maudlin reaction to the plight of the unfortunate individual who is presumedly doomed to an early death. *Topper*, an adaptation from the popular fantasy novel by Thorne Smith, explores the institution of high finance and contrasting life styles of the rich. A high living couple, Marion and George Kirby, are killed in an automobile accident and return as ghosts to "do a good deed" for a millionaire banker named Cosmos Topper, who is uncomfortably entrenched in the work ethic and a staid social life. He is pressured into a swinging style of life by the Kirbys, which results in a drunken brawl and his arrest by the police. Shunned before by the elite of their social class because they are considered dull, Topper and his wife are amazed to find overtures for engagements from this group who view Cosmos' escapade fascinating and exciting. Such comments by the sophisticated comedy film of the thirties show that some significant brushes with satirical statements were being attempted by filmmakers in that decade.

Other conventions and codes of the family and society were deftly being attacked by director Preston Sturges, who combined light comedy and satire in some of his best films of the forties. By far one of his most interesting statements was made in the 1944 film *The Miracle of Morgan's Creek*. This work is a comic exposé of hypocrisy and mechanization in order to cover up the plight of an unwed mother—not usually for the benefit of the woman, but for the comfort of everyone else. Novelist-filmmaker Marcel Pagnol had used this subject, showing the French lower class's handling of the situation with incorruptible *savoir-faire* in the screen adaptations from the plays *Marius*, *Fanny*, and *César*, made between 1931 and 1936. Sturges, with his continental, urbane wit was creating a film before its time with *The Miracle of Morgan's Creek* when he handled a taboo that would not easily fade from the culture, even in the wartime period of sexual laxness found in the forties.

The heroine of the Preston Sturges movie and the object of social consternation is a young, naive woman named Trudy Kockenlocker, who in one night gets drunk and impregnated by a soldier on leave whose name she can't remember. The comic complications develop when her family, relatives, and some people in their small town attempt to resolve the "embarrass-

Sophisticated comedy of the 1930s, as exemplified by *Topper*, satirized the release from the work ethic and staid social life as Roland Young and Cary Grant enact a scene of settling down for more than one bottle of champagne.

ment." This original screenplay by Sturges, which exposes strain and possible change in a middle-class moral standard, proves to be one of the best brushes with satire during the period.

Less daring was the script of Charles MacArthur's adaptation of a story by Edwin Lanham lampooning the rise and near fall of a political party in *The Senator Was Indiscreet* (1947), a study of a blowhard, pompous, vacuous U.S. senator who wants to be President of the United States. Under the guidance of George S. Kaufman in his one directorial shot in Hollywood, the film is certainly irreverent, but as political satire it now appears relatively tame.

One other American work that illustrates Hollywood's flirty approach to social comment in the forties is *The Male Animal*, a work created in 1942. It was probably one of the best films that took a poke at college education. This adaptation from the stage play by Elliott Nugent and James Thurber takes a look at the overemphasis on sports in higher education and contains some strong comic attacks on those who would thwart the academic freedom to teach controversial subjects—showing some trustees of a college trying to block the free expression of an educator. Not as strong an attack on censorship as it could have been, it nevertheless was unique for the film drama of that period.

The popularity of the British film comedy gained momentum in the forties and continued into the mid-fifties with many well-crafted, droll works of dry wit and with sophisticated comedies that occasionally touched on important social issues. One such occasion was the adaptation in 1941 of George Bernard Shaw's stage drama *Major Barbara* to a screen version which the famous playwright developed with director Gabriel Pascal.

Employing the Shavian paradox, the film drama follows closely the 1905 stage play in exploring a religious sect's attempt to save souls and rescue people from poverty, with many interesting ironies evolving. Satirical points by Shaw evolve in his drama when leaders in the Salvation Army discover that to help the poor the group is taking money from a capitalist who manufactures instruments of war used to destroy people. Shaw, of course, delighted in using the Salvation Army to develop this dilemma and central conflict because the religious group not only is vehemently anti-war but also uses some of the organization and trappings of the military in their march as "soldiers for Christ." Unfortunately, this film version seems dated and even stodgy. Also, Shaw, with all his brilliant wit, has a type of satiric thrust that now seems genteel. He is gracious to all concerned in the end—as if he were engaged in a polite, evening debating society event at Oxford University.

But *Major Barbara* was only a prelude and not a mainstream film in a movement which would finally gain acceptance in the art theatre movie house of America in the forties and fifties. In post-war Britain a fresh new comedy movement emerged. Such vital works as *Whiskey Galore* (1949)—called *Tight Little Island* in the U.S.A.—*Kind Hearts and Coronets* (1949), *The Lavender Hill Mob* (1951), *The Man in the White Suit* (1951), and *The Ladykillers* (1955) were works that viewed some aspects of society with a comic, critical eye. Both *Kind Hearts and Coronets*, to be discussed in detail later, and *The Ladykillers* were irreverent works which dealt humorously with murder for profit. More general comments on human foibles, politics, and the free enterprise system were made by *Whiskey Galore* and *The Man in the White Suit*. *The Lavender Hill Mob* shows a trio of mild-mannered, respectable men struggling and almost succeeding with the big heist. With a more jaundiced view of human enterprises, the films that dealt with crime moved to not only irreverence but also black comedy. But the treatment is essentially light, and there is little that could be called corrective in the intent of these works. Furthermore, the relatively innocent nature of the acts and the warmth of the characters involved mute the possibility of making a clear-cut statement that could be labeled satire.

However, three adapted works from satirical literature did appear in the British cinema of the fifties: *The Beggar's Opera* (1953), *Man with a Million* (1954), and *Animal Farm* (1954). While the first two works softened the approach of the original, they proved to be significant steps in setting the stage for more films of the same type.

John Gay's *The Beggar's Opera* proves to be a rather difficult work to adapt for a twentieth-century audience. The eighteenth-century stage play, probably the first example of a musical since it incorporated popular tunes of the day, was a hit in 1728 because it had social commentary on the mores of that age. Director Richard Brooks does not give the work the resonance needed, but adopts a somewhat lighter tone than might have been intended. Nevertheless, the moments that depict the battle of the sexes and some of the satirical thrusts at marriage come through effectively. It is difficult to translate the pose of highway robber Macheath as he imitates the airs of the landed gentry and the political establishment before audiences in the United States, but Britons in the fifties could grasp this type of satire. Well-read critics and students of the drama might also catch the lampoon of sentimental literature of the period and the pokes at opera. As a film *The Beggar's Opera*, starring Sir Laurence

Melting down stolen gold bars, Stanley Holloway and Alec Guinness are part of the gang in the British comedy *The Lavender Hill Mob* (1951).

Olivier, proves to be good entertainment, and as a precursor of the 1963 screen adaptation of Henry Fielding's famous eighteenth-century novel, *Tom Jones*, the work paved the way and was more than merely the act of rubbing shoulders with satire.

The source for the British production of *Man with a Million* was a short story by Samuel Clemens, "The One Million Pound Bank-Note." The original story by the author who used the pen name of Mark Twain is tied to an elaborate ruse by a poor American, Henry Adams, who is given on a temporary basis a million-pound note by two wealthy brothers in England who want to see if a man with no means can con his way into high finance and high society with merely a piece of paper in his possession. Thinking Adams is a rich man, merchants eagerly give him credit; he is urged to lend his name to projects by financiers; and, finally, he is courted by high society. But these fickle groups vehemently reject him when they learn he is a fraud. This film version, adapted and elaborated upon by Jill Craigie, retains a good deal of the intent of the original story with some softening of the satire by an extended romantic entanglement. The short story does suggest Adams's concern for a young woman, but concentrates more on the bogus millionaire's acceptance by groups of the upper class in Britain.

More faithful to the original story, in this case, a novel, is the animated feature-length cartoon *Animal Farm*, a work that will be examined in detail when the comic attack on institutions is set forth. This movie proved to be a breakthrough. George Orwell's analogistic satire showing barnyard animals establishing what they believed to be an ideal government only to have it turn into a suppressive regime was rendered in the adaptation with amazing fidelity. A full-blown social comment had arrived on the screen in the fifties and would exhibit wider acceptance and growth in the sixties to make satire a significant movement.

CHAPTER 2

DEATH FOR PROFIT AND GRAVESIDE HUMOR

IT WOULD APPEAR THAT DEATH was seldom used as a subject for comedy let alone for satire until modern times. Greek and Roman comedy drama only brushed with the subject occasionally because the classical period of literature seemed to confine death to the serious drama. The ancients seemed to have a fear and reverence for death that didn't allow for much levity. Not until the sixteenth and seventeenth centuries in the popular dramas of the roving players of the *commedia dell'arte* did the subject become aired in an absurdist way. Previously, in medieval religious dramas some humor was achieved which depicted purgatory in an ambiguously humorous way. The pressure of the church to convert sinners was grim enough for a psychological escape value. Crude burlesques showing devils torturing condemned souls in the hell scenes of the dramas devised by village players developed into a type of dark comedy. Some sense of humor on the subject of death evolved much later from the situation in which the *commedia dell'arte* figure of Pierrot, the moon-struck lover, tries to kill himself as he pines over his lost love. The renowned French film *Children of Paradise* (1945) illustrated the Pierrot tradition as it was carried on into the nineteenth century. In this film poor Pierrot tries to commit suicide by tying a rope to a tree, only to be interrupted by a washmaiden who wants to use the rope for a clothesline. A genteel fellow, he forgoes his passion to kill himself in order to help the woman. Skit descriptions of the antics of such a clown in the *commedia dell'arte* of hundreds of years ago also indicate there was a routine where the suicide prone lover fails in all methods to dispatch himself and finally resorts to the unlikely act of trying to tickle himself to death. But this routine by the comedian existed more on an absurdist level of comedy—a way of release from the death threat which did not offer a clear social statement.

Death for profit and graveside humor seemed to come into vogue in the nineteenth and twentieth centuries. As a novel created in 1889 and a film adapted from the work in 1966, one of the best examples of this development was Robert Louis Stevenson and Lloyd Osbourne's *The Wrong Box*. Before this unusual handling of graveside humor is explored, some other examples of the film medium's handling of death need to be cited: *Nothing Sacred* (1937), *Arsenic and Old Lace* (1944) and *Kind Hearts and Coronets* (1949), plus a few films created in the sixties and seventies.

The slow degenerative death from radium poisoning would hardly seem a likely subject for humor. A young woman named Hazel Flagg in the plot of the movie *Nothing Sacred* was presumably afflicted by such a malady when she worked in a factory which used the dangerous substances to illuminate the dials of watches. With such a questionable concept for comedy, Ben Hecht wrote one of the most original, sophisticated comedy films of the thirties that took a poke at society—his target was both journalism and the readers of the medium. He attacked the sob sister manifestation: People who wallowed in a gratifying, personal cry over the plight of an individual who was more unfortunate than they.

In brief, the complications of *Nothing Sacred* develop when an editor assigns a reporter, Wally Cook (Fredric March), to develop stories on the plight of the dying woman, Hazel Flagg (Carole Lombard), by inviting her to New York. Even though she has found out from her physician, Dr. Downer (Charles Winninger), that the medical report was in error, Hazel doesn't want to forgo her New York adventure and deceptively maintains she is still fatally poisoned by radium. Lombard, probably the best sophisticated comedienne of the thirties, deftly delivers a line in the movie to reporter Wally Cook with all the airy gaiety needed to show her determination to have her fling in New York: "I'm not going to go to bed until I have

As Hazel Flagg, Carole Lombard reveals that she has been feigning a fatal illness in the 1937 *Nothing Sacred.* Standing behind her are the editor (Walter Connolly) and reporter (Fredric March) who have released sob sister stories on her plight.

convulsions and my teeth start falling out." After a series of stories in the newspapers that make her a celebrity, she is easily recognized as she engages, with Wally, in what people think is her last fling in a New York night club. Noticing the patrons of the club moping and shedding tears over her plight, the cynical reporter dislikes the wallowing in bathos and remarks:

> WALLY: [Disgustedly] For good clean fun there's noth-
> ing like a wake.
>
> HAZEL: Oh, please, please, let's not talk shop.

Thus, death is handled with a dark comedy touch. This touch is somewhat lightened under director William A. Wellman's hand, but the death-for-profit motive reigns when the newspaper enthralls its readers with Hazel's adventures in New York and the impending doom that hangs over her head. In a more modest way Hecht's dialogue displays some of the bitterness of that used by the Restoration wit of William Wycherley in such plays as *The Country Wife* (1675) and *The Plain Dealer* (1676). But, of course, the British dramatist was a skilled satirist while the twentieth-century screenwriter Ben Hecht more often dips his pen in quinine rather than acid. Hecht's lampoon of society remains more on the level of a wisecracking observer commenting on a world engaged in a con game. The opening titles indicate his view of a metropolitan center devoid of any integrity:

FIRST TITLE: This is New York
                      Skyscraper Champion
                      of the World . . .

SECOND TITLE: Where the Slickers and
                      Know-It-Alls peddle gold
                      bricks to each other . . .

THIRD TITLE: . . . And where Truth,
                      Crushed to earth, rises
                      again more phony
                      than a glass eye . . .

At the end of *Nothing Sacred* the public remains duped even though Hazel's ruse is discovered by the newspaper editor (well played by character actor Walter Connolly with the use of exasperation comedy). Wally and Hazel embark on their honeymoon incognito and unrepentant, obviously disdainful of a society engaged in the folly of sentimentality. This last touch indicates what some might call the amoral ending similar to that used in British Restoration comedies and reinforces the view that the drama by Ben Hecht was attempting social satire.*

---

*An investigation of a preproduction script by Hecht at the Museum of Modern Art Film Library in New York shows that the author had some tougher, hard-hitting lines of a political nature (i.e., on the Red baiters of the time) and even more dark comedy on death—evidently portions that were cut during the production to lighten the total work.

More than any other sophisticated comedy of the thirties this film with an original scenario was uncompromising in handling significant comment on the society of the times, specifically, a manifestation of the media of that age—sob sister journalism. The adaptation of the 1941 stage comedy *Arsenic and Old Lace* by Frank Capra in a 1944 release was novel in its use of death and killing in a humorous way, but the profit motive or con game does not become an integral part of the plot as so often happens in a socially significant comedy film that uses death and avarice as its subject. The three-and-a-half-year run of one of the best box-office stage dramas illustrates how the public loved black comedy even in the forties. The creation of a playwright who is essentially a one-play author,* Joseph Kesselring, the work obviously had a clever, intriguing idea that made it famous. Two sweet, elderly, maiden sisters dispatch itinerant old men sympathetically by offering them elderberry wine laced with arsenic. They have a brother who is even more insane than they are, who readily buries the bodies in the basement because he believes he is Teddy Roosevelt dealing with yellow fever victims who have been working to build the Panama Canal. Humor is achieved by the women's twisted logic and understated attitude toward their acts of violence. They are merely engaged in a well-meaning gesture of sisterly love—their euthanasia is a way of giving the unfortunate old men peace.

Arsenic and Old Lace was an American play that was innovative for its time. It was created in a decade when the taboo of euthanasia was much stronger than it is today. Capra does a competent rendering of this stage play by handling his actors well (with some excellent performances from Cary Grant, Raymond Massey, Peter Lorre, and Josephine Hull) and moving the comedy at his characteristic vigorous, lively pace. However, the play itself is essentially all fluff, even with its enjoyable dark comedy. There is greater social significance, although not strong satirical comment, in such Capra classics as *Mr. Smith Goes to Washington* (1939), *Meet John Doe* (1941), and *It's a Wonderful Life* (1946).

---

*Kesselring wrote three other plays for the Broadway stage, but they were relatively ineffective works.

An adapted work from Roy Horniman's novel *Israel Rank* by Britain's Ealing Studios in 1949, *Kind Hearts and Coronets*, would seem to provide the social views that *Arsenic and Old Lace* lacked. As in the American play, a number of people are killed to provide a dark comedy basis, but these murders are for profit, executed in a cool way and not by some twisted mind that wants to help others. The protagonist, Louis (Dennis Price), commits seven murders in order to achieve a title and an inheritance from a line of eight intended victims. Alec Guinness, in a *tour de force*, plays all eight of the victims—even a woman, a suffragette named Lady Agatha d'Ascoyne. Humor is achieved from the deaths because they are often in ludicrous situations and tied to the obsessions of the victims. Lady Agatha, for example, engages in a balloon ascension to shower leaflets urging the women of Britain to fight for their rights. Louis observes her from a window and takes careful aim with a bow and arrow. He cleverly states to himself a variation on a verse: "I shot an arrow in the air; she fell to earth in Berkeley Square." One of the intended victims actually is not dispatched by Louis. The Admiral Lord Horatio d'Ascoyne dies, as Louis describes in voice-over narration, from "A certain confusion of mind, unfortunate in one of his rank" (from the scenario in *Masterworks of the British Cinema*, Harper & Row, p. 231). He gives an order to move his ship to port (left) when he should have said starboard (right) and rams another ship, sinking both vessels. Obstinate to the last (the captain of the ship insisted he probably meant starboard, but he, the admiral, maintained his orders were correct), Horatio, without registering any emotion, stands like a rock on the bridge as the ship goes down. The last shot of this scene shows his hat floating in the waves as the ship sinks. What we often call English understatement in humor reigns in the film, and it is a delightful piece of dark comedy. Satire of a sort does exist, but it has very little sting. Most of it is directed at the pomposity and pretension of the upper class and, occasionally, at the effeteness of the male in high society and respected professions.

Satire with more bite was created in *Monsieur Verdoux*, a work by Charles Chaplin, two years earlier in the United States. His 1947 original work (and, therefore, not a major consideration for this study) now holds up much better than the highly

Before its time *Monsieur Verdoux* (1947), with Charles Chaplin and
Martha Raye, featured a dark comedy Bluebeard who murdered for profit.

touted *Kind Hearts and Coronets*. It was created at the beginning
of a cold war period with Russia and a growing conservative
trend in America, when the victory of World War II was swelling
national pride. Chaplin's philosophical tract at the end of the
film, indicating that we are living in criminal times when war is
a natural outgrowth of corruption, was an unpopular and even
horrifying view to most audiences at the time. His sophisticated,
comic Bluebeard, a murderer of widows for profit, stated

bluntly: "One murder makes a villain—millions, a hero." It was too strong for the forties; this view would be more acceptable in the sixties when the establishment began to be criticized for dealing in a questionable "peace action," as Vietnam was euphemistically labeled by political and military leaders.

Chaplin's Henri Verdoux is the perfectly sane killer, not like the sisters of *Arsenic and Old Lace*. Each murder of a widow incorporates situations that make it comic. Much is made of the dapper little fellow's stalking of the victims as he courts them and figures out a way to do them in. One of the funniest sequences is his encounter with the widow played by boisterous comedienne Martha Raye. He takes her for a romantic ride in a rowboat in order to develop a feigned drowning incident and nearly ends up the fatality of the excursion on the lake. After each murder Chaplin shows this unusual lover-killer counting, with uncanny dexterity, the money he has gained from the struggle. As a running gag there is usually a container with a wet sponge to lubricate his fingers to zip through a pile of franc notes. There is only the shade of the little tramp of *City Lights* (1931) and *Modern Times* (1936). As indicated in the illustrations above, much of the work could be taken on the level of the 1944 *Arsenic and Old Lace* and the 1949 *Kind Hearts and Coronets* if it were not followed with Henri Verdoux's explanation of his views on mass murder. British film critic Roger Manvell gave a rave retrospective evaluation of *Monsieur Verdoux* in 1955 when he stated that this work has much of the quality of Swiftian satire. Manvell writes:

> Verdoux is at war with society . . . the natural man dehumanized by the unnatural cruelties which are slowly strangling the civilized world. He bears the comic exaggeration of the satiric form, like Swift's characters or those of Molière. [*The Film and the Public*, Penguin Books, pp. 166–170]

Chaplin is, I believe, given a bit more credit than he deserves from Manvell. However, the film is superior to many works of the sixties which handled the Bluebeard theme. Such contrived comedies as *Five Golden Hours* (1961), starring television comedian Ernie Kovacs, and *Arrivederci, Baby* (1966), starring

Tony Curtis, were potpourri dark humor works with protagonists who were sleazy Don Juans, attempting to kill rich widows
whom they had married for their money. Unlike the Chaplin
work of 1947, these works often merely play footsie with murder. Curtis, playing a very unconvincing teenager in *Arrivederci,
Baby*, does cause the death of a husband who is in his way, but
he, like Kovacs in *Five Golden Hours*, does not have much luck
getting rid of the unwanted woman.

The importance of death to further one's fortune becomes
even more sappy when Shirley MacLaine plays the kookie
femme fatale who does well at outliving a number of husbands
in *What a Way to Go!* (1964). A direct killing of men emerged
in the plot of *The Girl Most Likely to . . .* , a film surprisingly
created for television in 1973. A novel work, partly authored by
comedienne Joan Rivers, this film depicts a woman (played by
Stockard Channing) who kills four men for revenge because
they took her only as a sex object to be humiliated, although she
is an ugly duckling. Emerging as a swan after extensive plastic
surgery, she lures them, as a beautiful black widow spider, to
their death. In one of the most innovative ploys to rid herself of
one of the men, she gets the most athletic one to take a dive
from a plane for a sexual thrill. Naturally, his parachute is faulty,
and he is foiled in his attempt to achieve high dive bliss. *The Girl
Most Likely to . . .* is not exactly satire, but effective dark comedy.

Many other films that handled murder and death in a humorous way could be cited, but the two that focused on the subject
of death in the sixties that were the most successful were adaptations from novels: *The Wrong Box* by Robert Louis Stevenson
and Lloyd Osbourne and *The Loved One* by Evelyn Waugh.

Both the novel and the adaptation of *The Wrong Box* employ
graveside humor. Satirical dimensions develop because the
works explore the machinations of relatives to obtain an inheritance. The greed of the potential benefactors becomes so strong
that these avaricious people are shown in the worst light. They
feign concern for the health of a relative when, in reality, they
hope for his death. The premise of the satire would seem to be
more severe than that of *The Loved One*. The Waugh novel does
present the greed of the funeral director, which provides a less
scathing comment than the greed portrayed in *The Wrong Box*.

One of the most fascinating aspects of the Stevenson-Osbourne novel is that it might be considered an early example of dark comedy since it was created in 1889. The Victorian author who became famous for such youth-oriented works as *Treasure Island*, *The Black Arrow*, and *Kidnapped* (also, *A Child's Garden of Verses*), had breadth in his creative skills. Robert Louis Stevenson moved in other directions—he liked the macabre. He created the Gothic horror novella *Dr. Jekyll and Mr. Hyde* and, of course, the dark comedy *The Wrong Box*. A foreword to this satirical novella indicates that Stevenson and his collaborator realized they were treading on the sensitive middle-class morality of the times: "The authors can but add that one of them is old enough to be ashamed of himself, and the other young enough to learn better."

The satirical approach to the basic story material was strong for the period, but the authors inject a spirit of play tone, a wry tongue-in-cheek narrative which mutes some of the invective spirit or attack so that this grim subject is softened for Victorian taste. The scenarists Larry Gelbart and Burt Shevelove, who became established writers with their book for the 1962 musical *A Funny Thing Happened on the Way to the Forum*, follow suit—they retain the strong spirit of play in their adaptation. But the screenwrights have drastically altered the basic plot of the last two-thirds of the novel, employing a mere plot thread from the source. The mix-up of two boxes, one containing a statue and another a body (mistakenly thought to be that of an uncle who was in a train wreck) still holds to the original narrative line. There is also a great deal of manipulation to conceal the supposed death of their uncle by two nephews who are slated to inherit the fortune of the old man if he outlives his brother. Many of the novelistic complications which show the body being shifted from place to place, discovered and then disposed of, only to reappear again, evidently were thought to be overly complicated by the adapters—a type of farcical development that has some of the earmarks of the stage farce of the late nineteenth century.

Gelbart and Shevelove simplify and focus the plot in a way they think will be more appealing to a twentieth-century audience. The last portion of the film, especially the climactic sequence, becomes a frantic, conniving, and, finally, a physical bout, with the nephews attempting to grasp the inheritance from an executor. They forcefully grab the box containing the money and race off, driving a horse-drawn hearse. Using a beer wagon and another hearse, the police and other relatives engage in a mad dash to apprehend the thieves. Since this portion of the film departs so drastically from the original and employs a broader type of humor, it might be considered the weakest portion of the adaptation. Some critics might fault the work for using a lower type of humor and appealing to an audience that indiscriminately enjoys slapstick chases. (A similar, broader type of comedy was also tacked onto the adaptation of *The Loved One* by Terry Southern, a change that will be discussed later.)

While adapters have used heavy hands with the climactic portions of *The Wrong Box*, they've dramatized the opening, basic situation of the novel faithfully as they depict the establishment of a lottery called a tontine, with boys between the ages of six and ten as participants. Their fathers put money into a trust that will, with investment, add up to a large sum in seventy years. The sole survivor of the group will win the tontine. The novel's distinctive use of humorous asides can be illustrated by the forecast of a hollow victory:

> The proceeds are fluttered for a moment in the face of the last survivor, who is probably deaf, so that he cannot even hear of his success—and who is certainly dying, so that he might just as well have lost. [Stevenson and Osbourne, *The Wrong Box*, 1925, Charles Scribner edition, pp. 3–4]

This type of wry comedy, of course, does not work in a dramatization unless the adapters choose to employ a narrator making comments on the action via the "voice-over" action.

The difference between the novelistic narrative and the dramatic mode of telling the story becomes apparent as the adapters relate the deaths of members of the tontine. The novel states the process dryly:

> In the year 1840 the thirty-seven were all alive; in 1850 their numbers had decreased by six; in 1856 and 1857 business was more lively, for the Crimea and the Mutiny carried off no less than nine. There remained in 1870 but

five of the original members, and at the date of my story, including the two Finsburys, but three. [*The Wrong Box*, pp. 4–5]

In vignette fashion the film shows ten deaths over a span of years. Comedy generally evolves when a dignified but dense person strikes a heroic pose in a way that causes his death, or a pompous person becomes a victim of a ridiculous accident. With great dignity, his sword raised, a military officer who is standing in front of one of his troop's own cannons, orders his men to fire. He repeats the order when the men, realizing the situation, look perplexed. The men finally obey and he is killed. As Queen Victoria confers knighthood on a distinguished gentleman, she evidently places the sword a bit too heavily on his shoulder. Out of camera's view a body is heard to fall. The queen declares: "We are frightfully sorry, Sir Robert."

These Monty Python types of vignettes help to set the tone of the dark humor in this expository portion of the film which follows with the revelation of the status of the Finsbury family and the characters in the drama.

Woven into the refurbished plot of the co-scenarists are the characters of one of the surviving brothers, Uncle Joseph Finsbury (played skillfully by veteran British actor Ralph Richardson) and his nephew Morris Finsbury (well handled by comedian Peter Cook), with fidelity to the source, the novel. In the film version Joseph retains the facets of the would-be intellectual who is merely a packrat lover of facts—a pedantic old fool who does not realize he is one of the most boring persons in the world. To a cart driver who gives him a ride after he has escaped from the train wreck and the nephews he detests, Joseph delivers one of his frequent, impromptu lectures: "Do you know how often the word *whip* occurs in the Old Testament? One hundred and (if I remember exactly) forty-seven times" (*The Wrong Box*, p. 35). He then rambles on to tell the hapless listener how many million letters and thousand verses are in the Bible, plus the various editions of the work. The cart driver becomes distressed by this flood of useless information which Joseph so enjoys. Like most people the driver recoils from this pedant, and only the relatives who stand to gain from an inheritance tolerate the old man's deluge of facts.

As in the novel the nephew Morris fills the role of the comic villain in this version of *The Wrong Box*. He encounters frustration after frustration as he attempts to set up himself and his brother to gain the fortune, the tontine. He finds that what he thought were the mutilated remains of his uncle have been misdirected. The mix-up of boxes (the body and a statue) causes Morris great agony—expressed in comic terms. Thinking Joseph's brother about to die, he hopes to keep the news of what is supposed to be the dead Joseph concealed until the ill and older brother, Masterman Finsbury, dies. Overstatement in humor develops often in the novel when Morris realizes that his great expectations have been thwarted: "Great God!" cries Morris, bounding into the hansom like a Jack-in-the-box. "I have not only not gained the tontine—I have lost the leather business!" (*The Wrong Box*, p. 68). The distress of Morris provides many hilarious moments in both the novel and the film. Striving to maintain his dignity under the stress of many reversals, he is finally reduced to sniveling and pleading at the end of both novel and film. After all the confused situations that have caused him to labor so diligently yet in vain, he declares he is a poor orphan who deserves consideration. In the movie version, when it is revealed that Uncle Joseph is actually alive, Morris still has hopes. But the novel, with a different portrait of Masterman's heir, Michael Finsbury, shows this shrewd relative taking over some of Uncle Joseph's liabilities and a second right to the tontine fortune. The comic villain is foiled in a traditional ending.

Gelbart and Shevelove have taken considerable liberty with the Michael Finsbury of the novel. In the film version, Michael (played by Michael Caine) is an innocent medical student. The writers turn the character into a romantic lead—a light comedy portrait. His timid wooing of a young girl, Julia, whose guardian is Uncle Joseph, creates a type of comedy that is only briefly treated in the novel. The source creation shows Michael as a dapper, con-artist lawyer who constantly thwarts the many mechanizations of Morris. The film Michael takes no direct action against Morris. Furthermore, the novelistic Michael is a Victorian gay blade with a devil-may-care attitude who in the most distressing circumstances, such as getting rid of the body in the wrong box, wants a friend to go out with him for a drink.

Obviously, this character change from novel to film produces a lighter tone in many portions of the movie. Only the naive Julia of the novel comes close to being an exemplary character. All other potential heirs are conniving to obtain their fortunes by almost any means.

However, the attitude of characters toward death and a body that is shifted about from person to person remains one of the darkest elements in both the novel and the film. Whenever one of the characters in this complicated plot of mistakes and misalliances has the body dumped on him, he fears the law will implicate him and he gets rid of it. Even Michael in the film version gets rid of the body by placing it in a piano and having it carted off. Each man who takes such an action pretends to be an honest man—a person who should report the situation to the police. But these self-proclaimed men of integrity never do. Both the novel and film focus on this type of hypocrisy and thereby expose human nature in the comic terms of satire.

In a moment of self-examination the novelistic portrait of Michael wryly reveals that he finds his questionable dealings humorous: "I have sometimes thought I would like to try to behave like a gentleman myself, only it's such a onesided business, with the world and the legal profession as they are" (*The Wrong Box*, p. 187). But the screen Michael has been cast in a different mold. He would never engage in this type of cynical reflection—even as he gets rid of the wrong box, he naively takes action by following a suggestion of a servant.

The concept of a warped sense of integrity is, therefore, somewhat muted. Nevertheless, the satire tied to the concept of greed still is maintained in the film version of *The Wrong Box*. For the mass audience the concept of propriety at all costs does come forth in many aspects of the screen version. Part of the extension of the characters' attempts to appear moral in a romantic relationship develops with the attraction between Michael and Julia, an innovation the screenwriters lifted from the novel in which Julia develops an affair with a lawyer friend of Michael's. There is a great struggle with emotions that lean toward lust, and attempts on the part of both lovers are made to dignify their sexual appetites. When Gelbart and Shevelove extend this portion of the novel, they seem to be showing us some of the cobwebs of Victorian morality that, to a degree, still clutter our own minds.

There is an added dimension in the novel that touches on this odd morality of the past—one that still plagues us today. We still have censors who would make sure that all our literature and performing arts are free of any impropriety. The depiction of what some call "evil deeds," such people maintain, might be imitated. The authors of the novel use this first person, seemingly detached, tongue-in-cheek observation:

> In a really polite age of literature, I would have scorned to cast my eye again on the contortions of Morris. But the study is in the spirit of the day; it presents, besides, features of a high, almost a repulsive, morality; and if it should prove the means of preventing any respectable and inexperienced gentleman from plunging light-heartedly into crime, even political crime, this work will not have been penned in vain. [*The Wrong Box*, p. 172]

Again this type of narrative reflection shows what is often thought to be the province of the novel to create comedy by humorous philosophical asides—in this case to poke fun at what George Bernard Shaw labeled "middle-class morality." Such asides have some of the quality used by Henry Fielding in *Tom Jones*. And John Osborne's adaptation of this work in 1963 retained some of the flavor of the novel by using the disembodied voice of a narrator (voice-over action, as it is called) to make such comments on the action.

Since film director Bryan Forbes had a script which avoided this technique, the dramatic action carries the comedy. Reviewers generally favored *The Wrong Box*, except for an occasional detractor such as Stephen Farber, who also did not like Forbes's serious works, *The L-Shaped Room* (1963) and *King Rat* (1965). But Farber even admits, "As usual Forbes has assembled a good cast . . . but. . . . " The critic then accuses the creator of directing erratically "with sticky fingers in many fashionable pots—black comedy, Victorian parody, knockabout Lesterease farce" and dismisses the movie as mere entertainment to please "the Swingers" (Farber, *Film Quarterly*, Winter 1966–67, p. 63). Such underrating of comedy during the sixties was not uncommon.

With historical perspective *The Wrong Box* does gain stature. Actually, Forbes pulls together these comedy elements from the "fashionable pots" into a unified whole and with a distinct style; furthermore, he obtains from his actors a quality of "ensemble acting"—a feature of dramatic performances often associated with the best stage productions. Actors Richardson, Caine, and Cook work well with each other. Forbes produces some splendid scenes, using one of the great British film actors, John Mills, who plays the older brother of Uncle Joseph. In one of his early roles for films, music hall comedian Dudley Moore turns in a solid performance as an effete rake and brother of the villainous Morris Finsbury. There are two short scenes which allow Peter Sellers, an established leading film comedian by 1966 (the year of this film), the fascinating depiction of a degenerate, alcoholic physician who readily dispenses poison to kill hated or burdensome relatives and a fake death certificate for the nefarious plans of Morris. To this dark portrait of moral and professional deterioration, Sellers adds a note of pathos when he occasionally states, "Of course, I was not always as you see me now." This cameo portrait of decadence is an invention of the adaptors— the novel has Morris only contemplating that he may need a "venal doctor" who will give him a death certificate (*The Wrong Box*, p. 70). It is an addition that fits the tone of the original work and, for these particular scenes, gives the movie a darker cast than the novel.

While seldom shown on television, *The Wrong Box* is available on video tape and is worth viewing by people who like dark comedy with the death theme; this film ranks high and is on the satirical level of *The Loved One*. In 1966 Bosley Crowther, who did not like *The Loved One* the year before, did not worry about the alterations that evolved from the adaptation of *The Wrong Box*. He found the total film delightful and concluded his review with this observation: "Mr. Stevenson and Mr. Osbourne can rest contented that their story has been expertly vandalized." (*New York Times*, July 20, 1966).

Since there was a favorable acceptance by critics of the Stanley Kubrick film *Dr. Strangelove or: How I Learned to Stop Worrying and Love the Bomb* in 1964, a film scripted by Terry Southern that displayed many of the features of the developing black comedy trend, it is little wonder that filmmakers looked to Evelyn Waugh's 1948 novella, *The Loved One*, as a source for a major motion picture. This satire examines the funeral business, Hollywood, America's taste for the gaudy and superficial, the Miss Lonelyhearts (advice to the reader) type of journalism, and expatriate British actors trying to maintain a Victorian dignity in a land they consider primitive. But almost unanimous rejection by the critics was framed in the same tones of indignation which they professed that satire should have. Robert Hatch of *The Nation* attacked Terry Southern and his co-scenarist Christopher Isherwood as vulgarizers because they "turned Evelyn Waugh's brief, witty, tough attack upon American mores, as exemplified in the country's funeral rites, into a loose-lipped, leering, cute-boys-together campground" (*The Nation*, November 1, 1965, p. 316). The reviewer for *Newsweek* set forth the view that satire should be offensive, as disgusting as Swift's "A Modest Proposal," but he believed the movie failed in its excesses, deviations, and parody of the source so that this movie version, as he states it, "never earns the right to be scabrous" (*Newsweek*, October 18, 1965, p. 122).

The view that a writer who attempts satire and doesn't achieve it must be censored for his failure can be questioned. It would appear that some "social redeeming value" test has been applied by the critic as he or she views comedy. Fortunately, not all critics of the film did agree that it was a poor work. Arthur Knight of the *Saturday Review* seemed more magnanimous: "*The Loved One* is gallows humor, which may not be to everyone's taste. But it is certainly the longest and boldest step up from conventional film fare ever to come from a major American studio" (*Saturday Review*, October 23, 1965, p. 75).

There seems to be a major flaw in the picture which could more properly be called a poverty of invention by director Tony Richardson and his adaptors when they attempted to provide a more dramatic and farcical climactic sequence. The adaptors evidently were trying to appeal to a mass audience when they updated and overplotted the last portion of the original story line. As it has been indicated, *The Wrong Box* suffered a similar popularization fate.

In *The Loved One* writers Southern and Isherwood depict the Reverend Harry Glenworthy, entrepreneur and owner of the elaborate cemetery called Whispering Glades (a parody of the well-known Forest Lawn establishment that seems to be a self-lampooning world in real life), as a religious con man who sees more money in senior citizen condominiums than in the funeral business. He has discovered that people are living longer and that his enterprise will not realize the financial growth it needs. So he wishes to convert the property to real estate. Glenworthy (played by Jonathan Winters) states in the film: "Got to be a way to get those stiffs off my property!" A plan is developed to achieve a heavenly touch that would be the opposite of interment—rocket the corpses into orbit. Film critic Bosley Crowther sees this portion of the film as going "into an orbit of witless inanity" (*New York Times*, October 12, 1965, p. 57).

If the concluding sequence goes this far astray or produces the inanity Crowther believes, how could the work be considered a major achievement in the black comedy film of the sixties? It is the case of enough strong parts to equal a solid whole. Many threads of the novel and a great deal of the dialogue are retained. Some added elements work—even though a purist, one who believes little should be added or altered by the adaptation, might not agree. Some humorous sexual intrigues between the leading young couple, Aimée Thanatogenos (played by Anjanette Comer) and Dennis Barlow (enacted by Robert Morse), receive extended treatment, but there is enough suggestion in the original work to make this type of addition valid. Waugh's indication that Aimée's mind is out of joint continues to be supported throughout the novella and is reinforced by Dennis's comic understatement after she commits suicide. Talking to his rival in love, Joyboy, he asks: "Of course, I never thought her wholly sane, did you?" (*The Loved One*, Dell edition 1966, p. 179). When Waugh first fully describes her, he concludes with, "Her eyes greenish and remote, with a rich glint of lunacy" (*The Loved One*, p. 67). Screenwriters Southern and Isherwood add a sequence showing her living in flaky bliss, completely unaware, in a hillside house that is slowly crumbling as the earth slides from under it—a contemporary phenomenon in the hills of Hollywood.

Aimée's strange relationship with Mr. Joyboy, especially their professional relationship, produces dark comedy in both media and illustrates the way in which the film often follows the

Rod Steiger as head mortician courts his cosmetologist, played by
Anjanette Comer, in an adaptation of Evelyn Waugh's novel *The Loved
One.*

novel closely. As Mr. Joyboy (enacted mincingly by stocky Rod
Steiger), head mortician for Whispering Glades, works on the
facial features of the corpse of Sir Francis (Dennis's uncle) to
achieve the proper look to make him presentable to all who
would view him for the funeral, this would-be artist of his
profession produces a smile on the dead man's face. Aimée
observes, "But, Mr. Joyboy, you've given him the Radiant Childhood smile" (*The Loved One*, p. 82). Mr. Joyboy counters with
the view that he just can't help it because he is sending Sir
Francis to her. Mr. Joyboy woos Aimée, a cosmetologist for the
establishment, through the expressions on the faces of the
bodies he sends her. *Reductio ad absurdum* in comedy evolves

when Aimée observes that her mentor and potential husband finds the arrival of a dead infant a unique challenge to his artistic abilities. "You do love children, don't you, Mr. Joyboy?" (*The Loved One*, p. 85). In a grotesque way it would appear that Aimée thinks this proper, meticulous creature would make a good husband. "Off to baby," he declares as he leaves her. This situation and many of the lines of Waugh are reproduced in the movie. In a narrative form which allows the reader his or her own images, such material is strong enough. The visual dramatization becomes even stronger. Bosley Crowther found much of this to be "morbid ribaldry." In his *New York Times* review he objected to "too much kidding around with corpses, too much clowning in the embalming room. . . . " (*New York Times*, October 12, 1965, p. 57). But, it should be realized, most of this type of material is taken directly from the novel.

The critic may be right if he is accusing Tony Richardson of using a rather heavy hand in developing this satire. But a close reading of Waugh's novella will show that the author was pulling out the stops; he found the excesses of Forest Lawn outrageous and wrote an elaborate feature article for *Life* on this enterprise before he was inspired to do a novel on the subject (Waugh, "Death in Hollywood," *Life*, September 1947, pp. 73–84). Almost all of the dark comedy films of the sixties that approached satire were criticized as works that were offensive or, at least, in bad taste. But the essence of satire is the use of invective comedy that strikes out at the mores of society. It is an attack, and such an attack will always offend someone.

Waugh found in his Forest Lawn parody, Whispering Glades, a microcosm of the self-delusion, wish-fulfillment, naiveté, and ethnocentricity in the American culture. When Aimée writes for advice to the lovelorn columnist, she complains that a foreigner (Dennis) "*is very distinguished looking in an UN-American way and very amusing when he is not being irreverent. Take the Works of Art in Whispering Glades Memorial Park, he is often quite irreverent about them which I think an epitome of all that is finest in the American Way of Life*" (*The Loved One*, p. 122).

This passage from the novel is more direct in its satire than the film, but the film illustrates the view that our value system is often superficial and bound to vague sentiments. The movie Dennis tours the many sections on the grounds of this strange cemetery, viewing with amazement the odd combination of sensuous Greek statues, cute cupids, and animal statues. The Mortuary Hostess in the book explains one of the sections of the "park": "Then there is Lovers' Nest, zoned about a very, very beautiful marble replica of Rodin's famous statue, the Kiss. We have double plots there at seven hundred and fifty dollars the pair" (*The Loved One*, p. 54). So the film does visualize, as is its province, much that is set forth in the novel. Haskell Wexler's photography of the statues, with the musical score by John Addison, lets the audience know they are witnessing a bizarre world.

Many of the standard threads of the novella's plot are faithfully rendered by the adapters. The development of a strained, comic triangle affair which Aimée has with her two potential husbands (or, at least, steady boyfriends) seems to be effectively translated from the novel to the film. This is well coordinated with the lampoon of the Ann Landers type of journalism. In a brilliant bit of casting Tony Richardson employs Lionel Stander to play the role of the Miss Lonelyhearts writer. Called the Guru Brahmin in the novel and film, actor Stander portrays the chain-smoking lush with gravel-voice sarcasm. His comic movements as a drunk are enhanced by the fact that he has a body like that of a football linebacker who has gone to seed. As the Guru (who is identified in the novel as Mr. Slump) dictates advice to Aimée, he writes a sweet, sympathetic letter to help her choose between her two boyfriends. Suffering from a hangover, he is not happy with the quality of his writing and tells his assistant, "Hell, I feel awful this morning. The girl sounds like a prize bitch anyway" (*The Loved One*, p. 140). The movie has similar invective remarks, and when the misanthropic Guru becomes disgusted with Aimée's letters which show her affections vacillating from letter to letter, he crushes her with his final bit of advice. He suggests that she jump off a high building (*The Loved One*, p. 171). It is one of the darkest moments in *The Loved One* because Aimée does commit suicide when she hears this recommendation to solve her problems. In the novel Mr. Slump cuts Aimée down via the phone; in the film she seeks him out as he drinks in a bar. He gives the advice to her face-to-face.

The triangle threads of the story are not as dark in the film version of the incidents involving Aimée and Dennis. There is a little more of the spirit of play as Dennis woos her. However, this comic spirit becomes bizarre when he meets her on the grounds of Whispering Glades. With the imagery of monuments to the dead in the film, these rendezvous take on a darker cast. The adaptation shows Dennis reciting poetry to her in the various locations of the cemetery. In the novel he sends her poetry he has transcribed from the *Oxford Book of English Verse*, claiming he is the author. When Dennis tries to seduce Aimée in the cinema version, he makes his move near a recreational park-like portion of Whispering Glades. Aimée points out, as she struggles, that he is "unethical"—a word she often uses in the novel. Aimée in Waugh's work obviously uses the term "unethical" to mean "immoral" and writes to the Guru that Dennis *"wants unethical things and is so cynical when I say no we must wait"* (*The Loved One*, p. 150). The adapters become more blunt by having her write, " . . . and tonight he tried to blank and blank with me" with Aimée indicating this was part of being cynical and not concerned with things that are sacred to her. Aimée's naive view of love and marriage is fully exploited by the adapters and seems to be in the spirit of the source novel. Southern and Isherwood give Dennis a more aggressive sexual nature than Waugh does. However, Robert Morse portrays the role with a tone of the boy genius experimenting with his manhood.

The purist might object particularly to a rather sharp switch in the character of Mrs. Joyboy (the obese actress Alyliene Gibbons plays the role). In the novel this dominating mother is a carping malcontent—a shrew. Waugh takes a satirical poke at the son as he describes her:

> The mothers of great men often disconcert their son's admirers. Mrs. Joyboy had small angry eyes, frizzy hair, pince-nez on a very thick nose, a shapeless body and positively insulting clothes. [*The Loved One*, p. 135]

The film mother is a contented cow of a woman who relishes a television food commercial almost as much as she does the real thing. She is the epitome of gluttony—a woman who would happily gorge herself to death. Her obsession seems to become, in the hands of the scenarists, a substitution for sex. The lasting cinematic image of Mrs. Joyboy that becomes etched in our mind is a wallow in a whole refrigerator load of food. In her desperation to satisfy her gluttony, this mountainous woman accidentally pulls the refrigerator and its contents on top of herself. Instead of being distressed, she refuses to be rescued, for she is too busily engrossed in an eating orgy.

An objectionable addition tied to a switch in character? Perhaps it would be to a purist. Yet, it seems to illustrate Evelyn Waugh's disturbing view of the excesses of our American society. Also, the scenes involving Mrs. Joyboy do not seem to alter the basic movement of the source's plot.

The movie tampered only slightly as it used the original material, showing the strange way we treat our dead (a comment that is universal) when Dennis composed his only original poem—a eulogy to his uncle, Sir Francis:

> They told me, Francis Hinsley, they told me you were hung
> With red protruding eye-balls and black protruding tongue
> I wept as I remembered how often you and I
> Had laughed about Los Angeles and now 'tis here you'll
>   lie;
> Here pickled in formaldehyde and painted like a whore,
> Shrimp-pink incorruptible, not lost nor gone before. [The
> Loved One, pp. 101–102]

Here is a savage comment on the embalmer's lack of art and the hypocrisy of those who remark, "Doesn't he (she) look natural?"

The movie version of The Loved One does seem to retain much of the author's original purpose. It should be realized that in the attempt to make a motion picture appeal to a wider audience, Hollywood has traditionally softened satire. Even upbeat endings have been added. Lonelyhearts (1958), adapted from Nathanael West's Miss Lonelyhearts, inverts a tragic confrontation between the protagonist and an irate husband. An unlikely reconciliation develops as a denouement of the drama. An updated version of Elmer Rice's play The Adding Machine (1923) in 1969 never comes to grips with the depersonalization of humankind in a mechanized society. Granted, the original satire may have been overstated; nevertheless, the adaptation seems to skirt the issue by making the conflict more of a personal problem for the hapless man named Zero.

Some film adaptations, such as *Catch-22* (1970) and *Slaughterhouse-Five* (1972), seem to need a reading of the novel to fully appreciate the film. *Catch-22* has a narrative line that has been drastically altered by the adaptor Buck Henry—so altered it is difficult to follow (Vincent Canby, *New York Times*, June 25, 1970, p. 181). The psychological switches in time of the protagonist of *Slaughterhouse-Five* (from present to past to future, in many variations) seem easier to follow if one has read the book. *The Loved One* is, even with its changes and additions, a self-contained unit. The dark comedy *The Wrong Box* (1966) has the same trait. Adaptors Larry Gelbart and Burt Shevelove have condensed, rearranged, and come close to mutilating the original novel by Robert Louis Stevenson and Lloyd Osbourne. Yet, the work stands on its own. Along with *The Loved One* it remains as an example of one of the best comic films to come from the whole sixties dark comedy movement.

While both movies, *The Wrong Box* and *The Loved One*, are flawed works, especially the climactic portions of these adaptations, they represent not only two of the best efforts in the dark comedy genre, they show the medium coming to grips with satire. The creations written and directed by Mel Brooks and Woody Allen from the late sixties, continuing through the seventies and into the eighties, are films people loosely label satires. But these movies, while they contain elements of black humor, are in a light vein. The works are spoofs of movies and fads of the time that lack the bite, penetration, and significance to be in the same league with *The Wrong Box* and *The Loved One*, works that will stand the test of time.

CHAPTER 3

WAR AND HOLOCAUST FOR SOME PAINFUL LAUGHTER

DIRECTOR STANLEY KUBRICK BEGAN HIS assault on the social institutions of government and the military in the sixties with a satirical thrust that would be repeated in the eighties using a similar attack on authority in the film *Full Metal Jacket*. The earlier work, *Dr. Strangelove or: How I Learned to Stop Worrying and Love the Bomb*, released January 30, 1964, provided the springboard for a new film comedy—a film that may be called the quintessence of dark comedy and, possibly, the most significant cinematic satire of the decade. No other anti-war comedy film of that period and the succeeding decade would be as favorably received critically and popularly. Granted, *M*A*S*H* in 1970 would prove to be more popular, make more money, and spawn a long-running television show, but the precursor has remained in a league by itself. And, while it might seem odd that such a controversial film would make any money at all, *Dr. Strangelove* made a profit of five million dollars after being produced for a million and a half dollars.

Director Stanley Kubrick and screenwright Terry Southern molded Peter George's novella *Red Alert** into a brilliant movie. The filmmakers switch the tone of a basically serious work (with a number of ironic undertones) that explores the bungled efforts of the United States Strategic Air Command's fail safe operation with nuclear weapons that results in holo-

---

*Novelist George used the pseudonym Peter Bryant for his Ace Books (1958) version of his work, but he has a screen credit with Kubrick and Southern using his own surname.

caust. They turn the story into a savage, black comedy statement on the plight of modern civilization under the stress of annihilation. George's narrative reveals his purpose when he states in the Foreword:

> Most important of all, it is a story which could happen. It may even be happening as you read these words. And then it really will be two hours to doom. [Peter Bryant (George), *Red Alert*, Ace Books, Inc., 1958, p. 5]

But, as serious as this foreword seems to be, the total novella on which the movie adaptation is based contains strong irony that even approaches satire. The portrait of Brigadier General Quinten, a SAC base commander of the 839th Wing, evolves in the novella into a study of an insane, bellicose bigot. The crew members of the B-52 bomber (ironically called *Alabama Angel*) develop into an examination of a group of men who engage in misplaced genuflection to authority and patriotism. They see themselves as heroes, carrying out a holy war of retribution by turning their jet toward Russia to bomb an Intercontinental Ballistic Missile Base. Mistakenly they think the United States has been attacked when, in reality, the hawkish Quinten has launched the first strike in order to obtain (he thinks) "peace on earth." So the basic story material and the portraits of the men have, at least, ironic leanings toward satirical comment.

Before sealing off all communications to and from his base, Quinten phones SAC headquarters in Washington, D.C., and reveals that he was responsible for this unprovoked attack on Russia:

> "Sure, the orders came from me. They're on their way in, and I advise you to get the rest of SAC in after them. My boys will give you the best kind of start. And you sure as hell won't stop them now." [*Red Alert*, p. 34]

The film adaptation of *Red Alert* reproduces this message with some added remarks which magnify and extend the madness of the maverick general who is called in the movie General Jack D. Ripper (skillfully enacted by Sterling Hayden). Filmmakers Kubrick and Southern add the kind of "start" the lunatic has given the U.S. Forces: "1400 megatons worth." And, to

move his wackiness to the point of comedy, the adapters end
the message with this declaration:

> "God willing, we will prevail in peace and freedom from
> fear and in true health through the purity and essence of
> our natural fluids. God bless you all." [From the film *Dr.
> Strangelove . . .*]

The Commander for all SAC bases in the movie, General
"Buck" Turgidson (well-handled by George C. Scott), indicates
that his staff is trying to translate the meaning of this puzzling
statement. Of course, the movie audience has learned that
Ripper believes that when fluoridation of water was introduced
in the United States in 1946, it was a Communist plot to sap the
"precious bodily fluids" from the American male. Thus, the
filmmakers make sure that the hawkish general is more unhinged than in the source, *Red Alert*.

But the madness of Quinten's fear that Communists are
infiltrating was fully established before it was translated to the
screen. He warns his troops that the base may be approached
by hostile forces:

> "I'm going to give you three simple rules. The first is to
> trust no-one, whatever his uniform, whatever his rank,
> who is not known to you personally. The second is anyone
> or anything that approaches within two hundred yards of
> the perimeter is fired on. And the third—if in doubt, fire
> anyway. I would sooner accept a few casualties through
> accident than lose the whole base and personnel through
> over-caution." [*Red Alert*, p. 36]

He concludes with the jingoistic ploy of appealing to the
men's position to defend the families of America. It is the same
line that has been fully embraced by the would-be heroes of the
Alabama Angel. And these men have great pride in the accom-
plishments of American industry and ingenuity. When a Russian
missile hits the plane and the craft keeps plugging away on its
mission, engineer Federov in the novel announces proudly,
"Take a lot more than that to kill a fifty-two" (*Red Alert*, p. 101).
Ironically, the captain of the plane rationalizes away the fact
that the plane's radio, because of the hit by the missile, will not

receive messages from air command. "There's nothing anyone would want to tell us we don't already know" (*Red Alert*, p. 143). However, everyone is frantically trying to stop the attack. With a heroic pose, as if he had seen too many "gung-ho" air force movies, such as *Twelve O'Clock High* (1949), the wounded pilot of the novel, Captain Clint Brown, gallantly flies only 200 feet above the terrain to avoid flack and to suicidally set off the bomb at "ground zero." His last thoughts on the possible destruction of life mold into upbeat, patriotic rationalizations: "What they were doing was surely right, and they could answer for it without shame" (*Red Alert*, p. 167). The irony of these last thoughts as he dies, his hands on the controls, before the crash and explosion of the plane plus the nuclear bomb leans toward satire. The crew members do not know that their sacrifice was not only in vain but that their actions in following orders were, indeed, very wrong.

An effective metamorphosis of the pilot and leader of the B-52 crew, a stroke of genius in character development and casting by the filmmakers, occurs in the movie where this portrait becomes Major T. J. "King" Kong, played by Slim Pickens.* The character still retains the do-or-die patriot fervor but emerges with disarming hayseed and cowboy images—creating ironies that contribute to the satire of *Dr. Strangelove*. Kong's dedication is often punctuated with folksy asides and observations. Reading off the contents of a kit to be used by each airman in case he has to bail out over Russian territory, he states:

> "Survival Kit Content Check. In them you will find: one forty-five caliber automatic; two boxes of ammunition; four days concentrated emergency rations; one drug issue containing an anti-biotic, morphine, vitamin pills, pep pills, sleeping pills, tranquilizing pills; one miniature combination Russian phrase book and Bible; one hundred dollars in rubles; one hundred dollars in gold; nine packs of chewing gum; one issue of prophylactics; three lipsticks, three pairs of nylon stockings. Shoot, a feller could have a pretty good weekend in Vegas with all that stuff." [From the movie *Dr. Strangelove* . . .]

---

*It has been reported that Peter Sellers was to enact Kong as his fourth role in the movie, but was too ill at the time to handle the assignment.

In contrast to much of the movie emphasis involving the struggle of man with machines (communication devices, electronic maps, computers, etc.), Kong offers his homey views on the crippled airplane as if he were dealing with a limping horse to get himself through the desert in the Old West of the nineteenth century. His obsession and zeal (molded after the dogged efforts of the leader in *Red Alert*) are obvious as he zooms to the target with his plane flying low to avoid Russian radar. But Kong does not die with his hands on the controls. A bizarre, heroic act, which seems to smack of writer Terry Southern's wacky sense of humor, again shows Kong transposing machine to animal. Like the old-fashioned do-it-yourself leader he tries to disengage the hydrogen bomb from the damaged drop system. Astride the bomb as he unjams the system, he rides the bomb down as if he were in the saddle of a bucking bronco at a rodeo. He shouts in triumph, "Yahoo! Whahoo! Whahoo!" Proudly he rides to his and the world's annihilation.

One crew member wonders, just before the explosion, "What about Major Kong?" As in the novel, self-sacrifice and heroism are ironically futile gestures and unconscious immoral acts against civilization.

Three contrasting roles enacted by Peter Sellers, Group Captain Lionel Mandrake (Howard in the novel), President Muffley (merely called President in the source work), and Dr. Strangelove (a film story innovation—not used by novelist Peter George), also show interesting switches to promote satire. As in the novel the group captain is an assistant and confidant of the hawkish general who, on his own volition, launches a first strike on Russia. This character, realizing the gravity of the situation in both novel and film, questions the general's actions and effetely tries to remedy the international crisis by attempting to reason with the madman. Sellers plays the role as a British officer who has been assigned to the SAC 349th Wing. Humor is often achieved by his understated reactions to potential catastrophe as he struggles to maintain a British, tight-lipped, uplifted-chin decorum to find some way of reversing his superior's orders. An example of this cool, understated humor is evident when General Jack D. Ripper of the movie asks Mandrake if he has ever been tortured because he, the general, fears his base is being invaded by Communists (actually U.S. troops)

In *Dr. Strangelove* . . . Peter Sellers plays the title role of the sadistic scientist and social engineer.

who will torture him into revealing the call-back code for the planes that he has sent to bomb Russia. Mandrake recalls that he was tortured by the Japanese when he was captured in World War II:

> "I don't think they wanted me to talk, really. I don't think they wanted me to say anything. It's just their way of having a bit of fun—the swines. Strange thing. They make such bloody good cameras." [From the movie *Dr. Strange-love* ...]

Film critic Robert Hatch (*The Nation*, February 3, 1964, p. 127) seems to err in his interpretation of Peter Sellers's role as the President of the United States. "President Muffley is the embodiment of the American executive ideal—a man whose sole quality is a talent for deciding what other men should do—and the fiendish notion here is to project such a man into a moment of ultimate crisis where any decision is irrelevant." Bosley Crowther, on the other hand, seems morally indignant when he is troubled by a film which projects "discredit and even contempt for our whole defense establishment, up to and even including the hypothetical Commander in Chief" (*New York Times*, January 31, 1964, p. 16). The dichotomy of interpretation regarding this portrait can be realized if one closely observes Sellers's enactment. He pulls from the novel some of the sincerity of a man trying to do the best with an almost impossible situation; yet, he infuses the creation with some of the plain-folks, common man image of a President Harry Truman or President Dwight Eisenhower. With uncanny mimicry Sellers flattens his speech patterns to reflect the American dialect of the Midwest—Missouri or Kansas. With the aid of Kubrick-Southern-George, he creates a fine comic character with dimension. No wonder there is some confusion in critical examination of this character. President Muffley's idiom and folksy chatter, like Major Kong's, creates humor by seeming incongruous in such a grave situation. One can witness his well-meaning struggle with the drunken Premier of Russia, Dimitri Kissoff, when he phones him about the actions of a SAC base commander who has gone insane:

"Hello. Ah . . . hello. Hello, Dimitri. Listen, eh, I can't hear too well. Suppose you can turn down the music just a little? That's much better. Yes. Fine. I can hear you now, Dimitri. Clear and plain and coming through fine. I'm coming through fine too, eh? Good. Then. Well, then, as you say, then, we are both coming through fine. Good. Well, it's good that you're fine and I'm fine. I agree with you, it's great to be fine. [Laughs.] Now then, Dimitri, you know how we've always talked about the possibility of something going wrong with the bomb. The bomb, Dimitri. The *hydrogen* bomb. Well now, what happened is, ah, one of our base commanders—he has a sort of—well, he went a little funny in the head. You know, just a little funny. And, ah, he went and did a silly thing. Well, I'll tell you what he did. He ordered his planes to attack your country. Well, let me finish, Dimitri. Let me finish, Dimitri. How do you think I feel about it? Can you imagine how I feel about it, Dimitri? Why do you think I'm calling you? Just to say hello? Of course I like to speak to you. Of course I like to say hello. Not now, but any time, Dimitri. I'm just calling up to tell you something terrible has happened. It's a friendly call. Of course it's a friendly call. Listen. If it wasn't friendly, you probably wouldn't have got it." [From the movie *Dr. Strangelove* . . .]

Muffley gets more direct and informs the premier of Russia that they will give him all the defense systems of the bombers and will do everything possible to help Russian forces to shoot them down if the planes cannot be recalled. As he concludes his conversation, a type of small-town, neighborhood bickering can be observed as truth and fiction seem to merge—nations and their leaders seem to be as petty as feuding children:

"I'm sorry too, Dimitri. I'm very sorry. All right, you're sorrier than I am. But I'm as sorry as well. I am as sorry as you are, Dimitri! Don't say that you are more sorry than I am for I'm as capable of being just as sorry as you are. So we are both sorry. All right? All right." [From the movie *Dr. Strangelove* . . .]

Comic license allows our novelists, playwrights, and filmmakers to take such pokes at authority. And the Kubrick-Southern-George adaptation of *Red Alert* rakes over the image of the scientist, one of our most sacred cows of the highly technological age of the twentieth century. Dr. Strangelove, the third comic portrait of Peter Sellers, is the most scathing, black comedy characterization in the film. While other characters in the film are depicted as insane, stupid, effete, small minded, petty, bigoted, or jingoistic, and even a combination of such traits, Dr. Strangelove is sketched broadly as a sadistic, fascist scientist. He seems to be a cross between the real life portraits of Dr. Wernher von Braun, a United States affiliated retread of a Nazi V-2 rocket specialist, and Dr. Henry Kissinger, a political expert with formidable academic credentials who would later prove to be a philosopher with political influence and an inclination to social engineering.

In the film, when Strangelove learns that the Russians have a Doomsday Machine (a type of super atomic bomb), ready to go off automatically if the country is attacked, he gleefully philosophizes: "The whole point of the Doomsday Machine is lost if you keep it a secret. Why didn't you tell the world?" Russian Ambassador de Sadesky tells him it was about to be announced. Dr. Strangelove's own name might suggest that this is a man in love with violence and international manipulation. The moral questions are forgotten because he represents the amoral application of his science to control the world for any big power with which he is affiliated.

His physical traits are viciously caricatured into a cartoon version of a twisted mind in a twisted body—he is a grotesque. A paraplegic in a wheelchair, he has one bionic arm (probably his own invention) that periodically whips and gyrates out of control. When it runs amuck, it may choke its own inventor or snap into the classic Nazi salute to Adolf Hitler. Speaking with a heavy German accent, he has a perpetual leer—sardonic and, occasionally, almost satanic. His advice on human survival as the holocaust approaches has the perverted passion of a mad laboratory scientist engaged in his own evil but brilliantly conceived experiment:

> "Mr. President, I would not rule out the chance of preserving the nucleus of the human specimen. It would be quite easy, eh, eh, at the bottom of some of our deeper mine shafts. Radioactivity would never penetrate a mine some

thousands of feet deep. And in a matter of weeks sufficient improvement in drilling, space could easily be provided. . . . " [From the movie *Dr. Strangelove* . . .]

When asked how long people would have to stay down in the shafts, the scientist calculates with difficulty as his bionic arm goes awry, but he comes up with the view that it would be "possibly one hundred years."

"It would not be difficult, Mein Fuhrer! Nuclear reactors could—I'm sorry, *Mr. President*. Nuclear reactors could provide power almost indefinitely. Greenhouses could maintain plant life; animals could be bred and *slaughtered*. A survey would have to be of all the available mine sites in the country, but I would guess that dwelling space for survival of a hundred thousand of our people could easily be provided." [From the movie *Dr. Strangelove* . . .]

When asked by the President who would be selected for survival, the scientist delights in the thought of genetic engineering by indicating that a computer could be programmed to select for "youth, health, sexual fertility, intelligence, and a cross section of necessary skills." He also makes sure that top level leaders, governmental and military, are included to foster the principles of leadership and tradition.

All ironic aspects of the novel *Red Alert* pale in comparison with the adaptation's most ludicrous irony at the end of the film when Dr. Strangelove seems to be cured of the neurological damage that has made him a cripple. In his enthusiasm for solving the possible "mine gap" between the United States and Russia (a posited view of General Turgidson, who believes the Russians might have a similar survival plan), he rises from his wheelchair and walks like an automaton for several steps, pensively saying, "I have a plan. . . . " Then he realizes he is walking and shouts with joy, "Mein Fuhrer, I can walk!" This savage Terry Southern touch is evident as the viewer sees the body of the most warped mind being cured as if by a miracle. And, then, the Doomsday Machine goes off.

Dr. Strangelove or: How I Stopped Worrying and Learned to Love the Bomb remains the richest anti-war film of the decades of the sixties and seventies, but not much more space can be given to this work without neglecting other films that also made important social comments on war. Two overall observations, however, need to be examined briefly to round out this evaluation. The structure of the film shows a link with *Red Alert* while certain sexual themes depart from the source. Three locations, the cabin of the B-52, the SAC military base, the conference room for the President and military officials, operate in parallel actions in concurrent time to develop tension in both the novel and film. While the crew of the B-52 in *Red Alert* often think of girlfriends as they yearn for home, their explicit sexual attitudes depart very little from the genteel handling of such material in the war movies of the forties. *Dr. Strangelove* provides a breakthrough for more direct references to the physical act. Critics such as Andrew Sarris (*Village Voice*, February 13, 1964, reprinted in Sarris' *Confession of a Cultist*, pp. 122–124) detected sexual symbolism in the first shots of the movie which this critic calls "the aerial copulation-fueling," as the B-52 receives the necessary stimulus to keep flying. While it might sound like excessive Freudian analysis, it can be seen as valid when it is realized that this clip of stock footage is accompanied by a popular song, "Try a Little Tenderness." However, this comic point is still obscure to the average viewer. "Buck" Turgidson's obsession with a girl who is more of a playmate than a secretary during a crisis also provides a comic comment. This general seems more interested in his personal appetites than in the fate of the world. General Jack D. Ripper, the madman, misinterprets his "loss of essence" after the sexual act as the effect of fluoridation. And, finally, Dr. Strangelove, with the detached demeanor of a pimp or whorehouse madam, dreams of his brave new world in the mine shafts with an abundance of women to each man. All these sexual concepts in the movie show a more direct handling of the material without the coyness exhibited in three previous decades of film. Other films that explored love, marriage, and the family would follow with this bolder approach.

Two British films, Richard Lester's *How I Won the War* (1967) and Richard Attenborough's *Oh! What a Lovely War* (1969) are, respectively, adaptations from novel and stage which deserve less attention than the Stanley Kubrick work. Both are flawed efforts and both, for different reasons, had only a slight effect on the moviegoers of the period even though they were made during the growing rebellion over the Vietnam conflict.

The 1967 Lester film seems to be a precursor to Kurt Vonnegut's novel *Slaughterhouse-Five*. (The film adaptation by George Roy Hill will be examined in detail later.) While no direct influence seems to be detectable, many interesting parallels are evident. Patrick Ryan's 1963 anti-war novel of the same title as Lester's film, *How I Won the War*, has as its leading character Ernest Goodbody, a naive lieutenant who commanded a platoon as they engaged in a number of misadventures—misfired or botched military engagements. Like Billy Pilgrim of Vonnegut's 1969 novel, the protagonist of this work, Lt. Goodbody, never learns anything from his experiences. In these two novels the leading characters have a cloud over them. Everyone who is around them seems to suffer. But Goodbody as drawn by Patrick Ryan is an active, however inept, jingoist; Billy Pilgrim in Vonnegut's work remains passive—the fall guy who gets it "in the neck" along with others and doesn't seem accountable for the misfortunes that descend wherever he is present. Goodbody comes out unscathed, whereas Billy becomes a mental cripple. With an unbendable mind, the lieutenant of Ryan's work actually comes out believing he has won the war when, in fact, he has done more to lose it.

Structurally, Ryan's novel *How I Won the War* is simple in comparison with the Vonnegut work. A first person reflection, it does employ some flashbacks and digressions by Goodbody because the narrative line follows the war memoir design. Charles Wood's screenplay for Richard Lester becomes almost as complex as the Vonnegut novel when it becomes "unstuck in time." Evident in the movie are several narrative lines with a recurrent presentational style. That style, contrasting with an accompanying realistic style, seems to be borrowed from the theater of the absurd, vaudeville, the documentary film, and stage expressionism. Like Lester's 1969 *The Bed Sitting Room*, an absurdist view of the aftermath of World War III, this film probably proves to be confusing to most viewers, except the most sophisticated ones who would be familiar with the stage dramas of Samuel Beckett, Eugène Ionesco, and Jean Genet.

Lester and his writer Charles Wood darken the vision of Ryan's *How I Won the War* by depicting the nonheroic deaths of the entire platoon except for one man—the man who was the coward of the group. And, the hapless lieutenant of the film is more of a schmuck—a dense idealist constantly espousing king and country morality and one who does not seem to have the education and breeding exhibited in the novelistic portrait of the protagonist. Although some shades of the novel persist in the adaptation, the novel fits more in the mold of the twentieth-century novelists Evelyn Waugh and Aldous Huxley—satirical fiction from the classical models of the past. Patrick Ryan's protagonist in the novel, and in the film, follows in the vein of Voltaire's *Candide*. Goodbody has some of the traits of Candide: the eternal optimist whose faith is never shaken under a deluge of adversities that would turn the average man into a cynic.

Richard Attenborough's *Oh! What a Lovely War* proves, in retrospect, to be a less effective work than Richard Lester's anti-war statement. Lester attempted to expose the follies of heroic and jingoistic attitudes; he also wanted to attack the conventions of the mainstream war genre. Attenborough, operating with source material that incorporated many elements of the musical theater, seemed to embrace the techniques and moods of the sophisticated, lavish British musical film genre of the late sixties, such as *A Funny Thing Happened on the Way to the Forum* (1966) or *Oliver!* (1968). But *Oh! What a Lovely War* was of humble birth and would suffer from the Pygmalion treatment.

The stage play was derived from a radio special entitled *The Long, Long Trail*, produced by the BBC in 1960 (*Film Facts*, Vol. 12, 1969, p. 386) and later adapted by Britain's new directions theater under the guidance of entrepreneur-director Joan Littlewood at London's Royal Court Theatre in 1963. This anti-establishment type of theater emphasized unique approaches to the art and often used works with strong social commitment. *Oh! What a Lovely War* used a few conventional stage sets and costumes—drawing on presentational styles of the past, the improvisational mode of the *commedia dell'arte* and the British Music Hall. In the United States Megan Terry would launch a similar anti-war work, *Viet Rock* (1966), which, like the precursor, was a group effort of the actors, writers, and director—a type of theatrical experience that was vital and alive.

Some roots of this type of theater were derived from the German playwright Bertolt Brecht, best known for his stage plays *Three Penny Opera* (1928) and *Mother Courage* (1941), dramas with strong statements on people's inhumanity.

Richard Attenborough's sincere attempt to make a significant statement in his directorial debut with *Oh! What a Lovely War* received mixed reactions from critics. While some critics, such as Judith Crist in New York and Roger Ebert in Chicago, were intrigued by the message of the film, those who concentrated on the values of the original stage play, Andrew Sarris and Vincent Canby (both New York critics), found that the filmmakers were molding the material into a film in ways that muted the intent of the original work. In fact Lester's *How I Won the War*, produced two years previously, gained more respect from those who found Attenborough's effort arch and laborious. Some who had witnessed the modest, original theatrical play found the gargantuan effort of the 132-minute film (cut from 144 minutes) tedious.

But Attenborough's *Oh! What a Lovely War* suffers not only from production elephantiasis; it is overly smooth, slick, polite, and even pretty—hardly in the same mold as other anti-war films like *Dr. Strangelove*, *How I Won the War*, and *Slaughterhouse-Five* (1972). Charles Champlin in the November 16, 1969, *Los Angeles Times* (reprinted in *Film Facts*, Vol. 12, pp. 388–389) actually found that the work just missed "being fully the masterpiece it might have been" and pointed out that the work had a whole change of tone from its source. This, however, did not seem to disturb him when he wrote: "The fury, the rage of the stage version, expressed as savage satire, becomes in the film a gentler kind of sorrow."

Fortunately there are some moments of the film that are not submerged by overproduction. Many critics were impressed with Maggie Smith's recruiting song "I'll Make You a Man"—a song featuring a seductive black-widow-like tart who urges men to fight for king and country. Vincent Canby observes "as the men scramble to the stage to enlist, there is a quick close-up of Miss Smith who has turned into the War Whore—her eyeshadow grotesque, the skin across her face as taut as pink leather" (*New York Times*, October 3, 1969, p. 34). This is, of course, a firm, effective translation of the satire in the original

work. And it is to Attenborough's credit that the final staging of
this sequence of the film shows the women as the only ones left
as they walk in a field of crosses. The camera dollies back to
reveal the graves of thousands. And occasional scenes do capture the ironies present in the original stage production by using
contrapuntal, gay, rousing, or sentimental war songs which contrast with the horror of men wounded and killed. But Attenborough's adaptation never developed a filmic style and an
economy of execution that would clearly translate *Oh! What a
Lovely War* from stage to screen.

Probably the most overrated film that was, at the time of its
production, thought by the general audience to make an anti-
war statement was the 1970 *M*A*S*H*, a creation of director
Robert Altman and adapter-screenwriter Ring Lardner, Jr.
When viewed today the film reveals elements of black comedy
which were fresh when first presented but seem to age and
wither with time. With all its irreverence it was recognized by
many critics, even in 1970, as essentially a service comedy. With
its cutdowns of authority it doesn't go much further in lampooning the military establishment than *Kelly's Heroes*, made the
same year.

M*A*S*H is, at best, a service comedy masquerading as
satire. One can ask: What anti-war statement does the film really
make? The only view that seems to emerge with an attempt at
biting humor is that people engaged in war are not heroic. They
are even self-serving and hypocritical. But this is merely a
lampoon of the typical war movie, and since the Mobile Army
Surgical Hospital (from which MASH is the acronym) is behind
the lines, we can see barracks humor (practical jokes) inter-
spersed with dark operating room humor when a fresh batch of
wounded are "coptered" from the front. And, in a muted way,
the establishment also doesn't know what's happening in many
situations and is not "on top of it" in its leadership. More on the
burlesque level, this type of material is the main staple of the
genre, the service comedy.

M*A*S*H now appears genteel, as curious as this may seem.
Some of its daring, for the time, was the exposure of the religious
bigot Major Frank Burns, played by Robert Duvall. He is shown
to be a prig who is raging with suppressed sexuality. *New York
Times* critic Roger Greenspun pointed out (January 24, 1970,

p. 123) that this film was "the first major American movie openly to ridicule belief in God—not phony belief; real belief." But the filmmakers too often pull the rug from what might blossom into satire. Those who have seen the movie (not to be confused with the long-running television series) may remember that Major Burns is humiliated and revealed as a hypocrite when his sexual affair with "Hot Lips" is exposed. His amorous meeting with this woman is broadcast to the whole camp via a public address system when a microphone is placed under a bed to listen to the lovemaking. While the hypocrisy is revealed, it is reduced to a leering, cute practical joke. Other gags follow this as Major Burns's colleagues take verbal swipes at him by asking him if Nurse Hot Lips Houlihan is "any better than self-abuse."

M*A*S*H, like many satires and black comedies, deals with such taboo areas as death (taken lightly or for profit) and sexual deviation (again, taken lightly as nightclub comedy of license or as an exposure of social prejudice). This film deals with both in one situation of a sequence that shows the picaresque surgical duo, Hawkeye (played by Donald Sutherland) and Trapper John (enacted by Elliott Gould), trying to cure the base hospital's dentist from his morose fears of homosexual leanings. The demented dentist wants to commit suicide, and through a ruse the final feast and adieu to the world is arranged. Director Altman shows the feast as an image of a parody of Leonardo da Vinci's painting "The Last Supper." The theme song, "Suicide Is Painless," accompanies this derivative gag. Luis Buñuel employed such a parody in his 1961 *Viridiana* in a satirical way: a collection of outcasts engaging in plunder and a gluttonous orgy are transformed into an ironic pictorialization of the revered classic painting as the camera dollies back to reveal the derelicts in a similar pose. The copycat image is merely clever—the original, savage. And the sequence in *M*A*S*H* is concluded with a practical joke in reverse. The dentist does not die but is rescued on his deathbed by a nymphomaniac who proves he has all the conventional responses to be a fullblooded heterosexual—another cop-out for an essentially pregnant satirical situation.

Some attention has been given to *M*A*S*H* regardless of the quality of the adaptation or the quality of the film because it does represent a breakthrough of the times that would allow more significant films to be produced. The movement to present humor that went against the taboos was realized fully in this very popular film. The acceptance of these relatively new attitudes in a 1970 film was to have some social ramifications when a television version of the Altman-Lardner creation arrived on a previously more censored medium. Along with *All in the Family* the television series *M*A*S*H* would make some comic inroads into what was acceptable in the popular arts; thereby, leading to a more realistic, comic vision of our world.

M*A*S*H by Richard Hooker, Peter George's *Red Alert*, and Patrick Ryan's *How I Won the War* all received only passing recognition. But Joseph Heller's *Catch-22* was another matter. The publisher's publicity pushed the fact that five million people had purchased the book. Many critics, with reservations, saw this novel as a revisionist satire on World War II—the most significant anti-war novel, cast in the humorous mode, since Eric Remarque's serious treatment, *All Quiet on the Western Front*. Consequently, director Mike Nichols and screenwriter-adapter Buck Henry were taking on more than anyone could chew in their 1970 film version.

While the cinema adaptation received mixed reviews, some critics saw it as a faithful translation of the novel. After seeing the movie for the second time, and getting around to reading the novel,* Vincent Canby praised the filmmaker's approximation of the novel's intent (*New York Times*, June 28, 1970, section II, p. 1). One critic, Edmond Gross in *Harper's Magazine* (December 1970, p. 36), viewed the film as an improvement over the novel: "Nichols and Henry were intelligent enough to avoid being literal: as a result they could be faithful to the book. The book is long, the movie is short; the book was endlessly repetitive, the movie uses repetition sparingly; the book was sprawling, the movie is clean, tart, and elegant." This is not to indicate that these two critics did not find some faults in the adaptation, but they, more than others, seemed to see a successful rendition of the novel.

---

*In his June 25th initial review of the movie, Canby stated that a person had to read the novel in order to fully understand the film. By the Sunday edition recap he had read the novel, and he admits in the second review that he hadn't done so earlier. This writer, who has dutifully read the whole work page-by-page, has run upon a few honest friends who have admitted to skimming or, even, not finishing the long, involved work.

In the screen version of *Catch-22* the filmmakers rely on flashbacks to provide a structure that interprets Joseph Heller's complicated series of repetitions and a number of recollections plus forecasts that are not patterned as clear-cut flashbacks and flashforwards. Employing a third person omniscient point of view, the novelist often refers to some event that took place or will take place, thereby blending past and future with the present in a way that may be more complicated than need be. Many chapter headings are titled from the gallery of characters used in the work. But there does seem to be a chronological progression more clearly related to protagonist Yossarian's adversaries, Colonel Cathcart, Lieutenant Colonel Korn, Milo Minderbinder, and General Dreedle. When the narrative focuses on Yossarian, time is more subjective. Therefore, adapter Buck Henry wisely repeats one flashback that was the most traumatic and is used several times in the novel (see pp. 231, 341, and 445–446 in the Dell paperback version). It focuses on Snowden, the dying gunner on the B-25 bomber. This scene is used five times in the film version, with each repetition employing an extension from the first few lines of dialogue toward a full enactment of the incident in which Yossarian discovers he was "helping" by binding up a superficial wound when the gunner had almost been disemboweled by a flack fragment. The essential scene in the book reads as follows:

> Dobbs was weeping when Yossarian jammed his jack-plug back into the intercom system and was able to hear again.
> "Help him, help him," Dobbs was sobbing. "Help him, help him."
> "Help who? Help who?" Yossarian called back. "Help who?"
> "The bombardier, the bombardier," Dobbs cried. "He doesn't answer. Help the bombardier, help the bombardier."
> "I'm the bombardier," Yossarian cried back at him. "I'm the bombardier. I'm all right. I'm all right."
> "Then help him, help him," Dobbs wept. "Help him, help him."
> "Help who? Help who?"
> "The radio gunner," Dobbs begged. "Help the radio gunner."

In a scene from *Catch-22*, Yossarian (Alan Arkin) learns from Dr. Daneeka (Jack Gilford, *left*) the no-win rules of the military establishment, as indicated in the title of the novel and film.

> "I'm cold," Snowden whimpered feebly over the intercom system then in a bleat of plaintive agony. "Please help me. I'm cold." [*Catch-22*, p. 231]

This is a moment of horror that is repeated in the mind of the protagonist in both media, but the film medium profits from a stronger emphasis on this incident. Yossarian, one of the few sane airmen at his base, has a fear of death, and the story of the novel and the film centers on his struggle against military officialdom to get grounded.

There is an attempt by filmmakers Nichols and Henry to retain the best satirical situations and characters from the original source. The basic thrust of the novel's title is well dramatized. Captain Yossarian pleads with the base physician, Dr. Daneeka (a part played by Jack Gilford), that he should be taken off duty so that he would fly no more missions. "Can't you ground someone who's crazy?" asks Yossarian. The doctor explains that when he says he is insane, he is actually sane enough to realize he might get killed if he flies more missions. The Catch-22 of the military is that Yossarian is thereby fit for duty (*Catch-22*, pp. 46–47). Heller delights in this nonsequitur and use of circular, faulty logic. He employs it as one of the key types of confused thinking that makes a military establishment during war such a strange world. But he extends this to other situations. When Yossarian meets and begins to fall in love with an Italian prostitute, she mopes because she is sure that he will not marry her because she is not a virgin. He says he will—that it makes no difference. She then declares he is crazy to marry her. Yossarian finds himself in another Catch-22 situation. He declares: "You won't marry me because I'm crazy, and you say I'm crazy because I want to marry you? Is that right?" [*Catch-22*, p. 164]

The repetition of the satirical Catch-22 in Heller's made world of circular, self-destructive thinking provides a pattern for both the novel and the film. It is also a no-win world for the hapless comic hero, a type of Everyman with the sanity and integrity that are rare traits in an environment peopled with wacky, amoral creatures.

In both the novel and film the chief antagonist of Yossarian is Colonel Cathcart, a sadistic, pushy commander who keeps upgrading the number of missions his men must fly before they receive some leave or a change of duty. Critic Arthur Schlesinger, Jr., known for his work as a historian and political analyst, noted that the portrait of Cathcart seems to be a lampoon of authority during the Vietnam conflict:

> Played by Martin Balsam in the film, he is a grizzled maniac in his fifties, bearing a considerable resemblance to Lyndon B. Johnson. To remove any doubt in the matter, Colonel Cathcart is given a scene, not to be found in the book, where he receives a subordinate while sitting on a toilet—an unmistakable allusion to what is said to have been one of the less beguiling administrative habits of the former President. Thus Cathcart's escalation of his war seems to spring from the basic policy madness of Vietnam, not from the more complicated problem of military mad-

ness within a rational policy as in World War II. [From
David Denby, ed., *Film 70/71*, Simon & Schuster, p. 81]

Part of the reason for Cathcart's slave-driving tactics in both
the novel and film is his desire to achieve fame. He pushes the
chaplain to write some "snappy prayers" to be delivered before
his men fly a mission. He hopes that this will help him get a
spread in the *Saturday Evening Post*. He wants the prayers to be
upbeat and not so somber. In the novel he states:

> "The men are already doing enough bitching about the
> missions I send them on without rubbing it in with any
> sermons about God or death or Paradise. Why can't we take
> a more positive approach: Why can't we pray for something
> good, like a tighter bomb pattern, for example? Couldn't we
> pray for a tighter bomb pattern?" [*Catch-22*, p. 197]

All top-echelon officers are self-serving and vicious in *Catch-22*.
General Dreedle is played in the movie with the sweeping authori-
tarian style that Orson Welles might use if he were playing Big
Daddy in Tennessee Williams's stage play *Cat on a Hot Tin Roof*.
He gets disturbed when a subordinate who produces a minor
irritation as he inspects the troops cannot, by an updated twentieth-century code of military conduct, be simply taken out and shot.
In *Catch-22*, there is no game of the men trying to outsmart
authority—a fantasy of the fluffy service comedy genre.

But a lower-echelon officer, Lieutenant Milo Minderbinder,
probably creates one of the most interesting views of the war in
the whole gallery of Heller's characters. His position in the story
is even upgraded by Buck Henry's adaptation. The wheeler-dealer
con man comes into his glory in the times of war when food and
military supplies can be acquired and traded. Milo is a parody of
that type of parasite, and he even confiscates the B-52 crew's
parachutes and the morphine from the first-aid kits on the planes.

During a bombing raid with flak filling the sky, Yossarian
becomes panicky and reaches for his parachute only to find that
it has been donated to what Milo calls his M & M Enterprises.
In one of the movie flashbacks as the protagonist opens a kit
of morphine to ease the agony of the dying Snowden, he finds
it is gone. In the novel a note is in the kit that reads: "What's

good for M & M Enterprises is good for the country. Milo Minderbinder" (*Catch-22*, p. 446).

This third flashback in the novel and the film (the movie has five) provides an indication that Milo is a war profiteer who cares nothing about the men in his outfit. In the movie the kit contains only a coupon for so much stock in the Minderbinder-created firm. The allusion Heller employs in the novel harks back to President Eisenhower's administration when Secretary of Defense Charles Wilson, a former head of General Motors who was accused of vested interest, made the mistake of uttering a similar phrase, "What's good for General Motors is good for the country." Created in 1970 the movie could, of course, hardly expect many to catch such an allusion from the fifties political scene. Furthermore, in the novel Lieutenant Minderbinder forms a group of bombers to bomb the United States Air Force base through a contract with the Germans. His concept of free enterprise is carried by Heller to a *reductio ad absurdum*. Milo engages in an inversion of values that is more perverse than that of the mad SAC commander of the novel *Red Alert* and its filmed version, *Dr. Strangelove*. Milo, who declares that war is too important to be left to the government, is strangely not insane but perfectly logical in his insistence that the system should be reversed:

> "Frankly, I'd like to see the government get out of war altogether and leave the whole field to private industry. If we pay the government everything we owe it, we'll only be encouraging government control and discouraging other individuals from bombing their own men and planes. We'll be taking away their incentive." [*Catch-22*, p. 266]

The movie does have Milo bombing his own base but does not examine his philosophy of free enterprise. The film may be confusing the issue when it shows Minderbinder riding in a military vehicle in Rome, standing tall in the perfect pose of a young Nazi officer. While some critics, such as Edward Grossman in *Harper's* (December 1970, p. 38), see Jon Voight as miscast in the role of Milo, his demeanor and youthful guile contrast sharply and delightfully with the sinister demeanor of the higher echelon: Colonel Cathcart, Colonel Korn, and General Dreedle. In Heller's novel Milo's nonplus amorality produces some of the book's best satire.

Coming after and on the heels of the giant box-office attraction *M*A*S*H* in 1970, the movie *Catch-22* had difficulties achieving the popular success of the predecessor. *Catch-22* also couldn't live up to the high critical acclaim given to the novel. No one really cared about the source of *M*A*S*H*. Also, there was something slightly askew in Nichols's direction of *Catch-22*. The blends of the comic and serious elements are not clearly defined. In retrospect the handling is not as faculty as it seemed on first viewing. Even so, Nichols may have been consciously trying to make a great movie from what he thought was a great novel. The strain shows—especially in some of the scenes in Rome when Nichols seems to be engaging in polemics or a series of Fellini-type images. Nevertheless, there are enough qualities to the movie *Catch-22* to rank it with such films emphasizing anti-war statements as *Dr. Strangelove* and *Slaughterhouse-Five*.

The George Roy Hill screen version of Kurt Vonnegut's *Slaughterhouse-Five* has received increasing critical acclaim since its release in 1972. Much of the negative criticism of the film takes the form of swipes at the author for his lack of depth. Paul D. Zimmerman was probably one of the most severe when he wrote of Vonnegut's work: "He is the Rod McKuen of social philosophers, manipulating sentimental symbols in complicated patterns meant to give them profundity" (*Newsweek*, April 3, 1972, p. 85). Vincent Canby of the *New York Times* was more favorably inclined to the novel and the adaptation, but he questioned the effectiveness of the anti-war statement as presented and stated that he believes the work does little more "than increase our smug satisfaction with our own high-mindedness" (*New York Times*, March 23, 1972, p. 51). In a review that was favorable, Arthur Knight concentrated more on the character of Billy Pilgrim, with an indication that the protagonist of the story was crushed by both the Dresden fire bombings and by the near-fatal plane crash—a view that Billy was not a simple, but a complicated satirical portrait (*Saturday Review for Science*, April 15, 1972, pp. 10–11).

The key to understanding Vonnegut's novel and the film adaptation lies in the character of Billy Pilgrim, not in the amount of emphasis on the anti-war statement, although this is tied to the comic development of Billy. Void of his own philosophy, Pilgrim

In a scene from *Slaughterhouse-Five*, Billy Pilgrim (Michael Sacks) is interrogated by two malcontents, Weary (Kevin Conway) and Lazzaro (Ron Leibman), who believe him to be a German.

depends on hand-me-down homilies and reductionistic truisms. The most obvious was Billy's "framed prayer" on his office wall, which Vonnegut states was "his method of keeping going":

> GOD GRANT ME
> THE SERENITY TO ACCEPT
> THE THINGS I CANNOT CHANGE,
> COURAGE
> TO CHANGE THE THINGS I CAN,
> AND THE WISDOM ALWAYS
> TO TELL THE
> DIFFERENCE

[from *Slaughterhouse-Five*, Delta Book Edition, 1969, p. 52]

Vonnegut intends this to be a satire of the middle-class, middle-brow mind. In his fantasy world of his life with simple, loveable, sexpot Montana Wildhack on the planet Tralfamadore in space, Billy discovers a locket between her huge breasts "containing a photograph of her alcoholic mother—a grainy thing, soot and chalk" on the front of which is written Billy's favorite prayer (*Slaughterhouse-Five*, pp. 180–181).

One of the effective ironies of the novel and film is the fact that Pilgrim becomes a mental case under duress. It would appear that such a modest mind would not be this fragile, but it should be remembered that even a mere dog's mind snaps when teased and prodded too much. Heller's comic protagonist of *Catch-22*, Yossarian, is a much different character. He is the sane and moral one in the world of the insane and amoral. Yossarian is fully aware of the dangers of the erratic society about him; Pilgrim is a klutz, nearly a zero. His mind does not comprehend effectively the chaos and dangers of war. His strange lack of comprehension brings him luck while others around him are maimed or killed because they react directly to the dangers they face. His anesthetized brain and naivete bring him luck. It is a comic character of nature that in some ways harks back to Voltaire's *Candide*.

Movie critics occasionally seem to take diametrically opposing views on the protagonist in *Slaughterhouse-Five*. The American Film Institute sponsored publication, *Filmfacts* (1972, Vol. V), indicated in its reprint of a number of views that the "critic consensus" of the film was "6 favorable, 4 mixed, 6 negative" (p. 94). Charles Champlin in the reprint of his *Los Angeles Times* review of March 24, 1972, finds the film "perhaps not intellectually profound, but it is impassioned, warm, human and positive" (p. 95). On the other hand, Gary Arnold in the *Washington Post* (review of August 29, 1972), points to the scene in the movie when Billy Pilgrim meets his wartime mentor and surrogate father, Edgar Derby. "The movie desperately needs some indication of simple human companionship and fellow-feeling, but the scene is slanted to make both men look stupid and ridiculous" (p. 96 of *Filmfacts*).

Is there a fault in the tone given to the movie by George Roy Hill and screenwriter Stephen Geller? Possibly. Yet another reason for the diverse reactions might be the way critics as well as general audiences react to satire. Champlin, in his own curious way, finds actor Michael Sacks moving when he displays "homely and innocent vacuous charm" (p. 95). Arnold wants satire to have a heart.

It is possible that Kurt Vonnegut as the author of the original fable for our times has not been sharp enough in his satire. He grapples with war and not too solid middle-class values that were being questioned in the sixties. Joseph Heller, with all his excesses in *Catch-22*, was probably more successful in his bout with war and the American way of life. Heller attacks his subject with the relentless spirit of the bull in the ring; Vonnegut scurries around like a terrier annoying a rat. And, there is some virtue in the two approaches and the results achieved. There are qualities in the filmic adaptations that transcend much of the critical comment that developed when *Catch-22* and *Slaughter-house-Five* were brought to the screen in the early seventies. Both of these film adaptations, with settings in World War II, showed the influences of the anti-war feeling of the period. Using more direct approaches to the Vietnam conflict and its consequences at the end of the decade, *Coming Home* (1978), *The Deer Hunter* (1978), and *Apocalypse Now* (1979) have not proved to provide as clear anti-war statements as the predecessors *Catch-22* and *Slaughterhouse-Five*. The attitudes expressed in all three of these more recent works are personal and oblique. They are, of course, not satires, and as serious anti-war statements they still are no match for director Lewis Milestone's screen rendition of the classic anti-war novel, *All Quiet on the Western Front* (1930).

A second wave of Vietnam war films appeared toward the end of the next decade, the eighties. In 1986 *Platoon* became a box-office hit, and the next year *Hanoi Hilton*, *Hamburger Hill*, and *Full Metal Jacket* proved that filmmakers were taking a more direct, uncompromising look at the war that had caused so much embarrassment to the government of the United States. Only Stanley Kubrick's *Full Metal Jacket* launched a satirical attack on this so-called peace action.

Indirect, analogous treatments in 1970, *M*A*S*H* (the Korean war) and *Little Big Man* (the Indian wars of the nineteenth century), seemed self-contained, and many filmgoers did not make the connection. However, Kubrick's adaptation of *The*

Short-Timers by Gustav Hasford, with the title of *Full Metal Jacket*, became a direct satirical assault on the controversial Vietnam war. This 1987 creation elicited high hopes from critics who ranked the director's *Dr. Strangelove* and *A Clockwork Orange* as two of the best satirical movies of the last three decades. His earlier ironic, anti-war, anti-authority *Paths of Glory* (1957) also had received kudos.

The reception of *Full Metal Jacket* in the summer of 1987 was mixed. This is partly because the watchguards of Kubrick's work expected a stronger hot war parallel to the cold war *Dr. Strangelove* and partly because they seemed to be expecting a decline from the director of the 1980 near parody of the occult genre, *The Shining*, a work too ambiguous for their taste. Judgments on *Full Metal Jacket* misfired, with expectations or desires on the part of evaluators to have a one-barrel, anti-war shoot. Similar attitudes were expressed in reviews of Hill's 1972 *Slaughterhouse-Five*, a work not only on the futility of war, but also on middle-class blandness, lack of perception, and muted emotional reactions. The inhumanity of all wars cannot be comprehended by a society composed of such apathetic people as those who will merely go along unquestioningly with their leaders. Kubrick, using Hasford's novel, takes a similar double-barrel approach. As in *Dr. Strangelove*, authority is ridiculed. Authority bungles, promotes, and perpetuates—subjugates and dehumanizes the individual. Corrupt, self-serving leaders were the focus of Kubrick's attack in his first anti-war statement in the ironically titled *Paths of Glory*. This is a recurring theme in the director's work.

Full Metal Jacket, some journalistic evaluators claim, proved faulty because it lacked unity, a work divided into two parts. Part one, the boot camp training according to Richard Corliss and Roger Ebert, was so powerful that it surpassed and weakened the second portion, the war in Vietnam. Actually, this design may be the Hasford-Kubrick parody of the many World War II films that started with an elaborate training period when the men were united into one strong fighting machine and then a second portion when the bonded group achieved victory or died for their country while fighting the enemy. Also, if the critics had reflected more carefully, they might have seen that these divisions are united by the warped views and actions of authority as well as the cynical reflections of the protagonist-narrator, Joker. In the boot camp portion Sergeant Hartman (Gerheim in the novel) badgers the recruits with verbal and physical abuse until he thinks he has created a unified killing machine. But the hardships of war plus the many anomalies and ambiguities of the actions of Vietnam create confusion in the ranks. The published movie script illustrates this as Joker wears a peace button and paints on his helmet, "BORN TO KILL." When Joker is questioned by authority, the platitudes of leaders are satirized:

JOKER:	I think I was trying to suggest something about the duality of man, sir. The Jungian thing, sir.
COLONEL:	Whose side are you on, son?
JOKER:	Our side, sir.
COLONEL:	Don't you love your country?
JOKER:	Yes, sir!
COLONEL:	Then how about getting with the program? Why don't you jump on the team and come on in for the big win?
JOKER:	Yes, sir!
COLONEL:	Son, all I've ever asked of my marines is that they obey my orders as they would the word of God. We are here to help the Vietnamese, because inside every gook there is an American trying to get out. It's a hardball world, son. We've gotta keep our heads until this peace craze blows over. [From the script published by Alfred A. Knopf in 1987, p. 72]

With comic exaggeration this passage from *Full Metal Jacket* parallels some of the attitudes expressed by General Westmoreland and other officers engaged in the Vietnam conflict. As in the novel *The Short-Timers*, the leaders seem to be the only ones who believe in the mission, but the platitudes do not hold the men together. Lower authority figures lose control. Squad leaders flounder and make costly mistakes that lead to their own men's death. In the final sequence of the film adaptation, the most dedicated killing machine, Animal Mother, strikes out on his own to urge the squad members to kill a sniper. In a blind rush two members and the squad leader, Cowboy, are slaughtered. Animal Mother's seemingly heroic effort would be rewarded in the typical gung ho war movies of the forties; in this climactic scene it is satirized. The sniper turns out to be a Viet Cong girl of fifteen. Men are killed in an assault that proves to be no victory. Thereby, the futility of the squad's effort places this main combat sequence and the climax of the movie into a vein of satire far beyond the ironic combat scenes of such works as *Platoon* and *Hamburger Hill*.

Author Hasford maintained comic control of his material in *The Short-Timers* by the use of first-person narration of the total story by Joker, who sarcastically relates:

> Sunday.
> *Magic show.* Religious services in the faith of your choice— and you *will* have a choice—because religious services are specified in the beautiful full-colored brochures the Crotch distributes to Mom and Dad back in hometown America, even though Sergeant Gerheim assures us that the Marine Corps was here before God. "You can give your heart to Jesus but your ass belongs to the Corps." [p. 19, the novel from Bantam Books 1983 edition]

Adapters Kubrick, Michael Herr, and Gustav Hasford transformed this passage into a hard-hitting iconoclastic order by drill sergeant Hartman:

> Today is Christmas! There will be a magic show at zero-nine-thirty! Chaplain Charlie will tell you about how the free world *will* conquer Communism with the aid of God and a few marines! God has a hard-on for marines because we kill everything we see! He plays His games, we play ours! To show our appreciation for so much power, we keep heaven packed with fresh souls! God was here before the Marine Corps! So you can give your heart to Jesus, but your ass belongs to the Corps! Do you ladies understand? [p. 40, from the published scenario]

Herr indicated that much of the voiceovers he wrote in one version of the adaptation were cut, so that only a few are left in the movie. In the combat portion of the movie, Kubrick employs an innovative visual medium to compensate for the reflections of Joker as they existed in the novel. Some of the members of the squad are interviewed for television. The anomalies and ambiguities of the Vietnam war are exposed by the men's reactions:

> EIGHTBALL: They don't really want to be involved in this war. I mean, they sort of took away *our* freedom and gave it to the gookers, you know. But they don't want it. They'd rather be alive than free, I guess.

Joker's comments to the interviewer are, as usual, sarcastic and reflect similar views used in the novel:

> I wanted to see exotic Vietnam, the jewel of Southeast Asia. I wanted to meet interesting and stimulating people of an ancient culture and kill them. I wanted to be the first kid on my block to get a confirmed kill. [pp. 85–86, from the published scenario]

Another innovative addition to the movie version is the final march back to the base camp after engaging the enemy. What is left of squads reassembles as a diminished platoon. Instead of the victorious marine hymn which we have witnessed in so many World War II movies of the forties as the men march from the battle back—or as spirits snaking their way to heaven—the soldiers of *Full Metal Jacket* sing the Mickey Mouse Club song that they have heard from television. Besides a song that becomes a comic substitution, there is a line that may indicate a bizarre substitution for authority. The lyrics sung by the men goes "Who's the leader of the club that's made for you and me?" It is, of course, M-I-C-K-E-Y M-O-U-S-E. Also, there is a portion of the song that has the group holding a "banner high" for the Mickey Mouse Club—instead of the Marine Corps. One of the few voiceovers left from a cutting of the original scenario puts a cap on any possible romantic, heroic version of a hero going home to his loved one, and it indicates Joker's

A tense and serious moment from *Full Metal Jacket*, with squad members Cowboy (Arliss Howard, *left*), Donion (Gary Landon Mills, *center*), and Joker (Matthew Modine, *right*), as they try to flush out a sniper.

reflections: "My thoughts drift back to erect-nipple-wet-dreams about Mary Jane Rottencrotch and the Great Homecoming Fuck Fantasy" (p. 120, from the published scenario). It is a final comment that undercuts the heroic tradition of so many war movies.

Reflective evaluations in the future may upgrade a judgment on the importance of *Full Metal Jacket* when the Vietnam war film genre has run its course. It probably will join the ranks of the satirical film versions of the novels *Slaughterhouse-Five*, *Catch-22*, and Kubrick's other anti-war, anti-authority film, *Dr. Strangelove or: How I Stopped Worrying and Learned to Love the Bomb.*

CHAPTER 4

CORRUPT AND CRUMBLING INSTITUTIONS

THE ENDING OF NATHANAEL WEST'S NOVEL *Miss Lonely-hearts*, created in 1933, was powerful and ironic:

> God has sent him so that Miss Lonelyhearts could perform a miracle and be certain of his conversion. . . .
>
> He rushed down the stairs to meet Doyle with his arms spread for the miracle. Doyle was carrying something wrapped in a newspaper. When he saw Miss Lonelyhearts, he put his hand inside the package and stopped. He shouted some kind of warning but Miss Lonelyhearts continued his charge. He did not understand the cripple's shout and heard it as a cry for help from Desperate, Harold S. Catholic-mother, Broken-hearted, Broad-shoulders, Sick-of-it-all, Disillusioned-with-tubercular-husband. He was running to succor them with love. The cripple turned to escape, but he was too close and Miss Lonelyhearts caught him.
>
> While they were struggling, Betty came in through the street door. She called to them to stop and started up the stairs. The cripple saw her cutting off his escape and tried to get rid of the package. He pulled his hand out. The gun inside the package exploded and Miss Lonelyhearts fell, dragging the cripple with him. They both rolled part of the way down the stairs. [*Miss Lonelyhearts*, New Directions edition, first published in 1950, pp. 57–58]

The 1958 movie adaptation *Lonelyhearts*, once more removed from the novel by Howard Teichman's stage version, has an unlikely reconciliation between the embittered, cuckolded

Peter Doyle, and Miss Lonelyhearts (called Adam White by film adapter and producer Dore Schary). The husband of Fay Doyle, a woman who received advice to the lovelorn from Adam and, in a private talk about her problems, seduced the columnist, has learned of her unfaithfulness and threatens the young man in his newspaper office. Adam claims responsibility for the liaison and promises not to see the wife again. Peter Doyle breaks down and cries, unable to carry out his threat. Adam's newspaper editor and boss, William Shrike, observes the encounter and, uncharacteristically, seems to be touched by this sentimental reconciliation. Consequently, the end of the movie becomes the pure, softhearted liberalism of Dore Schary with not a shadow of the dark, ironic satire of Nathanael West. All the characters of the novel are star-crossed—fated to live out their troubled lives without rehabilitation. Furthermore, Miss Lonelyhearts of the original work writhes in mental torment with the illusion that he is Christ born to help diminish the anguish of the poor souls who write to him for advice. The rush to embrace and save the cripple ironically causes his destruction.

Schary's warped ending of West's creation would make it appear there is hope for the lonelyhearts—an inversion of the novelist's grim world. The screenwright and director Vincent J. Donehue substitutes the sentimentality of the soap opera for a poignant, nihilistic satire. Even the sardonic Shrike seems transformed into a man with a heart as he asks Adam White to stay with the paper because he has begun to see his potential after, even in the movie, he has nearly succeeded in crushing the young man's idealistic view of humanity. Shrike goes off to his wife, whom he has constantly torn down for her single act of infidelity that occurred years ago. In tender pantomime he picks up a single flower from a vase and wraps it in a piece of paper from a desk, as he leaves, evidently, to present this gift to his wife as a gesture of his love. Reconciliation in the final sequence of the movie is even illogical within the context of the adaptation as it strays far from West's skilled, anti-sentimental vision of society.

One portrait in the movie, that of Fay Doyle as played by Maureen Stapleton in her first screen role, rings true to West. Here Fay is a pathetic creature plagued with an impotent husband—a woman who becomes sexually starved. As with most conflicts derived from the original creation, reality is softened and sentimentalized in the film by suggesting, in this case, that a marital rift of long-standing has made Peter Boyle psychologically impotent. In an attempt to follow the novel more faithfully, the film shows Adam White submitted to Fay's advances in order to help her, only to be caught in a trap. She wishes more sexual favors, not a one-night stand; thus, she becomes a woman scorned. In her desperation she becomes vicious. While Ms. Stapleton is not given all the dimension of her counterpart in the novel (scenes that develop her character are deleted to make room for un-Westian domestic scenes revolving around the protagonist's girl, Betty, who becomes Justy in the movie), the actress provides subtle innuendo in her portrait. Even as she rages when she thinks the young man has loved her and left her, she adds gestures and intonations to give sympathy to this curious woman—one of West's most fascinating grotesques.

Robert Ryan's Shrike, if the ending of the film can be ignored, has many of the qualities of the character in the novel. He is, as his name symbolically indicates, that bird of prey impaling victims on thorns. Ryan handles the cynicism and the purple prose monologues with deftness. An example from the novel (not used in the film) shows that the character's somewhat too clever improvisational speeches may be more acceptable on the printed page of a novel with a style which departs from realism. Shrike suggests that Miss Lonelyhearts find solace by embracing art:

> "Art! Be an artist or a writer. When you are cold, warm yourself before the flaming tints of Titian, when you are hungry, nourish yourself with great spiritual foods by listening to the noble periods of Bach, the harmonies of Brahms and the thunder of Beethoven. Do you think there is anything in the fact that their names begin with B? But don't take a chance, smoke a 3 B pipe, and remember these immortal lines: *When to the suddenness of the melody the echo parting falls the failing day....* " [From the novel, p. 34]

Adapter Schary uses a similar type of witty monologue— something akin to but a bastardization of Restoration drama's cynicism and wit. When the movie protagonist is given his instructions for his feature column, he is told by Shrike:

> "Many of the readers of this newspaper write to us, with no encouragement, hopeful that among us are seers, prophets, angels who can answer questions signed Troubled, Worried, Anxious, Perplexed, Impatient. . . . "
> [From the movie *Lonelyhearts*]

Although it has the ring of West's dialogue, it is not as smooth flowing and contains more glibness than Shrike's novelistic monologues. The movie does retain some of the dark humor in suggesting that the advice to the lovelorn columnist not give certain advice. The novel states it this way: "Remember, please, that your job is to increase the circulation of the paper. Suicide, it is only reasonable to think, might defeat this purpose" (from the novel, p. 18).

The most risible portions in both the novel and the movie often come from the sardonic observations of Shrike and his parodies. Shrike lampoons the lovelorn column as a substitute religion. The protagonist of the novel has such a parody printed on white cardboard that reads:

> Soul of Miss L, glorify me.
> Body of Miss L, nourish me.
> Blood of Miss L, intoxicate me.
> Tears of Miss L, wash me.
> Oh good Miss L, excuse my plea,
> And hide me in your heart,
> And defend me from mine enemies.
> Help me, Miss L, help me, help me.
> In saecula saeculorum. Amen. [From the novel, p. 1]

But the 1958 film generally avoids religious references and parodies by making the protagonist Adam White into a fragile, milquetoast humanist. As hard as Montgomery Clift struggles with the portrait of the tortured soul (a type of character Clift often did well), he cannot suggest clearly that Miss Lonelyhearts has a Christ complex. The novelistic protagonist recognizes his own plight and states bluntly to his "sweetheart" Betty, "I've got a Christ complex. Humanity . . . I'm a humanity lover. All the

broken bastards . . . " (from the novel, p. 13). As this quote
indicates, the character in the original work has more insight
into his problems than the screen version does, and he is un-
happy with some of his idealism. He would often like to dismiss
his bent and escape. The movie touches somewhat on this phase,
in a much softer way, by having Adam say, "I'd rather ignore
them than laugh at them"—referring to the public who write
him agonizing letters.

By avoiding most of the religious connotations of the novel
the movie saps the basic story to make some satirical statement
on the crumbling of some of our institutions—the medium's
quick fix is to substitute psychoanalysis for religion. However,
the movie does touch briefly on religion when Shrike gives the
fledgling journalist advice on his job. He states bluntly that
Adam is an authority on the subject of mental problems. When
Adam objects but states that he has read Freud and Menninger,
Shrike suggests that he avoid a modern approach and instead
"use the psalms, prayers—the entire panoply of organized
magic." While this may have been a bold statement for the
fifties, it seems rather pale and dated today.

The movie fails in recreating the savage approach of West.
He was detached yet concerned in his satire. Not one glimmer
of sentiment entered the pages of the tight, short novel on a
would-be Christ who not only destroys himself when he tries to
help people but also destroys the very people he tries to aid.
This satirical theme was well handled by Luis Buñuel in *The
Nazarin* (1959), one year earlier the movie *Lonelyhearts* was
created. But in order to reach a mass audience in the late fifties,
filmmakers could not examine religion in a negative light. Hollywood would not frankly touch a theme that focused on the
degeneration of society, a diluted, homogenized moral view of
life linked to religion. Instead, the creators of *Lonelyhearts*
focused on the domestic crises of the Shrikes and Doyles and
on the misalliance of Miss Lonelyhearts and his girl. In the fifties
any negative reflection on religion was taboo in the United
States, and it would not be until twenty years later that it was
fully explored in John Huston's *Wise Blood*.

Dealing with a similar subject in 1979, *Wise Blood* was a
creation which proved that its adapters could do almost every-

thing right in the transformation to screen, while the 1958 *Lonelyhearts* has filmmakers who did almost everything wrong. Amateur screenwriters Michael and Benedict Fitzgerald were not going by veteran director John Huston's contemporary success in his field (he had not had any strong box-office creations in the decade of the seventies) or some negating factors of his age, but were obviously impressed with his reputation when they approached him to direct their adaptation of Flannery O'Connor's *Wise Blood*. In the past Huston often scripted or co-scripted his own films—such adaptations as *The Maltese Falcon* (1941), *The Treasure of Sierra Madre* (1948), *The Red Badge of Courage* (1951), *The African Queen* (1951), and *Moby Dick* (1956). He might have also been considered to direct *Wise Blood* because the director had handled two adaptations of other Southern writers, Tennessee Williams's *Night of the Iguana* (1964) and Carson McCullers's *Reflections in a Golden Eye* (1967). At 73 years of age, Huston directed *Wise Blood* as his fifty-fifth film.

Almost unanimous critical acclaim greeted the New York Film Festival presentation of *Wise Blood* in 1979. The praise continued through the commercial run of the movie in 1980. Evaluators were amazed by this faithful adaptation of the novel and expressed the view that the film captured the spirit and tone of the book.* A good deal of the dialogue and nearly every sequence (with the deletion of a few scenes) were employed in the movie version. If these journalistic evaluations and criticism, often relying on the perception of the moment and many times impressionistic, are valid, there might be little to do but rehash and post-judge the praise given to the film. However, reactions to the film raise some interesting critical points.

First of all, there are some earmarks of an almost flawless adaptation of an important work by Flannery O'Connor, and this would seem to counter the view that less important works or even inconsequential writings make better movies. Evaluators have been prone to see this manifestation with Sir Laurence Olivier's *Henry V* (1945) and *Richard III* (1956) because they expected more from his *Hamlet* (1948), or such critics are less

---

*But not all agreed. For a negative view of the adaptation, see Stanley Kauffmann's review, *The New Republic*, March 15, 1980. p. 24.

inclined to find fault when liberties are taken with a work they consider a secondary effort of a top-rated writer. Second of all, there is a tendency for some critics to want a purist translation from word to screen which is, of course, a nearly impossible task when the adapter moves from one narrative mode to another, the novelistic to the dramatic mode.

To the first critical view some evaluators may argue that O'Connor is not a major author and that her status and work could, at best, be classified with that of Nathanael West. No attempt will be made to get into such classifications or ranking since this study deals with satire, and both O'Connor and West are among our best satirists in the United States. Also, it should be realized that it is an area of literature that has produced only a few noted novelists and playwrights throughout the world. However, in his rave reflection on the second viewing of *Wise Blood*, Vincent Canby develops the view that "classics" are seldom well adapted and writes: "It's usually true that literary works of something less than the first order make the best films, not because they are second-rate works but because the levels of their perceptions and their lack of idiosyncratic style are less afflicted by the methods of cinema" (*New York Times*, March 2, 1980, Part II, p. 19). He then concludes that because some works being adapted are not so revered, the translator can make alterations on the works necessary "to bring them alive, not simply on film but as films."

The second concept, the purist's desire to see as faithful a translation of the work as possible, is a more interesting critical point since the Fitzgerald-Huston adaptation appears to be relatively pure in its approach because it seems to deviate less from the basic characters and situations in the story than so many film versions of novels.

A focus on two important characters in the work, Enoch Emery, a young man who tries to force his friendship on the protagonist, Hazel Motes, and Hazel's landlady, Mrs. Flood, who also attempts to force herself on the belligerent, atavistic leading character of O'Connor's tale, will reveal some changes in the adaptation.

Enoch, attempting to be Hazel's friend and even his disciple, is slighted by this adaptation. Enoch provides the source of O'Connor's title as he verbally tries to counter Hazel's superior, stand-off attitude. Enoch accuses Hazel of thinking he has "wiser blood than anybody else. . . . " But it is the opposite Enoch claims: "Not you, *me*" (*Wise Blood*, Faber and Faber, 1962, p. 59).

In both the novel and the film, Enoch does exhibit his desire to be recognized as perceptive. In a bizarre O'Connor touch Enoch leads Hazel Motes to a museum to show him the shrunken corpse of a South American native—an object that eventually becomes identified as a new Jesus in the twisted mind of the would-be disciple. Much of this sequence was dramatized well in the film, but the identification between those two deranged lonely souls remains obscure. Enoch is, to a degree, a manic version of Hazel, the protagonist, who morosely slips into the dark shadows of depression. While some of the wildness of Enoch's tangled visions are translated, they are hard to dramatize since the novel does more easily state what is going on in his mind. Much of the first portion of chapter five of the novel takes time to explore his voyeurism—his hypocritical downgrading of and lust for prostitutes mixed with his attraction-repulsion when he peeps at scantily clad proper women in their bathing suits. As a hyperactive portrait of some type of madness akin to Hazel Motes, the adaptation could have included several scenes to develop the dimensions of Enoch's character that were strong features of the book.

Reviewer Robert Hatch of *The Nation* recognized the cutting of some of the Enoch Emory scenes. He felt that Enoch was "peripheral to the film" (March 8, 1980, p. 283) and believed the character "personifies the loneliness of spirit that haunts all the characters." Nevertheless, Hatch concluded with the view that "the essence of the book blazes from the film."

Mrs. Flood, Hazel's landlady, is another character that loses some dimension in the transfer of O'Connor's work to the dramatic film. This character's mind is revealed by narrating her thoughts as she reflects on ways to bilk the young man out of the money he receives from a war-service-connected disability, and the description is further advanced by her on-and-off ruminations as to whether she should commit him to a mental institution or hold on to him for her own advantage. The movie adaptation, however, does handle effectively any direct verbal contacts she makes with him, such as her proposal of marriage and her pathetic expression of loneliness as Hazel is about to leave her. The ambiguity of her feelings for Hazel is more difficult to reveal in a dramatization. And, finally, the province of the novel can be illustrated as Mrs. Flood has final thoughts on Hazel's plight (and consequently her own) as she looks down at the young man on the couch who has been found near death by the police and brought back to her. She stares into his mutilated eyes (in his fanaticisms he has blinded himself) and thinks that the eyes "seemed to lead into a dark tunnel where he had disappeared." When Mrs. Flood shuts her own eyes, the narration continues: "She saw him moving farther away, farther and farther into the darkness until he was a pinpoint of light" (from the novel, p. 232).

This simple but effective vision of Mrs. Flood on the mental death (and as the author reveals to the reader, the real death) of Hazel illustrates the power of the novel to conclude the strange relationship between two characters—to show how one lost soul affects another.

The strength of the movie is not muted by the limitation of inner reflections. Unlike the compromising *Lonelyhearts* of 1959, *Wise Blood*, twenty years later, did not worry about offending the religious sensitivities of the audience. Protagonist Hazel Motes struggles with basic questions of Christianity and develops an almost total inversion of the standard concepts prevalent in a region of the South that has all the excesses of the Bible Belt fundamentalist religion. Hazel wants to start his own religion of "truth" by developing a "Church Without Christ . . . that church where the blind don't see and the lame don't walk and what's dead stays that way" (from the novel, p. 109; also in the film). In this satire Hazel meets a fake blind preacher; his nymphomaniac daughter, Sabbath Lilly; and a con man named Hoover Shoates (played by Ned Beatty), who wants to promote the fanatic Hazel whom he discovers preaching on street corners. Ironically, the "Church Without Christ" seems to have a following, but the power of Hazel's message often is negated by his misanthropy. Eventually, he becomes a martyr by finally blinding himself after putting sharp rocks in his shoes and tight barbed wire around his body. Part of the ironic humor is that the fanatic Hazel Motes becomes religious in his own way— seeming to follow the excesses of the past. Mrs. Flood discovers his strange practices and tells him that it's not natural and that people have quit doing such things. With his odd-ball logic he declares that since he's doing it, they haven't.

Much of the humor in both the novel and film is bitter and hardly laughable. The religious satire mentioned above moves on this level. John Huston evidently had much to do with the final product. Recognizing the mixture of the comic and serious in *Wise Blood*, he chose a focus which blended the two—wishing not to move too far to a comic emphasis. It can be argued that his interpretation may have de-emphasized the satirical aspects of the novel, that people can understand the least satirical moments better. But it is possible that Huston wanted to treat the work respectfully and did not want to cheapen it. If this is true, the approach to the work can be credited with a basic honesty. In this work there are no added gags to seek audience approval. Thus it was a long way from the typical approach of the Hollywood film industry in 1949 when it produced Mark Twain's *A Connecticut Yankee in King Arthur's Court* and Nikolai Gogol's *The Inspector General*, which were turned to mere film fluff. The satirical points in both works were chucked out and pleasant entertainments substituted. These works were political satires, but the industry wasn't interested in providing the audience something close to the original novel; *Wise Blood*, a labor of love, said something, however obliquely, about a significant subject—religion—and suggested that here was an institution that might no longer help humankind.

While O'Connor's 1952 novel displayed the crumbling of religion in our society, other satirists had been worried about the function of the political institution. Created before the big movement of films using dark comedy and satirical themes in the sixties and seventies was the adaptation of *Animal Farm* in 1954 from the George Orwell 1946 satire—a film realized on the screen as a feature animated work.

Movie cartoons, before *Animal Farm*, were generally considered entertainment for children. Not noted for even one-reel cartoons, the British adapted as a feature a very important novel of one of the influential writers of their country. Therefore, the adult cartoon was born long before America's Ralph Bakshi would move in this direction. Bakshi took the underground cartoonist Robert Crumb's adventure of a feline named Fritz to create the dark humor, X-rated comedy *Fritz the Cat*, a feature-length animated film. This 1972 work had serious as well as comic intent—attempting to satirize the follies of the decade, both the establishment of the sixties and the youthful foibles of those who came in conflict with authority in that decade. While it may have achieved the status of a burlesque using dark comedy, it was never satire. But it was far from the light feature animations of Walt Disney. Before Hollywood could achieve something close to satire, the tendency was to water down or even delete any social comment. The penetrating views of Jonathan Swift, a satire on politics, was turned into a light fairy tale when Dave and Max Fleischer created the full-length cartoon *Gulliver's Travels* in 1939. With only minor faults, *Animal Farm* was the first feature-length animation to concentrate on political satire.

Basically faithful to the source, this version of Orwell's allegory does seem to borrow some from the Disney style of animation and the inclusion of some cute animals to achieve humor. A duckling, for example, gets in the way, and a bit of knockabout humor is achieved as he struggles to help the animals harvest the crop after they have revolted and taken the farm from Mr. Jones, their tyrannical, drunken owner. Fortunately, this type of added humor is not obtrusive since it is seldom used. Also, the caricatures of the humans, such as Mr. Jones, are broad comic villains who are only tangentially employed by Orwell; the movie, in an attempt to dramatize the plight of the suppressed animals, extends the conflict between the barnyard creatures and their masters. Such an extension, however, does little to distort the original unless a viewer of the film demands a pure, pristine adaptation. Only the changing of the ending of Orwell's tale does some violence to the original.

Orwell's short novel concludes with a hanging ending. In his allegory the animals shake a tyrant only to see the rise of a new regime that apes the suppression of the former. Herein lies the profundity of the author's work. Many revolutions establish formative societies that benefit the people, but sometimes such states fall into the hands of leaders who impose tyrannical reigns. Orwell shows the pig leaders of "The Manor Farm" as developing an allegiance with men for profit—much of the spoils of the farm are being drained off in trade for the benefit of despot Napoleon and his fellow pigs. As the animals look into the farmhouse window, they see Napoleon playing cards with the human collaborator Mr. Pilkington. The work concludes: "No question, now, what had happened to the faces of the pigs. The creatures outside looked from pig to man, and from man to pig, and from pig to man again; but already it was impossible to say which was which" (from *Animal Farm*, New American Library, p. 128). The novel's ending is cynical, the movie's ending more optimistic because the animals revolt for a second time, charge the farmhouse, and destroy the building and their oppressors.

Despite these alterations, which change the tone of the novel as it is transferred to the screen, John Halas and Joy Batchelor (both producers and directors) have achieved most of the satirical points George Orwell developed in the book. As a result they have produced one of the most significant film satires of the twentieth century, an age which has seen the rise and fall of dictators bent on conquering the world—especially fascist regimes that have promised the people a fuller life under a form of nationalism that gives broad powers to the State. The nostrum of the society led by the pigs in *Animal Farm* more directly satirizes the Communistic political system. The animals are promised equality, but the panacea is altered by the leader to a qualification that once seemed to be an absolute: "All animals are equal but some animals are more equal than others" (from the novel, p. 123; also in the film).

Created during the Cold War with Russia, both the novel and the film contain many situations that parallel the development of the USSR as a major power in the twentieth century. Much of the jargon of Communist rhetoric against alternate political systems is parodied: "workers unite" is turned to "animals unite," the animals call each other "comrade," and a great deal of code word rhetoric is used when the animals celebrate ritualistically the rebellion that supposedly liberated them from slavery. But Orwell's allegory has enough universality to apply to all tyrants. The head pig is named Napoleon, suggesting he is a symbolic figure for all countries and ages. Napoleon's use of vicious dogs as a type of police force to ferret out and kill dissenters seems to apply more to Hitler's SS troops because most audiences of the film and readers of the novel picture a similar secret police force in Russia as being more subtle in its tactics, while the end result may be the same. The movie stresses the action of the police force more than the book does; however, there is a clear-cut Russian lampoon when the animals in the film sing a freedom song composed by Matyas Seiber, who also scores the total movie. There is a distinct Russian flavor to what the book calls the "Beast of England" song (pp. 22–23) in the screen adaptation. Orwell writes with tongue-in-cheek when he calls the melody of this song "a stirring tune" that was something between the song "Clementine" and the song "La Cucaracha" (from the novel, p. 22).

The film also profits from the use of animation to provide a special emphasis. Journalistic critic Bosley Crowther recognized this aspect of the production when he reviewed the movie in 1954:

> The theme is far from Disney, and the cruelties that occur from time to time are more realistic and shocking than any of the famous sadism that has occurred in Disney films. The business of Napoleon bringing up puppies to be his own special pack of killer dogs, the liquidators of those who oppose him, is, for instance, blood-curdling stuff. . . . The shock of straight and raw political satire is made more grotesque in the medium of cartoon. The incongruities of recognizable horrors of some political realities of our times are emphasized and made more startling by the apparent innocence of their surrounding frame. [*New York Times*, December 30, 1954, p. 14]

Viewed today, *Animal Farm* has lost only a degree of the power it had in the fifties. The occasional abstract cartooning effects, which were developed by the Disney staff in *Fantasia* (1940), *Dumbo* (1941), and *Bambi* (1942), prove to be particularly effective during moments of physical combat such as the first rebellion against farmer Jones and the counter-rebellion of the barnyard animals against the tyrant Napoleon.

In 1979 a satire with a less scathing exposé of politics coupled with business, *Being There* by Jerzy Kosinski, was brought to the screen, with the author of the novel adapting his own work. The protagonist of Kosinski's story sets forth his views on gardening, which people mistakenly take as a profound philosophy of business and political trends. This character, Chance, states very simply:

> "In a garden growth has its season. There are spring and summer, but there are also fall and winter. And then spring and summer again. As long as the roots are not severed, all is well and all will be well." [From the collection *Seven Contemporary Short Novels*, Third Edition, 1982, p. 455]

Chance is, of course, speaking of his experiences as a gardener—one of the few bits of information he has gathered in his lifetime since he is mentally deficient—a moron and an illiterate. But he does have another source to draw upon for conversation. He is a recluse who has been protected from the world by a wealthy man. Chance has developed an addiction to television and measures the real world by what he has been able to assimilate from TV. When he bluntly states he does not read newspapers (he can't read), but watches prominent figures in politics and business on television, the press interprets his remark to mean that he is too busy with his work to bother with newspapers. Some of his direct, simple statements, plus his life-cycle-of-plants statement (mistakenly taken as a metaphor), make leaders in finance and government believe he possesses a superior mind. With this basic situation Jerzy Kosinski has created a penetrating satire that exposes the superficial attitudes and actions of the leaders in our society.

More than any film satire created in the decades of the sixties and seventies, *Being There* achieved much power in its final production. This can be attributed largely to the skill of the leading performer, Peter Sellers. The contributions of Hal Ashby, known for his dark comedy *Harold and Maude* (1971), and Kosinski are obviously strong, but the performance of Sellers, possibly the best of his career, helped make the whole situation plausible. All the actions and reactions of Chance are taken from his dream world that he can control with the flick of a switch, the TV channel changer. In the novel the mental states of Chance can be probed. When this hapless creature must leave his position as gardener for a rich man and wander for the first time in the real world, Chance's view of it is expressed:

> So far, everything outside the gate resembled what he has
> seen on TV; if anything, objects and people were bigger,
> yet slower, simpler and more cumbersome. He had the
> feeling that he had seen it all. [From the novel, p. 442]

This mental state cannot be fully reproduced in the movie adaptation without a use of voice-over narration. As the protagonist wanders in the big world, comic wonderment is developed in the movie without displaying the bad taste that could be present if some comedian like Jerry Lewis were handling the scene. His broad comic portraits of the retarded are gross when we consider today's sensitivity to their plight. Sellers imparts the proper tone to this vacuous creature's reaction to the world and even gives a touch of sympathy for Chance's struggle. With a bit of innovation that departs from the novel, the movie Chance stops an obese black woman he sees walking in a crowd and asks her for food. He does this because in the mansion where he worked, a black servant always brought him his meals. Newly arrived in the real world, he thinks all black motherly types must be conveyers of food. Chance says: "Excuse me. Very hungry. Give me some lunch" (from the movie). The black woman indignantly turns away from him and keeps walking down the street.

The protagonist of Kosinski's story by chance (probably the significance of the comic hero's name) once more is folded under the wing of a rich man, this time a tycoon named Rand, played by the late Melvyn Douglas, who received an Oscar for his performance. Chance's views of the growth of the garden impress the businessman and eventually are conveyed to the President of the United States. Rand ecstatically reacts to Chance:

> "Very well put, Mr. Gardiner—I hope you don't mind if I
> call you Chauncey? A gardener! Isn't that the perfect
> description of what a real businessman is? A person who
> makes a flinty soil productive with the labor of his own
> hands, who waters it with the sweat of his own brow, and
> who creates a place of value for his family and for the
> community. Yes, Chauncey, what an excellent metaphor!
> A productive businessman is indeed a laborer in his own

vineyard." [From the novel, p. 449; with similar dialogue in the film]

Chance's name has been developed by Rand, who switches the meek fellow's identification of himself as "Chance, the gardener" to Chauncey Gardiner. Also, his identity is further confused by his physical appearance. This simple laborer on a rich man's estate was allowed to wear the cast-off clothes of his employer and guardian. The cyclic nature of fashion makes Chance look as if he were dressed in the latest creation as a dapper man of the world. But most of all, the deception is made complete by the protagonist's seeming air of detachment and lack of concern. It is taken as the "pure cool" of a man with brains of superior dimensions.

In the movie *Being There* Sellers proves to be a master at portraying this air of detachment in a way to convince those too tied up in power struggles to see they are misinterpreting almost everything Chance says. They take his simple statements as profound in a world engaged in over-speak—a deluge of words that hinders communication and is often purposefully designed to be misleading and deceptive. Herein is the core of Kosinski's view of society, the sharpness and penetration of the satire. *Being There* also exposes the clingers to the society of big business and big government. Those sycophants—"yes men" and leeches to power figures—are also lampooned by Kosinski in both the novel and the film.

A long feature article under the Show Business section, called "Sellers Strikes Again" by movie reviewer Richard Schickel (*Time*, March 3, 1980, pp. 64–73), revealed that Peter Sellers, having read the novel in the early seventies, yearned to play Chance and saw the role as an "opportunity to bring his career to its culmination" (p. 64). According to Schickel, the ingenious portrait of Chance was probably created by the actor who was the master of impersonation—so much so that his real personality was never fully realized or developed. So many of his other comic portraits were comments on character types while Chance was closer to the real Peter Sellers, trying to find his place in the world. Whether this is true or not, there is little doubt that Sellers merged himself in the role more than in any other of his career. As we view the movie today, we seem to see

In *Being There* Peter Sellers portrays Chance, a low IQ gardener who mistakenly becomes a counselor for a tycoon and the President of the United States.

an actor no longer commenting on his role—in *Being There* he *is* Chance. Consequently, this film may develop even higher critical acclaim in the future.

Another film that focuses on the corruption in political and business institutions was developed in 1979: *Winter Kills*, an adaptation of Richard Condon's 1974 novel. When compared with the more subtle *Being There*, produced the same year, *Winter Kills* appears broader and heavy-handed. A millionaire, Thomas Megan, who has his hands in politics so that he can achieve more control and power in all phases of his financial empire, is etched in zany, burlesque strokes—a portrait far from the suave, genteel tycoon Rand in *Being There*. Megan of *Winter*

Kills, played with zest by John Huston, is a vulgar, self-centered capitalist who will stop at nothing to achieve his goals. It is possibly a deviant portrait patterned after the real-life patriarch Joseph Kennedy. Richard Condon's wild tale of power politics operates on some of the same levels of paranoia that can be witnessed in his earlier work *The Manchurian Candidate*, a work adapted to film in 1962, with direction by John Frankenheimer. Condon's 1974 fantastic fabrication draws from the many investigations and far-out speculations on President Kennedy's assassination. This novel attempts satire but more often ends up with ironic situations, some broad comedy and pasteboard characterization. The drawing of the millionaire Thomas Megan comes close to cartoon caricature. This can be illustrated as Condon has the seventy-year-old codger tell his son Nick how he dislikes some of his associates:

> Take Nolan, an army General, my roommate at Notre Dame. I made that son-of-a-bitch, just because he happened to get assigned to room with me in a jerkwater Midwestern college. But let anybody come to him from Texas with a hard-luck story and he'd cut off my balls to help him out. All right. Take Cerutti. Cerutti is not only the best research-and-development mind in the world outside of two Japs and a Swede who can't speak English, he is a full professor I bought right out of Yale, the big time. All right. He's sick. He can't stand people around him. So I made it possible that he didn't have to earn a living like every other rope-puller in the world. Sure, he's very smart, imaginative with the best analytic mind except three guys who I couldn't communicate with. I pay that reclusive little prick two hundred and fifty thousand dollars a year to handle all investigations for me and make them come out right, and I bought him a whole fucking island to himself so he wouldn't have to look at people. So what happens? He thinks I'm just a little Mick on the make. He thinks he's *superior* to me. [From the novel, Richard Condon, *Winter Kills*, New York: Dial Press, 1974, p. 10]

Author Condon gets most of his humor from this character, and the movie, aided by Huston's performance, follows suit. To show how director William Richert changes the tone of the original novel when he shows the death of this international financier, the concluding portion of the book and film need to be examined. In the novel Thomas Megan becomes a raving madman when his son Nick confronts his father with information he has received placing responsibility on Megan for the death of the older brother, Tim Megan, who was the President of the United States. The father threatens to lock Nick up and give him a prefrontal lobotomy; he goes to the ledge at the top of a fifty-story building and declares he will shout to the world to expose the conspiracy of a son who "bribed police and a crooked doctor" who "plans to take over my fortune on trumped-up charges so fantastic that they cannot be believed by any honest, freedom-loving, right thinking American" (from the novel, p. 304). The novel describes the fate of Thomas Megan as he slips on the edge and grabs at the folds of a gigantic flag which starts ripping. Megan is terrified and asks for help from his son, but the flag gives away and he falls to his death. In the adaptation by director Richert, who also wrote the screenplay, the son tries to reach down to help his father, but the old man tells him he'd be a fool to help because he'd be carried to his death also. The movie Thomas Megan, by contrast, remains cool and detached when he shouts to Nick: "If you get out of this alive, take our money out of the Western world and put it in South America! Brazil!" As the flag rips and he begins to fall backwards, he repeats "Brazil!" as he stoically slides down the flag and to his death fifty stories below.

While adapter-director Richert leaves the character of Nick essentially the way it is drawn in the novel, a straight and non-comic figure, he takes liberties with Professor Cerutti, played by Anthony Perkins in one of his many roles as a mentally disturbed person. In the novel Cerutti volunteers the information that puts the finger on the father, but Richert stages this scene of revelation as dark comedy. Nick threatens the professor with a blackjack that will break his arm. Cerutti refuses and Nick wacks his arm. "You clown, you've broken my arm," the professor says with annoyance. Nick breaks his other arm. Like a dispassionate scientist Cerutti observes and comments on the process. Finally, however, he gives in and reveals the truth.

Another example of Richert's alteration in character to achieve dark comedy is his portrait of Z. K. Dawson, a rough

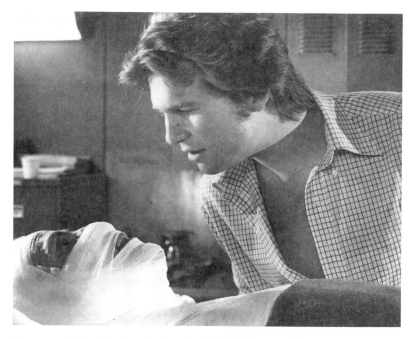

An unusual deathbed confession leads Nick Kegon (Jeff Bridges) to search for the assassin of his brother, the President, in *Winter Kills*.

old codger in the mold of Thomas Megan, another lampoon of the rugged individualist and capitalist by author Condon. He informs Nick that he had nothing to do with the assassination of the President because what Tim Megan did for him was good for his business (his investments in the war industry). "Your brother was a crisis-eating President. That is the only way that kind knows how to convey the illusion that he is accomplishing something—which he wasn't" (from the novel, *Winter Kills*, p. 96). Filmmaker Richert has Dawson spout a similar line but gives Dawson some of the character of the Hawkish John Birchite. Sterling Hayden as Dawson appears to be executing another version of his Jack D. Ripper from Stanley Kubrick and Terry Southern's *Dr. Strangelove or: How I Learned to Stop Worrying and Love the Bomb*. In the movie Dawson confronts

Nick, who is driving a small car, while he (Dawson) is in an army tank conducting his private war maneuvers on his ranch. Sterling Hayden has a beard and a demeanor that make him appear like the Old Testament God of Wrath or the abolitionist John Brown from a Thomas Hart Benton painting. He rages: "What are you doing on my field messing up my games?" After giving Nick a spiel on the fact that he profited from the brother's presidency and could have bought him off with his fortune if Nick's father hadn't already put Tim Megan in his pocket, Dawson chases Nick off his ranch by having his armored vehicle pursue his compact car and shoot at him as part of his war games. It is a wacky situation that seemed more in tune with a type of black comedy that was prevalent in the late sixties and early seventies—a type of anti-establishment movie comedy that was not in vogue by the end of the seventies.

William Richert's handling of Richard Condon's *Winter Kills* doesn't clearly have the bite of satire. The father's involvement in the conspiracy is softened by having Thomas Megan declare that he was caught up in the mechanization of the system of spying and corporation intrigue developed by Cerutti. The novel has the tyrannical millionaire fly into a tirade when he finds President Tim Megan viewing his role as one to help humankind:

> "It went to his head. . . . Front pages with his name everywhere he looked. It all turned him into a flag-kisser, for Christ's sake. He was all right for almost one year, then the whole razzle-dazzle turned his head. He peed all over his quotas. He decided to teach the niggers to read. He began to think we were all living in a democracy. He double-crossed me while he double-crossed himself. And I had every right to put out a life I had created in the first place. That's logical, isn't it?" [From the novel, pp. 302–303]

Furthermore, the movie version has Megan logically say when he is accused of putting out a contract for the death of his son so he could preserve his empire: "Wasn't money. For shame on you. . . . I'm the king of thieves but not a killer." Actually, there is vagueness in both novel and film regarding the father's role in the murder—much of it because both versions are overplotted and full of loose ends. What was intended to be satire is obscured by a maze of intrigue. A poignant statement on power politics and industry was attempted, but never fully realized.

Some lack of clarity in the satirical view on the depersonalization of the individual in the American industrial world was also evident in the adaptation of Elmer Rice's 1923 expressionistic play *The Adding Machine*. Both the source and the film adaptation, created in 1969, do not come to grips with the subject. The drama reflected some of the typical liberal cant of the teens and twenties—that people were being dehumanized by a mechanized society. Playwright Rice's protagonist, a man called Mr. Zero, possesses mathematical skills which make him a valuable employee, but in the name of efficiency and progress he is fired and replaced by an adding machine. The theatrical work provides a bitter and hardly laughable type of humor when it shows that a society of Zero's peers, all of whom are designated by numbers not names, has developed even entertainment into a mechanized ritual. They all live petty and pathetic existences. Rice provides a rather fuzzy satirical concept in his plot line after Mr. Zero kills his boss, is executed for his crime, and is condemned to operate an adding machine in the hereafter. At the end of this drama Zero is forced to return to the world of the living as a baby—his soul is to be recycled. The boss in this afterlife tells him: "The mark of the slave was on you from the start" (from the play, *The Adding Machine*, p. 268, in *The Theatre Guild Anthology*, first published in 1936 by Random House). Since Zero is a recycled slave from the beginning of time, Rice confuses the depersonalization of modern civilization by making a man who had troubles from the start—one who could not escape his destiny which seemed preordained by his inferiority. This ending is retained by the movie adaptation, created and directed by Jerome Epstein.

Nevertheless, the play and the film versions show the fate of the common person in a large city society gone sour by regimentation. Thus, in an indirect way it does satirize modern civilization. Using the expressionism that had its roots in the German theater of the teens, *The Adding Machine* poses cynical reflections on the fate of the individual such as those revealed in Georg Kaiser's play *From Morn to Midnight* (1916). Expressionism, a minor mode in the theater and the novel, often reveals the inner thoughts of individuals or groups directly to the audience in a highly stylized way. In fact, the adaptation of *The Adding Machine* retains the inner thought monologues and the intertwined mental reflections with a type of dialogue which reflects direct communication between characters. For example, when Zero is condemned to die for killing his boss who dismissed him after twenty-five years of faithful services, he delivers an inner thoughts monologue as an apologia:

> "Sure I killed him. Why didn't he shut up? If he'd only shut up! Instead o' talkin' an' talkin' about how sorry he was an' what a good guy I was an' this an' that. I felt like sayin' to him: 'For Christ's sake, shut up!' But I didn't have the nerve, see? I didn't have the nerve to say that to the boss. An' he went on talkin', sayin' how sorry he was, see? He was standin' right close to me. An' his coat only had two buttons on it. Two an' two makes four an'—aw, can it! An' there was the bill-file on the desk. Right where I could touch it. It ain't right to kill a guy. I know that." [From the play, p. 249]

In the stage directions of this scene, which takes place in court, the jurors sit with folded arms and appear not even to see, let alone hear, Zero. A similar scene with no reaction from the jury exists in the movie version, with this monologue from *The Adding Machine* well delivered by Irish actor Milo O'Shea, noted for his portrait of Bloom in the 1967 film version of James Joyce's *Ulysses*.

Adapter-director Epstein errs in the screen version by writing a discordant prison scene with Mrs. Zero, played by comedienne Phyllis Diller, as she complains to her condemned husband about all the trivial problems in her life. It achieves a type of dark comedy but does not fit well with Rice's original conception. Epstein also changes the Elysian Fields, a portion of the hereafter that is pleasant, to a seaside amusement park with some added contemporary comment on the alternate life-styles of the late sixties. Fortunately, Epstein does show Zero, forever the grubber with an obsession for work, rejecting this world of pleasure because he finds it immoral, thereby retaining some of the satire on a society that crushes *joie de vivre* from the life of those who accept the code of the work ethic as the dominant one to govern their attitudes. Even so, the film shifts the satirical social statement to Zero's personal problems in *The Adding Machine* about midway into the story and recovers only slightly when the movie retains the play's conclusion by showing Zero sent back to the world of the living to start another pointless existence.

It would appear that the education institution would escape the sting of satire because so many filmmakers used the salve of sentiment to depict the plight of teachers. From the 1939 *Goodbye, Mr. Chips*, adapted from the famous, popular novel of James Hilton, to the 1967 *To Sir with Love*, the devotion and trials of the teacher were more often presented sympathetically. Even by 1967 the comic treatment of the big city slum school in the United States in the film *Up the Down Staircase*, starring Sandy Dennis, gave no evidence of the subject being treated satirically—the film eventually evolved into a sweet, sentimental treatment. But in Britain three works—*If . . .*, *The Prime of Miss Jean Brodie*, and *The Decline and Fall of a Birdwatcher*— seemed to break the predominantly saccharine embrace of the educational institution. All three of these films were created in 1969 or were released in the United States that year; all three deal with the English public school; and all three moved in the direction of satire with varying degrees of success.

Of more concern to this study of film satire is the last-mentioned work, *The Decline and Fall of a Birdwatcher*. This work was adapted to screen by Ivan Foxwell from the 1928 novel by Evelyn Waugh—a significant first novel by one of Britain's leading satirists of this century. The actual title of the novel is *Decline and Fall*, a story of a young man, Paul Pennyfeather, who is unjustly expelled from Oxford and forced to take employment as a teacher in an inferior public school in Wales. The employment agent who arranges his job interview with the headmaster of this establishment bluntly informs the protagonist that his agency classifies institutions as "Leading School, First-Rate School, Good School, and School," and concludes, "School is pretty bad" (from the novel *Decline and Fall*, Little, Brown and Company's republished, 1977 edition, p. 14). Naturally, poor Pennyfeather is hired as a teacher in that lowest category—"School."

Waugh's novel shows irreverence not only toward the public school system (actually, a term that means the United States' equivalent to a private school), but also toward the snobbery, pretentiousness, and hypocrisy of the upper class. The penal system and religion also are dealt hard knocks. The overall design of the novel shows all these institutions interlocked. A key to the humor of the novel's interwoven social criticism is provided when educational and penal inhabitants are compared by a former, fussy schoolteacher named Prendergast who has taken over as prison chaplain. He complains to Pennyfeather, who has also left the profession of teaching, "Criminals are just as bad as boys" (from the novel, p. 223).

A Waugh-type aphorism appears in the movie version that shows a similar parallelism in the social satire. Paul Pennyfeather reveals how he can accept prison life for the sake of an older woman who has taken him for her lover. She is a high-fashion lady of questionable character, a comic femme fatale who has let Paul take a prison rap for her elaborate enterprise that deals in an international chain of brothels. He explains how he can adjust to his life behind bars:

> Anyone who's been to a British public school will feel comparatively at home in prison. It is only those brought up in the gay intimacy of the slums who find prison soul destroying. [From the movie, *Decline and Fall of a Bird-watcher*]

While this kind of remark from the Candide-like Pennyfeather seems inconsistent with the character that Waugh tries to establish in the novel, the film dramatization moves along in a way that this might not be noticed.

The adaptation of *Decline and Fall* is generally faithful to the development of the plot and character as it was set forth by Waugh in his first novel. There is, surprisingly, a certain amount of condensation of this short work. But only a few minor characters are deleted, and some lengthy monologues, which probably work better on the printed page, are deleted or condensed. What is missed in the film by one who has read the novel are the pub scenes, which depict the con man teacher Captain Grimes talking with the protagonist. The novel shows a camaraderie

developing between the apprentice teacher and the nearly degenerate veteran teacher. Grimes's endless confessions of how
he has a tendency to get, as he states it, "in the soup" are
humorous. As a way of condensing, the movie adaptation moves
some of these conversations to the teacher's rooms in the
school. Grimes explains that the system will never let a person
down. When he is dismissed from a job, he always gets a recommendation so he can find another position. As he states this in
the book and movie: "They may kick you out, but they never let
you down. I've been put on my feet more than any living man"
(from the novel, pp. 32–33).

This study in incompetency and questionable hiring procedures has been transferred from novel to screen. The actual
running of a school in the movie is more sketchy than the novel's
chronicled inadequacies of the boys' school run by Dr. Augustus
Fagan. This headmaster of the institution engages in grandiose
speeches as if he were a more educated version of Micawber
from Charles Dickens's novel *David Copperfield*. Many of the
deceptions and mechanizations of this delightful character, well
enacted by Donald Wolfit, are retained in the movie, but some
of the reflections of Dr. Fagan have been cut. Even though this
educator and his institution exist in Wales, he shows a disdain
for the people of the land and delivers his view of the evils that
lurk in the land:

> "I often think that we can trace almost all the disasters of
> English history to the influence of Wales. Think of Ed-
> ward of Carnarvon, the first Prince of Wales, a perverse
> life, Pennyfeather, and an unseemly death, then the Tu-
> dors and the dissolution of the Church, then Lloyd
> George, the temperance movement, non-conformity and
> lust stalking hand in hand through the country, wasting
> and ravaging. But perhaps you think I exaggerate? I have
> a certain rhetorical tendency, I admit."

Dr. Fagan then observes that Wales is a country that has
produced no art or drama and concludes: "They just sing" (from
the novel, p. 83). This is very colorful humor, but movies depend
on an international market, and Ivan Foxwell as adapter probably believed that such fascinating digressions, while they developed the character of Fagan, were too local. It became

necessary to delete this satire on the prejudice of the Britisher who wants to maintain his superiority.

About midway into the movie Paul develops a yearning for a Mrs. Margot Beste-Chetwynde. Since this woman and her friends are benefactors of the boy's school, the satire on high society becomes linked with education. An affair is initiated by Margot when she has her fourteen-year-old son engage Penny-feather as his tutor during school vacation periods. Paul is smitten by the mature sexuality of Margot. He readily accepts the post and becomes one of many of Margot's lovers. Since the novel and the subsequent film are stories of initiation of youth, comedy is achieved by showing the reactions of a naive person to a sophisticated, complicated world. Eventually, though, Paul will learn and be a con artist like everyone else—a thread of the plot Waugh used in his 1948 novel *The Loved One*.

The basic weakness of the movie version of *Decline and Fall* is the director's interpretation of the protagonist or the actor Robin Phillips's inability to handle comic reactions. Director John Krish seems to have Phillips play the role as straight as possible, without capturing the confusion and wonderment of a youth caught up in a corrupt world. He cannot fully cope with or change his destiny, hence the author's use of the term "decline and fall" for the title. The casting director should have provided this production with the talents of an actor like Michael Crawford, a British comedian who played some very funny leading men—young naive men. For example, he played Hero in *A Funny Thing Happened on the Way to the Forum* (1966) and Goodbody in *How I Won the War* (1967).

Most journalistic critics of the late sixties did not see the portrayal of the protagonist as a basic flaw in the production of *Decline and Fall of a Birdwatcher*. Vincent Canby of the *New York Times*, however, did recognize this deficiency when he wrote: "Robin Phillips is appropriately handsome and passive, but without any real comic dimension" (*New York Times*, January 27, 1969, p. 26). Both Canby and Hollis Alpert gave credit to the production for being faithful to the original: "It is as good a satire as I have seen lately," wrote Alpert (*Saturday Review of Literature*, February 15, 1969, p. 50). But quite a few critics (Canby and Alpert were among them) felt the work suffered by being updated rather than being set in the late twenties.

It is difficult to tell whether the updating of Waugh's *Decline and Fall* did produce a distortion that adversely affected the final creative product. Waugh's satire seems to avoid temporal elements and social fads. Much of his comic attack on education and society concentrated on inadequacies of institutions and the follies of people that will never be wholly corrected or resolved. The novelist, even at the age of twenty-five, with many of the weaknesses of a young writer, nevertheless displayed a keen grasp of absurdity in many human efforts. Fortunately, the movie presents enough of Waugh's world in a way that makes it one of the better film satires.

Probably one of the most curious attempts at film satire in the sixties was the screen version of the British theatrical piece by Spike Milligan and John Antrobus called *The Bed Sitting Room*. Richard Lester directed this film in 1969—a work that retains some of the characteristics of music hall comedy sketches and the absurdist drama of Samuel Beckett, a combination that is not as odd as it may seem since Beckett's plays have some facets of the popular theatrical forms. Without some background by reading or witnessing the absurdist theater of the fifties and sixties, the average moviegoer probably became lost in an incomprehensible maze of non sequitur situations. In 1960 there was some acceptance by the British public of this theatrical mode when playwright N. F. Simpson created *One Way Pendulum*, a comedy about an eccentric English family, with each member engaged in some wacky hobby or obsession, but this subject was literally closer to home.

The Bed Sitting Room takes place in the rubble of the aftermath of World War III. People live in a huge junkyard—sleeping in carcasses of automobiles, vans, and a subway train; rummaging in heaps of debris and mudpits for clothing and food. In this wasteland the incredible happens. Through a bizarre type of nuclear fallout mutation, a man named Lord Fortum, enacted by Ralph Richardson, turns into a portion of a house; hence, the title: the metamorphosis is into a "bed sitting room." A woman (played by Mona Washbourne) of a wandering family, who is simply called "Mother" by the authors, gets lost from her kin as they travel through the gigantic plain of junk and starts to cry. She reaches just below her ample breasts and pulls out a drawer in her stomach to obtain a handkerchief—a gag with

shades of a Salvador Dali painting. Bulging-eyed Marty Feldman, playing a female nurse, periodically pops into view, trying
to help people who are ill, generally botching his errand of
mercy. These are only a few examples of a film filled with the
kind of madness that Richard Lester was able to pull off in a less
surrealistic world of the Beatles creation, *A Hard Day's Night*
(1964) and *Help!* (1965). While Lester communicated his intent
to create an anti-war satire in *How I Won the War* (1967), *The
Bed Sitting Room* remains an obscure curiosity. There does seem
to be a satire on the rigidity of the British temperament; despite
the devastation each person tries to carry on as he or she did
before. An official merely called Inspector (Peter Cook) combs
the landscape suspended from a primitive balloon, informing
people that they must keep moving and avoid congregation
because they will offer a better target for the bomb. Since all
nations seem to have been reduced to rubble, his orders are
pointless. A physician, Bules Martin (Michael Hordern) continues to practice medicine, with a door frame and a couch for an
office—ludicrously trying to carry on in ankle-deep water as if
the conditions were the same as those before the atomic bombs
dropped. However, Lester's rendering of these scenes fails to
make a unified point. Even with an excellent cast of such skilled
actors as Ralph Richardson, Michael Hordern, Mona Washbourne, Peter Cook, Dudley Moore, Spike Milligan, and many
more, the comedy does not rise from the trash heap in which
the scene is set.

    While *The Bed Sitting Room* may have intended to show the
degeneration of all institutions in British society, a more effective approach to such a theme in the American society was
realized in the 1974 *The Day of the Locust*, an adaptation of
Nathanael West's 1939 novel. John Schlesinger, best known for
directing *Far from the Madding Crowd* (1967), *Midnight Cowboy*
(1969), and *Sunday, Bloody Sunday* (1971), was, according to
interviews that have appeared in film journals, enthusiastic
about the project and worked closely on the screen version of
West's work with Waldo Salt, a writer who also adapted *Midnight Cowboy* for the director. Although *The Day of the Locust*
was considered by literary critics to be one of the best satirical
novels on the world of Hollywood, the results achieved by the

director and adapter are not as much as most critics hoped for, but were significant enough to achieve a great deal of attention.

Critic Jay Cocks expressed succinctly part of the deficiency that exists in the screen version:

> Salt's adaptation follows West's novel closely in most of the plot details. It misses what is most crucial: West's tone of level rage and tilted compassion, his ability to make human even the most grotesque mockery. The novel, a series of interrelated sketches, does not have the strong narrative that lends itself best to film adaptation. So this movie has trouble finding focus. [From *Time*, May 12, 1975, p. 58]

As Cocks suggests, the virtue of the author as a satirist lies in his ability to attack the flaws and failures of people yet allow the reader some identification with the lonely souls in his well-honed tales. A key to this unique type of satire can be found in the text of *The Day of the Locust* as West provides philosophical reflection on the plight of those seeking a better life:

> Once there, they discover that sunshine isn't enough. They get tired of oranges, even of avocado, pears and passion fruit. Nothing happens. They don't know what to do with their time. They haven't the mental equipment for leisure, the money nor the physical equipment for pleasure. Did they slave so long just to go to an occasional Iowa picnic? What else is there? They watch the waves come in at Venice. There wasn't any ocean where most of them came from, but after you've seen one wave, you've seen them all. The same is true of the airplanes at Glendale. If only a plane would crash once in a while so that they could watch the passengers being consumed in a "holocaust of flame," as the newspaper put it. But the planes never crash. [From the novel, *The Day of the Locust*, New Directions paperback, pp. 177–178]

In this passage West reflects on those who come to the would-be promised land only to experience boredom to the point that they believe they have been "cheated and betrayed." West concludes: "They have slaved and saved for nothing" (p. 178). When the author explains the inner rage of the mass, the satire takes on an interesting dimension: these people are the ones who become not only vicarious sadists, they are a mob with the anarchic power to destroy civilization.

One of the leading figures in *The Day of the Locust*, Homer Simpson, would seem to be the least likely person to have this inner rage. A former hotel bookkeeper from the Midwest, his illness prompted him to come to the coast; as West states it, one who "seemed an exact model for the kind of person who comes to California to die" (p. 79).

The movie Homer, well played by Donald Sutherland, seems to reflect best the one who eventually gives way to an inner rage and, ironically, also becomes a victim of the mob. A reflective, critical examination of the film by Edward T. Jones indicates how director Schlesinger assists Sutherland in developing a disturbed mental state in one of the scenes:

> When Schlesinger lets his audience be taken by visual rather than verbal surprise, he is closest to finding a cinematic equivalent for West's style. One such instance is the superb analogy established between Donald Sutherland's Homer Simpson and a lizard. As the displaced Iowan sits in his dilapidated lawn chair, staring at the lizard, the creature stares back at him as if in recognition of the obviously shared physical resemblance and, more deeply, of a primordial brotherhood. Meanwhile, an orange falls from a nearby tree with a hollow sound, suggestive of an abyss beneath the surface of the earth which will shortly also look back at Homer. The sequence is original with Schlesinger and Salt, but it is thoroughly Westian in spirit and form. [*Literature/Film Quarterly*, Summer 1978, pp. 224–225]

The director also shows the inner tension of Homer in various awkward social situations by showing close-ups of his large hands—showing the character as not quite realizing what to do with his hands. This is most evident when this middle-aged man meets and develops an affection for Faye Greener, a seventeen-year-old bit player who wants to be a star. He becomes very anxious, inwardly disturbed, to the point that he squeezes and breaks a glass that he has in his hand.

The downfall of Homer in the novel and movie results from his relationship with two youths: Faye, who consents to a live-in arrangement at Homer's house that does not include a sexual relationship; and a child, Adore Loomis, an androgynous brat whom his mother hopes to turn into a moppet star. Homer's relationship with Faye turns sour as she becomes bored with the kind but shy man and, during a wild party in Homer's house, she readily ignores him and goes to bed with another man. In utter despair when he discovers Faye's infidelity, he packs his bags to leave Hollywood. Wandering down the street toward the bus station, Homer is caught in the crush of the crowd attending a Hollywood premier showing of a film, an event with many visiting stars. Having taunted Homer before, the boy Adore verbally mocks him again, and because the adult ignores him, throws a rock which hits Homer. Homer's inner rage breaks forth and he chases the child. When Adore trips and falls, Homer insanely stomps up and down on the child. When the crows sees this horror, they rush the madman and claw and beat him to death.

This apocalypse which forms the climactic sequence of the novel focuses on people fighting and struggling. The movie shows people running amuck to the point that property is burned and the world seems engulfed in flames—a holocaust that is symbolic of the collapse of civilization.

While some critics might fault the filmmakers for this melo-dramatic extension of West's climax, I believe it is necessary to visualize in broader terms the vision of impending doom developed by another leading character, Tod Hackett, an artist. Tod in both the novel and film engages in sketching and painting images of people whose faces reveal their inner being. And he develops a vision of what he calls "The Burning of Los Angeles." Following the novel, the movie employs expressionistic visions as Tod gets caught in the middle of the riot and has his leg painfully crushed and broken in the crunch. His mind reeling, he pictures the mob marching mindlessly for some crazy cause, and in the text West concludes: "No longer bored, they sang and danced in the red light of flames" (p. 184). As Tod is being taken to the hospital, the final lines of the novel state:

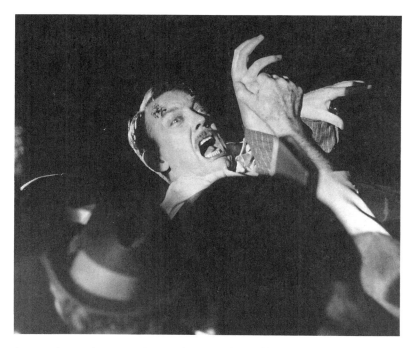

A crazed crowd at a movie premiere attacks and kills Homer Simpson (Donald Sutherland) in a climactic sequence of *The Day of the Locust.*

> The siren began to scream and at first he thought he was making the noise himself. He felt his lips with his hands. They were clamped tight. He knew then it was the siren. For some reason this made him laugh and he began to imitate the siren as loud as he could. [From the novel, p. 185]

The Day of the Locust as a movie would have more lasting emotional impact with this ending, but the filmmakers, having established more of a relationship between Tod and Faye than West allowed in the book, chose to incorporate a resolution in pantomime, showing Faye returning to Tod's apartment which he had vacated, as if she were concerned that the young artist had departed from Hollywood.

This extended ending and the interpretation of Faye in the film seem to be the most serious digressions and misrepresentations of the novel. Using Karen Black for the role of Faye Greener was questionable casting. Ms. Black was thirty-three at the time of the film's release, and it became obvious to most viewers that she was not the seventeen-year-old Faye Greener, an aggressive, promiscuous young woman whom West described as "taut and vibrant" (p. 94). Schlesinger indicated in an interview (*Literature/Film Quarterly*, Spring 1978, p. 113) that he tested younger actresses, but found that it was hard to get the depth that West achieved in this fascinating depiction of a woman. He, therefore, opted for an older, more skilled performer. Unfortunately, there are few scenes when Ms. Black can convincingly play the self-centered nymphet that destroys Homer and eludes the embraces of Tod Hackett.

Director Schlesinger is more successful in the casting and handling of most of West's grotesques: Abe, the pugnacious, whoremongering dwarf (Billy Barty); Harry Greener (Burgess Meredith), the father of Faye and out-of-work vaudeville comedian who sells phony elixir door-to-door with a dance and magic act for each potential customer; and Adore, the vicious, androgynous child (Jackie Haley). These characters are slightly extended and given a bit more dimension than in the source, but they fit well into the gallery of Westian eccentrics. Added to the personae by Salt is an Aimee Semple McPherson-style evangelist (Geraldine Page), who proves to be in tune with West's cynical description of the many freakish religious cults that existed in California during the thirties. In the novel Tod Hackett attended many Hollywood "churches" looking for models for his drawings. For anyone acquainted with such sects, the parody is close to the original:

> He visited the "Church of Christ, Physical" where holiness was attained through the constant use of chestweights and spring grips; the "Church Invisible" where fortunes were told and the dead made to find lost objects; the "Tabernacle of the Third Coming" where a woman in male clothing preached the "Crusade Against Salt"; and the "Temple Moderne" under whose glass and chromium roof "Brain-

Breathing, the Secret of the Aztecs" was taught. [From the novel, p. 142]

Screenwriter Salt invents a sequence with an evangelist named Big Sister who tries to cure the ex-vaudevillian Harry Greener of a long illness. He becomes thoroughly engaged in the attempt at a miracle, for it puts him back on stage. As the evangelist pulls him from his wheelchair, forcing him to stand, we witness a subjective view from Harry's mind as he pictures himself once more a clown before an appreciative audience. This innovative portion of the movie version adds rather than detracts from West's satire.

As has been stated earlier, *Time* critic Jay Cocks may be right in his view that *The Day of the Locust* strays from the novel by not achieving the "level rage and tilted compassion" of West. Some of the examples that have been quoted from the novel reveal the author's ability via the written medium to make philosophical observations. These philosophical observations seem to me to be the deciding factor in achieving the gamut of Westian satire. The adapters would have had to resort to voice-over narration using passages from the book to achieve more dimension, but they chose not to use a technique which was often used in thirties and forties adaptations. Nevertheless, the Schelsinger-Salt version does translate much of the tone of the original work. A person need only turn to the 1959 adaptation of *Miss Lonelyhearts* to see how far the film's sentimentalization of West goes to mute and even negate the attack of this satirist.

The Day of the Locust remains as the culmination of the corrupt and crumbling institutions of our country. West had a broader vision than some readers of the novel and viewers of the film might think. With agony he seems to see the collapse of civilization, not just the demise of a would-be idyllic life-style or the ravages of Hollywood that promote dreams to avoid reality. While some satirists concentrate on the flaws of the leaders as the corrupters, West's profundity is that he can see the seed of disaster in the followers, the disillusioned—those who live lives of quiet desperation.

CHAPTER 5

SEX, LOVE, AND OTHER MISALLIANCES

A *VARIETY* REVIEW CREDITED TO "MURF" on December 18, 1968, evaluating a spoof of the pornographic novel *Candy* as a screen adaptation, observed perceptively that "the emancipated screen" found filmmakers still unsure of themselves when they handled explicit sexual comedy. Odd as it may seem, the harsh-sounding, fricative, four-letter Anglo-Saxon word for sexual intercourse seemed still to be taboo in the 1968 film—even though avant-garde director Shirley Clarke retained the word as used by morphine addicts for a fix in the 1960 screen version of the play *The Connection*. But the word for all that was going on visually, "fucking," would soon emerge to offend some sensitivities of proper folk. By the late sixties it was possible in the United States cinema to simulate the sexual act and use almost all the blue language that had already been used in the novel, night club acts, and the legitimate stage. A decade and a half had passed since director Otto Preminger defied the production code by leaving in such terms as "virgin" and "pregnant" in the adaptation from the stage play called *The Moon Is Blue*, a 1953 work which was still in an age when the embrace of the lovers required the traditional fade to black.

Candy may have suffered not only because the film medium was self-consciously trying to handle racy material that had no firmly established tradition (filmmakers generally were used to innuendo), but also because of the inadequate directing by actor Christian Marquand. He seemed to have few qualifications for directing the film other than the fact that he appeared as a virile man with Brigitte Bardot in such works as *And God Created*

Woman (1957), a French film, and had directed *Of Flesh and Blood* (1963), a French-Italian production. Most reviewers of *Candy* evidently found the directing to be the basic weakness in this adaptation from Terry Southern and Mason Hoffenberg's popular lampoon of the pornographic novel. However, closer attention should have been paid to Buck Henry's screenplay.

Screenwriter Henry had co-scripted and received an Oscar nomination for the 1967 box-office hit *The Graduate*, based on a novel that more easily allowed for adaptation because it followed a narrative design that fit more easily with the dramatic mode. *Candy*, on the other hand, had many of the episodic and vignette characteristics of the pornographic novel—a series of adventures of the naive, hapless heroine who is sexually conned and assaulted by a variety of men. And, it should be noted, the black comedy writers who found this theme intriguing were not the first to handle such a parody. Nathanael West, who might be considered one of the godfathers of the movement, created a novelette, *A Cool Million*, as an inversion of the Horatio Alger, Jr., success story, in which both the hero and heroine are assaulted both physically and sexually.

Buck Henry errs most in his translation of *Candy* from novel to screen by casting aside the most basic motivation for Candy, the heroine, to rebel against her stuffy father, Mr. Christian. However, he retains the satirical facet of her personality which often sets her motives for yielding easily to men who seduce her. She gives sexual favors with the innocent air of a virgin to either the downtrodden or to older, lecherous men whom she admires for their feigned lofty ideals. Furthermore, Henry changes her father, to whom she constantly refers as "Daddy" by making him an effete social science high school teacher with a self-image problem instead of the proper businessman with stodgy, middle-class values. To further warp the focus of the Southern-Hoffenberg original expository basis for the sexual satire, Henry turns a phony liberal professor called Mephesto, who attempts to seduce Candy, into a visiting dipsomaniacal poet with Byronic poses and some of the quirks of a rakish Dylan Thomas. As in so many adaptations that employ guest stars, it could be that a more colorful character was devised so that Richard Burton might play a more dashing character rather than an overweight, lecherous college professor.

What Buck Henry cut and added in adapting the novel *Candy* may be said to be one of the basic problems that was at least recognized by the nameless *Time* magazine movie critic. What was basically a "satirical novel," as this evaluator stated it, bore the same relationship "in much the same way that an elephant might be based on a mouse" (*Time*, December 27, 1968, p. 56). It could be that *Candy*, while not a sex satire of the highest order, was, at least, one of the most vital, lively attempts in the black comedy literary tradition of the late fifties. As a narrative to be read, the novel at times exhibited a skill in handling conventional attitudes toward sex—holding such views of the uptight middle class to be foolish. The surrealistic vision of a father, horrified at the violation of his daughter and trying to protect her virginity, can be quoted as one of the most interesting passages in the novel. It is nearly untranslatable to the screen unless this vision were done on a surrealistic level; even then, the visual would be offensive when depicted. When Mr. Christian discovers his daughter in bed with the Mexican gardener, Emmanuel, his mental anguish bursts forth with bizarre images:

> It was not as though he couldn't believe his eyes, for it was a scene that had formed a part of many many of his most lively and hideous dreams—dreams which began with Candy being *ravished*, first by Mephesto, then by foreigners, then by Negroes, then gorillas, then bulldogs, then donkeys, horses, mules, kangaroos, elephants, rhinos, and finally, in the grand finale, by all of them at once, grouped around different parts of her, though it was (in the finale) *she* who was the aggressor, *she* who was voraciously ravishing *them*, frantically forcing the bunched and spurting organs into every orifice—vagina, anus, mouth, ears, nose, etc. He had even dreamed once that she asked him if it were true that there was a small uncovered opening in the *pupil of the eye*, because if it were, she had said, she would have room there (during the finale) for a miniscule organ, like that of a praying mantis to enter her as well! [From the novel, *Candy*, G. P. Putnam's Sons, 1964, pp. 45–46]

This is, of course, unlikely material to be translated from novel to film, but Buck Henry should have retained some of the father's traditional concern for the daughter's fate, which forms

This scene from *Candy* shows a guru (Marlon Brando) initiating a not-so-innocent Candy (Ewa Aulin) into ritualized sex.

not only a basis for Candy's defection from parental control but also the final irony of the narrative when Candy discovers that a Guru who is seducing her is her own father. As the dark comedy ending of the novel (also depicted on screen) wraps up the strange tale, Candy discovers the identity of her seducer and with "truly mixed feeling" exclaims: " 'GOOD GRIEF—IT'S DADDY!' " Thus, dark comedy embraced even incest—much as the pornographic novel had done—but in the case of this literary movement there was, at least, the attempt to satirize the mores of our society.

While *Candy* as a novel and a film makes most of its breakthrough in the ridicule of sexual attitudes in our society, some other targets are objects of derision. The growing popularity of

Eastern religions as guides for living is effectively linked with the central sexual parody, as a Guru named Grindle, enacted with only slight comic skill by Marlon Brando, seduces Candy while mouthing his feigned high ideals:

> I'm a doctor of the soul. I am certainly not interested in that silly little body of yours—it is the *spirit* that concerns us here. [From the novel, p. 204]

The hypocrisy of the games people play when dealing with their sexual urges has great potential in the novel and film at this point in the story. And, it should be realized, even Candy plays a game. It is convenient for her to pretend to embrace the ideals of those who are on the make. She has a strong libido masked by concern for others and a receptiveness for experiences that might prove to develop her total being. She is the archetypal groupie. Enacted by a Swedish actress named Ewa Aulin, the portrait of Candy is as sweet as the name but without dimension that would bring out the hypocrisy of this character in the movie.

Some of the actors seem to prevail despite director Marquand's inept handling of a botched adaptation of the novel. Walter Matthau, playing the hawkish general named Smight, enacts an added Buck Henry scene. He plays with coolness but firmness a lustful officer who has been forced to remain for weeks in an airplane that is filled with attack parachute troops— on guard to make a strike when trouble brews in various parts of the world. The dedicated Smight eagerly appeals to Candy to do her patriotic duty by providing him her charms. The liaison is about to be consummated as clothes of the pair are hastily removed; the attack comes at an inopportune time, as the ever-faithful Smight must immediately depart with his men— sans parachute. Often underrated as a comic actor, James Coburn enacts the grandstanding Dr. Kranheit, who performs a bloody brain operation* as if he were a matador going into the bullring; cheering hospital staff and interns enjoy his efforts. *Candy* also exhibits the talents of John Huston as Dr. Dunlap,

---

*Robert Altman is often given credit for the sanguine dark humor of the operating room in the 1970 *M*A*S*H*. *Candy*, of course, predates this war comedy.

who delivers another one of his scathing portraits of authority gone amuck. It is possible that director Marquand may have let these actors "do their own thing"; if so, these actors provide some spark to a plodding dark comedy that never reaches the depth of satire.

The adventures of a young, voluptuous woman in outer space on strange, exotic planets forms the basis for *Barbarella*, another 1968 film that employs a more sophisticated sex object than the naive Candy. But there is a similarity: both women are inclined to recline their sexually ample bodies at the drop of just about anyone's pants. Both heroines become involved in incidents that appear to be assaults, but rape is only suggested; it is more a game that male and female play. Both Candy and Barbarella are willing collaborators in the mock rape—typical male fantasy material that would become evident in the hard-core, explicit sexual scenes in such feature-length films as *Deep Throat* and *The Devil in Miss Jones* in 1972.

In the futuristic *Barbarella* film, the protagonist arrives on the planet Lythion only to find herself attacked by flesh-chewing mechanical dolls, remotely controlled by little girls of the planet who have an odd way of deriving pleasure from their games. Rescued by a virile hunter who has primitive ways, Barbarella learns the "old-fashioned way." Earth, it would seem, has found a substitute for sex by using exaltation-transference pills. Later in the film she meets another rescuer, significantly called Dildano, who Barbarella realizes might also want a reward for his heroic effort. But Dildano does not wish the label of barbarian and wants the hand-touching system with pills as a reward—to which Barbarella, who has developed a taste for the "old-fashioned way," dutifully consents. Visually the orgasm is depicted in a way that would pass the most prudish censor. It all amounts to a hair-raising experience—that is, Jane Fonda and David Hemmings are shown having the hair on their heads lifted up as if by static electricity as the climax is achieved. This parody of sexual substitution is extended to other mechanical means of sexual stimulus which must predict a grim future for the human and nonhuman aliens. At one point in the proceedings, a mad scientist, played by Milo O'Shea, puts the hapless Barbarella into a machine which he believes will induce a fatal sexual pleasure. Of course, she is not to be conquered in this department; she proves too much for the machine, and it blows up in series of sparks and smoke explosions. This colorful film was based on a cartoon strip by Jean-Claude Forest, published in Paris in 1964 in book form and reproduced in the United States during the underground cartoon development of the the sixties.

The genre of the pornographic spoof has its roots in male sexual fantasy, which is evident in both *Candy* and *Barbarella*. Furthermore, the story itself is mythical—a daydream. On the other hand, the personal, sexual confessions show mental reflection and daydreams in the realistic world, emphasizing serious psychological problems even when comedy is used extensively. Two novels, Philip Roth's *Portnoy's Complaint* in 1969 and Lois Gould's *Such Good Friends* in 1970, revealed respectively the sexuality of a man and a woman in their early thirties. Both show Jewish ethnicity but with universal implications, and both works are satires. While the Roth novel was brought to the screen in 1972 and the Gould novel in 1971, the more sensational and controversial *Portnoy's Complaint* should be examined first to obtain a perspective on the literary and film trend of the times.

When movie critics heard that a filmed version of *Portnoy's Complaint* was being planned, they were sure it couldn't be done. And, of course, they had reason to believe so. Philip Roth's brilliant, unusually long and well-sustained prose confession was unique for a literary work and seemed far removed from the dramatic mode. It was a popular success because its revelation of male sexuality was the most frank use of inner thoughts and fantasies that the public had witnessed in the art form of the novel. Many critics also realized that Roth's intent was on the other end of the spectrum from the sexual titillations that prompted the creation of Jacqueline Susann's *Valley of the Dolls* (released as a film in 1967) and Gore Vidal's *Myra Breckenridge* (adapted to film in 1970). In fact, these two movie adaptations received negative critical reaction, which caused Twentieth Century-Fox executives to be reluctant in developing a production of *Portnoy's Complaint*. When Richard Zanuck, who was to supervise the production of the Roth work for Twentieth Century-Fox, moved to Warner Bros., he took the property with him.

Warner Bros. seemed to make the same mistake with *Portnoy's Complaint* as the producers of *Candy* had done: a fledgling director was given the assignment. Granted, director Ernest Lehman was considered one of the top Hollywood writers by that time. His credits as a writer were impressive: *Executive Suite* and *Sabrina* (1954); *Someone Up There Likes Me* and *The King and I* (1956); *Sweet Smell of Success*, from his novella (1957); and many more. He was screen adapter and producer for the highly acclaimed *Who's Afraid of Virginia Woolf?* (1966). And he became the adapter, director, and producer of the ill-fated *Portnoy's Complaint.*

Given the basic difficulty of adapting a story that receives much of its richness from the first person confession of Alexander Portnoy to a psychiatrist named Dr. Otto Spielvogel, Lehman creates a script which appears to be adequate, although it lacks the depth of the novel. The skilled writer-adapter follows the basic incidents of the original rambling story and even tightens up the narrative in a way that is probably necessary for the drama. He stresses such key dialogue sections as Portnoy's lament:

> "Doctor Spielvogel, this is my life, my only life, and I'm living it in the middle of a Jewish joke! I am the son in the Jewish joke—*only it ain't no joke!*" [From the novel, Bantam paperback, pp. 39–40]

With only slight variation, writer Lehman remains faithful to such moments, but he errs in his ability to obtain the necessary anguish of "it ain't no joke." The oppressive, self-destructive guilt of Alexander Portnoy never is fully realized in the script or in the acting performances in the final production. To give the work bite and a satirical tone that exposes the sexual hang-ups that are both funny and tragic, the approach needs to be less glib in order to capture Roth's profundity in dealing with this subject.

Philip Roth sets forth a humorous definition before the narration starts which provides a key to both the humor and the satire of the book:

Portnoy's Complaint (pôrt'-noiz kem-plānt) *n.* [after Alexander Portnoy (1933–   )] A disorder in which strongly-felt ethical and altruistic impulses are perpetually warring with extreme sexual longing, often of a perverse nature. Spielvogel says: "Acts of exhibitionism, voyeurism, fetishism, auto-eroticism and oral coitus are plentiful; as a consequence of the patient's 'morality,' however, neither fantasy nor act issues in genuine sexual gratification, but rather in overriding feelings of shame and the dread of retribution, particularly in the form of castration" (Spielvogel, O. "The Puzzled Penis." *International Zeitschrift für Psychoanalyse*, Vol. XXIV, p. 909). It is believed by Spielvogel that many of the symptoms can be traced to the bonds obtained in the mother-child relationship. [Preface material of novel without a page number]

Some lampoon of psychiatry can be detected in this strange definition (such as the title of the article, " 'The Puzzled Penis' ") and the final concept of a "mother-child relationship"—a key to the inner conflict of Portnoy. The movie brings out some of the guilt that the youthful Alex suffers when he masturbates, material that was, of course, bold dark comedy for the time. But there seems to be too much smirking and leering in the presentation of this material, as if the writer-director embraces the heretofore taboo subject.

The guilt that lingers with Alex as a thirty-three-year-old is most directly developed in the movie when he engages in a *ménage-à-trois* with his girlfriend and an Italian prostitute. The movie also depicts a relatively mild orgy that is described as wild in the book. In both versions Alex goes into the bathroom after the incident and vomits. As an adult his guilt feelings smother any sexual enjoyment he might have. In the movie he ironically states that his mother would be happy at the reaction because he was having "too much clean fun." The novel diverts the act to the motherly advice of properly handling any mishap. Alex states: "My *kishkas*, Mother—threw them right up into the toilet bowl. Isn't that a good boy?" [the novel, p. 155]. It is more evident in the novel that any sexual pleasure takes on a sordid quality in the mind of Alex, who describes female organs grotesquely even when he reaches a sexual climax.

As critics of the movie pointed out, the movie never gradu-
ated visually from the fifties; even a romantic romp in the
country with his bedmate, Mary Jane, gives the picture a tone
unlike that of the book. The film contains little visual nudity or
suggestions of sexuality that were standard for the movies of the
late sixties and early seventies. Therefore, the film lacks the
necessary facets to reflect the novel's obsession with one subject. Writer-director Lehman concentrates on the language
used by Roth which seems to work contrary to that which might
have been a more tasteful rendering. By visually avoiding sex,
Lehman makes the movie seem like a lot of dirty talk grafted to
the sound track of an old-fashioned film.

Some critics found the performance of Karen Black as Mary
Jane (or "The Monkey," because of her unbridled sexual pas-
sions) as the only credible portrayal in the film. This may be true,
but also some credit is due to Jill Clayburgh as Naomi, a native
of Israel and a formidable outdoor woman who proves too much
of a challenge for Alex when he is bent on seduction. The
mother and father of Alex, enacted by Lee Grant and Jack
Somack, seem to be from vaudeville or television situation
comedy; they may as well be acting in another movie. By far the
most curious performance is that given by Richard Benjamin,
an accomplished comic actor who seems on target with his
protagonist in the 1969 film *Goodbye, Columbus*. His Alex
comes out as effete—a wimp and a *shlemiel* of a much lower
order than intended by Roth. Benjamin even seems uncomfort-
able uttering four-letter words, all of which must add up to
inadequate directing.

As indicated earlier, the script was adequate and might have
made the transition from novel to screen. Still, there is something important to the satire in the paradox of Alex's upbringing
by his parents. Roth gives Portnoy the insight to see his psychological problems springing from the paradox:

> Doctor Spielvogel, it alleviates nothing fixing the blame—
> blaming is still ailing, of course, of course—but nonethe-
> less, what *was* it with these Jewish parents, *what*, that they
> were able to make us little Jewish boys believe ourselves
> to be princes on the one hand, unique as unicorns on the
> one hand, geniuses and brilliant—like nobody has ever

Richard Benjamin in the lead role of *Portnoy's Complaint* reveals all to a psychiatrist.

been brilliant and beautiful before in the history of childhood—saviors and sheer perfection on the one hand, and such bumbling, incompetent, thoughtless, helpless, selfish, evil little shits, little *ingrates*, on the other! [From the novel, pp. 133–134]

Here is, of course, part of the conflicting attitudes of the parent that helps destroy Alex. It indicates some of the depth of the original work which is largely ignored by adapter-director Lehman. It also indicates some of the universality of Roth's theme; for it is not just an ethnic manifestation—many parents of various ethnic backgrounds handle their children in a similar way.

Some of the sins of the parents also press down on the brain of Julie Wallman Messenger in Lois Gould's novel *Such Good Friends* so that one might say here is the female counterpart of Roth's work—Julie's Complaint. Many of Julie's problems seem to be linked to the superficial values of the mother, her teen-age obesity, and her role as a woman which has been defined by men. Male comic villains, almost all sexual cads and self-serving machos, abound in the 1971 adaptation from Gould's novel. The roots of this dark comedy portraying the plight of a woman are interestingly handled.

The movie version with adaptation by Elaine May (under the pseudonym of Esther Dale) and direction by Otto Preminger had all the qualities of a sexual exposé of urban and suburban life that could be witnessed in the films *Loving* and *Diary of a Mad Housewife*, works created in 1970. In these movies, a trend developed toward a genre far removed from the romantic tradition of Charlotte Brontë's *Jane Eyre*. The woman is the victim of her husband's vices; he engages in extramarital sex as if it is his right, or he is overly obsessed with business so that a self-serving image of such becomes the only focus for the family. *Such Good Friends* presents an even darker, more sinister (yet comic) portrait of the husband.

In this 1971 work by Preminger and May, the husband is discovered to be a classical philanderer who is attempting to be a Don Juan or Casanova of the sophisticated urban society of our times. But the wife learns of his catalog of conquests only when he has become comatose in a hospital after a minor malady turns into a catastrophe in the hands of inept physicians. So dark humor looms as a heavy cloud over the plot complications as sex and death are mixed for humor. For example, Dyan Cannon as Julie Messenger utters vulgarities in her frustration as she leans over the intensive care bed of her husband and she pleads vainly for him to snap out of it:

> Come on now, Richard. It isn't funny anymore. It was a good joke at first, but it's beginning to wear thin. Listen. I apologize. . . . Look at me, you prick, or so help me God I'm going to divorce you. . . . Just look at me, Richard, and I'll never say anything more about needing all that air. I'll

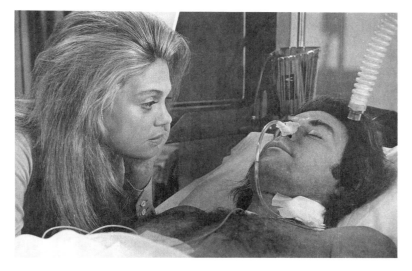

In *Such Good Friends*, Dyan Cannon decides to have a number of affairs when she learns her husband, who is dying, has been a philanderer.

gag the children. We'll go to Masters and Johnson and
fuck ourselves to mental health. . . . [From the film]

This dialogue was nearly two decades removed from language
used by Preminger, who, as it has been stated before, flaunted
his protest in dealing with the production code when he used
terms such as "virgin" and "pregnant" in the 1953 *The Moon Is
Blue*. But *Such Good Friends* would go farther than the prud-
ishly visual *Portnoy's Complaint* that brought the frank language
from novel to the screen. Preminger's film shows a simulated
sex incident confined mostly to nudity from the shoulders up,
with the more startling developments presumably occurring off
screen. It is a scene in which photographer Cal Whiting tries to
seduce Julie after luring her into excessive drinking and then
posing her for a private centerfold via a Polaroid camera. He
finds the sexual act difficult and has to give up. Julie has one of
her best wisecrack lines of the movie when she uses her maiden
name to indicate her teen-age troubles with sex: "Julie Wallman—give her a try—instant impotence guaranteed." On the

raucous level of a broader comic spectrum is Julie's seduction of her husband's friend and physician Dr. Timmy Spector, a scene that seems to be an update from Aristophanes' *Lysistrata* or from the golden age of the American burlesque theatre. Timmy, well-played by James Coco with a certain degree of male swishiness, has difficulties as he tries to undress in response to Julie's overtures. He is frustrated by a hypochondriac's phone call and the problem of discarding a laced girdle that he wears for vanity's sake without Julie noticing his actions. Coco deftly milks the most from this frustration and shows the proper amount of male lechery in a comic way.

While it might appear from the incidents and dialogue cited from *Such Good Friends* that the film had characteristics of the sexploitation movies of the period, the work attempted to satirize a society bent on fast living. The sexual mores of the group—even Julie's efforts to get even over the slowly dying body of her husband—show a superficial, desperate grasp for a type of *joie de vivre* existence based on false values—a point stressed by Lois Gould in her novel.

Reviews were mixed, but Molly Haskell in *The Village Voice* (January 6, 1972, p. 49) found *Such Good Friends* a valid, effective adaptation. She qualifies her appreciation of the movie's success in translating the work by indicating that even though the depth of the portrait of Julie Messenger was not fully realized, Preminger captured "the desperately, stylishly on-the-make world in which real emotion has no outlet and even despair curdles into a one-liner." She also sees sex as satirized: "For the most part sex is either brutal and joyless, with the orgasm obsession precluding all feeling, or it is the flip side of a record with almost anything—job, sportscar, sleep—taking precedent."

A contrary view, as it often happens with controversial movies, appears in *Film Comment* (September 1973, pp. 56–58), with evaluator Elliott Sirkin berating the efforts of Preminger and May for not capturing the intent of the author or the milieu of what he calls the "New Class New Yorker." He faults Elaine May for incorporating the same kind of heavy-handed blast at the bourgeoisie that she and her husband, Mike Nichols, used in their staged and recorded comedy sketches. Sirkin seems too severe in his criticism. Lois Gould does not really infuse much depth into her characters and they appear only slightly more elevated than the Jules Feiffer cartoon caricatures. It is possible that Sirkin, as I gather from the tenor of his reflections on the film, sees Gould's narrative as a more profound work than it is—that he sees it as a less laughable, more hard-biting mode of satire. Viewed now, after nearly two decades of confession novels and autobiographies, the Gould work does not hold up as well as Roth's *Portnoy's Complaint. Such Good Friends*, as a first novel, displays some of the excesses and glibness of a writer who has a keen sense of humor but has problems controlling the gift. Protagonist Julie's one-line rebukes of physicians and her inept lovers come too easily and too often in the novel. True, some are justified because they reveal her rage and even mask an inner agony, but such a bombardment leaves little room to see the rest of her character. Nevertheless, the book and the film proved to make inroads for their time into a more candid view of a woman's sexuality.

The medium of theater also made a contribution to the comic overview of one of our basic drives. What had been hawked by its publicity agent and producer as the first legitimate theater's all-nude revue, *Oh! Calcutta!* received a quasi-metamorphosis from one medium to another medium via a national closed-circuit telecast which was presented in large cities in September 1970. This enterprise, a type of photographed stage play with some filmed outdoor scenes, brought in a reported two million dollars. If one considers the cost of the video event to be ten dollars a ticket, maybe the gross was not as large as it would seem. This filmed version of a stage work resurfaced in the summer of 1972 without much critical or popular response. On the stage the revue had been produced by the well-known British drama critic Kenneth Tynan. It evidently was a popular piece since it ran from June 19, 1969, to February 25, 1971, at the Belasco Theatre for a total of 1,316 performances.

The consensus of most theater and movie critics, even for that time, was that in both media the revue was not bold enough and lacked the satirical impact to make this work an effective exploration of human sexual behavior. This seems odd since there were some skilled writers who contributed skits: Samuel Beckett, Sam Shepard, Jules Feiffer, plus such luminaries as John Lennon and Kenneth Tynan. Also, David Newman and Robert

Benton, creators of the screenplay for *Bonnie and Clyde* (1967), were contributors.

The total review, in both the theatrical presentation and the movie presentation has an uneven quality in its humor that amounts to only a mediocre effort. Nevertheless, some skits do stand out and show inroads into sexual humor which is legitimized—put on a higher plane in our society than previously as it existed in the nightclub act and the burlesque theater. Critics often cite the sketch "Was It Good for You Too?" reportedly written by Dan Greenberg, as one that explored the curious sadomasochistic relationship between the sexes. Another skit lampoons the Masters and Johnson experiments with sexual response by showing copulating couples wired for bodily reactions. As a man and woman engage in sex (simulated, of course), they are constantly distracted by a crew of scientists and technicians who resemble the Marx Brothers madly dashing around in the hospital examining room scene from a film *A Day at the Races* (1937). The deromanticizing of sex by the scientist seems a fit subject for a lampoon in this portion of *Oh! Calcutta!* The young man and young woman almost prevail over this experiment when they seem to fall in love and want to know each other's identity. The mad scientist, to keep the whole thing pure and objective, thwarts the couple by vehemently insisting: "No names!"

Some value in exposing past attitudes toward sex evolved from a piece called "Delicious Indignities, or the Deflowering of Helen Axminster," a burlesque of the euphuistic style of pornography of the eighteenth and nineteenth centuries, a possible contribution by Kenneth Tynan since it has such a British flavor. The most literary of all the sketches, this work shows the intended seduction gone sour—a subject for sex comedy that has existed throughout the ages. While the would-be seducer of Helen Axminster manages to get her suitably tethered by the wrists as she manipulates blinds on a window in his home, he accidentally sits down in a mechanical chair (designed as another entrapment device) and falls victim to his own plot. Unable to proceed with his plans, he is forced to listen to a long tale of the various seductions inflicted upon Helen, who is convinced she is still a virgin because she did not enjoy or wish the sexual act to take place. Because of the compromising situation in which they will be discovered, Helen forces him into a contract for marriage. He is crestfallen by her lurid tale and by the fact that he wanted to marry a virgin.

Another sketch in *Oh! Calcutta!* mentioned favorably by the critics is "Will Answer All Sincere Replies," a look at the swinging sexual world of the sixties. In this portion of the work a young couple try to spark the lull in their married sex life by receiving in their home experienced, older (and much to their dismay, gross) married swingers for the evening. The young man who suggested answering the classified ad comes out the loser as his naive wife enters into a *ménage à trois* with the older couple. Having ejaculated prematurely when he danced with the sexy older woman, the young man disgustedly plays solitaire as the trio (unseen behind a high-back couch) engages in an orgy.

As seen in most of these sketches, the man becomes the butt of the joke, which may indicate why some reviewers thought the supposedly liberated sex comedy of stage and screen was rather routine material—barely updated from the golden age of burlesque in theaters of the twenties and thirties.

While *Oh! Calcutta!* explored many of the taboos of our society's sexual mores, it completely neglected the hang-ups regarding homosexuality—a manifestation that is often clothed in our culture in such euphemistic phrases as "sexual preference" and "alternate lifestyle." The stage, novel, and film media have been shy and delicate in approaching the subject, even on a serious level. Considered vulgar by some segments of society for his occasional use of sexual humor, Charles Chaplin used homosexual gags in his two-reel short *Behind the Screen* as early as 1916 and incorporated such humor in the boxing sequence of *City Lights* in 1931. Comedy of this type generally pokes fun at what was thought to be deviant male behavior. When Hollywood employed the subject of homosexuality on a serious level, it was easier to tiptoe up to the subject with female homosexuality. The lesbian theme was dropped from *These Three*, the 1936 screen adaptation of Lillian Hellman's stage play, *The Children's Hour*, but reintroduced in the 1962 remake. European filmmakers would examine this type of love relationship with Claude Chabrol's *Les Biches* in 1968. The British stage play of Frank Marcus, *The Killing of Sister George*, brought to the

screen that same year, however, proved to be one of the first
examinations of lesbianism that used both a comic and sympathetic approach. In America, Mart Crowley would bring to
Broadway in 1968 *The Boys in the Band*, the first full development of the comic drama concerning male homosexuality that
treated the subject with understanding and compassion. This
drama was brought to the screen in 1970 by director William
Friedkin with minor attempts to open up the stage drama
presentation with a few exterior scenes and resulted in a work
with excellent performances by most of the original cast of the
stage play.

The Boys in the Band uses a mixture of the comic and serious
in a way that gives the appearance of satire, but the reigning
sympathetic treatment of the plight of the homosexual in the
play and movie seems to undercut satirical intent. The appearance of a satirical approach exists in the wit of the drama. The
main characters in the work are sophisticated New Yorkers who
have the skill of the clever philosophical observation that seems
to follow the long tradition of the British comedy of wit. When
Michael is trying to cut out drinking, he is asked by his current
lover, Donald, "And just how does a clear head stack up with
the dull fog of alcohol?" Michael replies: "Well, all those things
you've always heard are true. Nothing can compare with the
experience of one's faculties functioning at their maximum
natural capacity. The only thing is . . . I'd *kill* for a drink" (the
drama, *Famous American Plays of the Sixties*, Harold Clurman,
ed., Dell. p. 329). The ability to laugh at the faults within a
person's own psychological makeup becomes one of the most
enjoyable features of the drama, but sometimes this self-re-
proach becomes self-abasement that is painful. When Michael
complains to Harold, who arrives stoned, that he is late to his
own birthday party, Harold replies:

> What I am, Michael, is a thirty-two-year-old, ugly, pock-
> marked Jew fairy—and if it takes me a while to pull myself
> together and if I smoke a little grass before I can get up
> the nerve to show this face to the world, it's nobody's
> goddamn business but my own. [The play, p. 352]

One of the high points of cynical wit in the play and movie occurs when Harold attacks the sop often given to those who are unattractive, that true beauty exists in the soul. He is offered as a birthday present a dense, handsome young man named Cowboy. To the statement that beauty is only skin deep Harold replies:

> It's only skin deep and it's *transitory* too. It's *terribly* transitory. I mean, how long does it last—thirty or forty or fifty years at the most—depending on how well you take care of yourself. And not counting, of course, that you might die before it runs out anyway. Yes, it's too bad about this poor boy's face. It's tragic. He's absolutely cursed! How can *his* beauty ever compare with *my* soul? And although I have never seen my soul, I understand from my mother's rabbi that it's a knockout. I, however, cannot seem to locate it for a gander. And if I could, I'd sell it in a flash for some skin-deep, transitory, meaningless beauty! [The play, pp. 358–359]

Here is a penetrating revelation on the gay man's concern with being attractive to his own sex, which might be transposed to examine the priority that is stressed in our society's obsession with female beauty and youth. But Mart Crowley has only flashes of such profundity in *The Boys in the Band*. His approach is desultory, ranging over a wide variety of problems in the gay community. Furthermore, Crowley reduces his main characters to a wallow in self-pity in order to obtain sympathy for them. Satire fades as sentiment enters. Before the curtain falls on the play and the credits begin to roll in the film, we witness a scene that shows the seemingly invincible Michael in the middle of a nervous breakdown as he quotes the dying words of his father on the meaning of life: "I don't understand any of it. I never did" (the play, p. 395). The playwright was examining new ground—a subject that had not been as boldly handled before. In much the same way that Frank Marcus approached *The Killing of Sister George* in dealing with lesbianism, Crowley produces a hybrid drama—a curious combination of comedy and sentiment that almost wants to make some satirical comment on the so-called normal world. The characters seem to parody love relationships in the heterosexual, or "straight," world.

A more direct and what might seem to be a lower form of homosexual humor is employed in the movie adaptation of Terry Southern's *The Magic Christian*, a novel published in 1960 and brought to the screen in 1970. Since Southern had a firm hand in adapting his novel, the film story line does not deviate very much from that in the novel. A millionaire named Guy Grand engages in a number of expensive practical jokes which either puncture the propriety of proper folk or expose their greed. The assault on propriety employs a number of ruses which show what some might call deviate sexual behavior. The main ones employed in the movie are (1) In a legitimate stage presentation of *Hamlet* Lawrence Harvey, in a cameo appearance as Hamlet, breaks into a striptease routine as he renders the somber "To Be or Not To Be" soliloquy; (2) In a championship heavyweight boxing match, two boxers meet in a face-to-face confrontation only to break from the standard pugilistic pose, embrace, and kiss each other on the mouth (much to the annoyance of the crowd since they came for a bloodbath); (3) A nightclub act features two muscle men, one black and one white, who dance provocatively to a song praising the virtues of Mr. Universe; and, (4) What is thought to be an attractive woman singing "Mad About the Boys" in a bar and making advances to charm the older men eyeing her, turns out to be a transvestite. When the blond wig is removed, we can recognize Yul Brynner in a cameo role.

As it might be detected, the intent of three of these incidents (1, 3, and 4) is to lampoon the standard concept of the woman as the sex object. In this way, the humor does rise well above the standard nightclub homosexual gag. Incident number 2 shows male masculinity at its aggressive worst (or best, according to one's point of view) with a reversal gag that turns the bloodiest male sport into a gesture of homosexual love, thereby overturning the primitive image of "maleness" that has existed from ancient times. These examples from *The Magic Christian* show effective use of dark comedy, but do not add up to a sustained and significant statement about our society's attitudes on sexual behavior.

It is possible that one of the keys to successful satire lies in the role of the male in the relationship between the sexes since it would appear that the male has established and maintained so many of the traditional views. *The Magic Christian*, at least, pioneered with an attempt to lampoon male sexuality on the screen.

When the battle of the sexes goes to the point that little connection between man and woman exists or the relationship becomes very grim, some comic works display a misalliance that does not seem to have the promise of ever mending. Three films, *Happy Birthday, Wanda June* (1971), *Carnal Knowledge* (1971), and *The Battle of the Sexes* (1960), show the potential for a darker type of satire on human sexuality. A contemporary view on the mismatched relationship between the sexes in Kurt Vonnegut, Jr.'s stage play *Happy Birthday, Wanda June*, directed by Mark Robson, shows a chauvinist explorer and soldier of fortune, played by Rod Steiger, who returns to his wife after seven years of roaming. Expecting to find everything the same as when he left his wife, he discovers his domestic kingdom in disarray. His spouse has two other men courting her, and his son has conflicting views on his relationship with the adult male.

Happy Birthday, Wanda June shows the swaggering husband named Harold Ryan trying to reestablish his reign in what Vonnegut intended to be a parody of Ulysses. The wife is appropriately named Penelope. As this limp parody shows in an inversion of heroics, all the brute force and invective of the modern Ulysses fails to make this anti-hero master of the suitors, his wife, and his son. Vonnegut, who is also responsible for the screenplay, does not quite achieve the satirical thrust that he intended and ends up, at best, with dark comedy. This lampoon of Neanderthal male domination evidently puzzled *New York Times* critic Vincent Canby, who is generally more astute when it comes to interpretation of dark comedies. He holds the curious view that Vonnegut's statement that he does not create villains means we are to "sympathize with this mastadon at the moment of extinction" (December 10, 1971, p. 50). While the work does cast a strange light on the fading Harold Ryan, I believe this character is the butt of the joke, and one of his rivals, Dr. Norbert Woodley (played by George Grizzard), is the sensitive male who should receive the sympathy. But this ambiguity of interpretation indicates that Vonnegut has not achieved his goal. Director Robson, who seemed to be on the skids as a filmmaker at this time, does little to correct the problem.

Carnal Knowledge is a film with an effective original screenplay by Jules Feiffer and direction by Mike Nichols. It proves to be one of the grimmest misalliances of the sexes. Feiffer chronicles the sexual lives of two men, Jonathan and Sandy, from their college days to middle years. The film explores some of the changing mores of the sexes over a period that is roughly from the forties into the sixties. Jonathan, with the obsession of a long distance swimmer or a mountain climber, remains fixed in his attempt to seduce all women. He becomes convinced that all women are out to demasculinize him or, as he crudely puts it—they are all "ballbusters." At the same time it would appear that his buddy, Sandy, with all his strained sincerity, accompanied by unfailing naiveté that keeps him in the dark, might find a firm traditional relationship with a woman. But he, too, ends up disillusioned, divorced, and lost in the world of the sixties. Sandy, a role effectively enacted by Art Garfunkel, affects mod clothing as a middle-aged man and believes he might have found the right woman when he starts living with a frail seventeen-year-old hippie. Jonathan (played well by Jack Nicholson), forever the con man, must move from woman to woman as he searches for a quick sexual fix. Condemned to a type of earthly hell, he becomes impotent—the opposite of his self-image as a stud. Molly Haskell who, as it has been mentioned, favored the woman-oriented comedy *Such Good Friends*, draws a rather strange conclusion from this Feiffer-Nichols film. While most critics view it as a significant portrait of a destructive, second-rate Don Juan, she states in her book *From Reverence to Rape* that Jack Nicholson's Jonathan ends up being appealing to the male viewer. She writes:

> We get an image that purports to indict the men but that insidiously defends them, not least through the satisfaction they take in degrading the women. In the relationship between the filmmakers (Nichols and Feiffer) and their protagonist, we get the indulgent view of the artist toward his creation, the mother toward her child. Thus Nicholson is a bad but charming boy, whose "bad"ness, when it is not an asset, is a product of wicked society and evil women,

while his charm is all his own. And finally, for all his problems, he is a typical "neat guy," and as such he scores with the men if not with the women. . . . *Carnal Knowledge* . . . remains closer to the locker room than to the bedroom. [*From Reverence to Rape*, Holt, Rinehart, and Winston, 1974, pp. 360–361]

It is a questionable interpretation, unless one believes that a male like Jonathan in real life might find the character appealing. It probably is possible to find some men like this and some like Harold Ryan in Vonnegut's *Happy Birthday, Wanda June*, but they are surely part of a dying race. Given the subject of her book, Haskell may be engaging in a type of special pleading in her attempt to construct the image of women as reflected in all films. Also, she found no positive or exemplary woman to expose Jonathan thoroughly or set him in his place. But the bent of Feiffer's character needs to be examined. Jonathan would not date or marry a formidable woman. As the sardonic final scene of the movie shows, he is forced to go to a prostitute who, with a prearranged scenario, must engage in a lengthy monologue of how great he is in order to lift not only his ego but also his penis.

It is necessary to turn to a more traditional battle of the sexes to show the ultimate in a traditional misalliance that says a great deal about the role of sexual stereotypes in our culture. From James Thurber's short story "The Catbird Seat" Monja Danishewsky devised a screenplay called *The Battle of the Sexes* that extended the work to provide a more elaborate portrait of Mrs. Barrows and Mr. Martin in their power struggle. This British movie depicts the woman as a relatively sophisticated American—a part enacted by Constance Cummings—and the man as a mild-mannered, tweedy Scotsman, portrayed by Peter Sellers. This deviates from the story by Thurber because he painted the portrait of a gross, assertive woman with pushy qualities that would be reprehensible in either a male or female. The comic cartoonist-writer sketched the antagonist in broad strokes which almost paralleled some of the famous cartoons the humorist had published in the *New Yorker*.

In the short story she is a bullish creature who speaks by comparison as loudly as Martin speaks softly. Constance Cummings, in playing the role of Mrs. Barrows, presents an attractive woman who looks almost twenty years younger than her own age when she played the part. Nevertheless, she gives an excellent performance in *The Battle of the Sexes* by imparting to the role an edge of crassness mixed with self-assuredness and charm. Hardly the Amazon Thurber had in mind, the character nevertheless seems to work and provides an excellent foil for the perplexed Mr. Martin. The portrait of Mr. Martin, the underling in the office staff who takes a dislike to the dictates of Mrs. Barrows who has the ear of the boss of the firm, evolves into a man with a little more craft than that of the short story character, but he is still a mouse of a man and a bungler. The final assault on Mrs. Barrows with effete murderous designs becomes comic in Peter Sellers's hands. In this film role reversal, comedy works with all the taste that the British film comedy can muster. The rendering of the comedy is in the hands of the skilled Charles Crichton, a filmmaker noted for *The Lavender Hill Mob* (1951).

The Battle of the Sexes comes close to satire as far as film comedy goes, with an extension of the story showing the man struggling for the traditional ways and the woman attempting to run the business with more modern methods. Almost symbolically the man stands for the older ways and the woman the newer. Martin, of course, wins the battle with a ruse that makes the boss question the sanity of Mrs. Barrows. It is a comic reversal similar to the one Thurber used in "The Unicorn in the Garden." The victory of Martin in *The Battle of the Sexes* does not have the invective of the Thurber short story ending. Adapter Danischewsky shows Martin going up to a tearful Mrs. Barrows, who has lost her job, and offering her a single flower. It is, of course, an in-joke, using James Thurber's cartoon expression of a man making an overture to a woman. This ending mutes the thrust of the total story, and it would appear that reconciliation is possible in the battle of the sexes. The voice-over narrator explains that Martin has won the battle but not the war.

In both literature and film the relationship of the sexes is difficult to satirize in the twentieth century. Of the films I have examined that are adaptations, it seems that the 1971 *Such Good Friends* and the 1960 *The Battle of the Sexes* come closest to being satires instead of merely dark comedies. These two works, as movies, are closer to the classical mold of satire. In a sense they are more direct and less burdened with psychological concerns. Both *Portnoy's Complaint* and *Candy*, even with psychological concerns, seem to have some potential for satire, but the executions of these movie productions prove inept. We seem to be grappling with a difficult period in our sexual mores—an overconcern with meaningful relationships. It is all a painful process if one views the self-help books that are ground out regarding the subject. To find a free-flowing, less self-conscious, and even a more natural bent in the satirization of love and sex in literature, we need to turn to such works as *Lysistrata*, *The Tales of Decameron*, and *The Country Wife*—all products of the past. To lift the yoke of Victorian prudery seems to be a Herculean task. Although we have come a long way in our ability to satirize the plagues of war and death, we have a long way to evolve before we can satirize our sexual nature.

CHAPTER 6

ROGUES, CON MEN, MADMEN, AND ASSORTED DEVIANTS

IN THE SIXTIES AND SEVENTIES an interesting protagonist appeared more prominently than before in the film drama: the picaresque character who was engaged in an almost innate attack on society. This character, more often a man than a woman, seemed to be born with an anarchist's spirit; a colorful combination of rogue, rake, rascal, con man, vagrant, madman, he sometimes evolved into a first-class artist and philosopher who listened to a different drummer. With all the traits of a self-centered, noisome show-off, such a type, it should appear, would be too obnoxious to be worthy of our attention. But within this rogue was the quintessence of the free spirit that we would all like to be and the devil-may-care charm that often helped expose the foibles of a culture with oppressive, impossible-to-live-by values. Occasionally, this picaresque persona would have an almost Christ-like facet that would lead to his own destruction. For example, in Joyce Cary's *The Horse's Mouth* and Ken Kesey's *One Flew Over the Cuckoo's Nest*, developed protagonists Gulley Jimson and Randle Patrick McMurphy had such a trait. Not all leading figures of such stories have this characteristic, but it would seem that most deviants in these tales are subjects for society's crucifixion. Also, these rogues are fascinating because they possess personal traits often ranging between the enigmatic and ambivalent in a way that tells us much about the complex nature of human beings. Some of the most interesting films to use such a protagonist are *The Horse's Mouth* (1958), *Tom Jones* (1963), *A Fine Madness* (1966), *The*

Magic Christian (1970), *One Flew Over the Cuckoo's Nest* (1975), and *The World According to Garp* (1982).

Probably one of the best examinations of the creative artist, without sentimentality or over-romanticized reflections, was developed by Joyce Cary in his 1944 novel and brought to the screen in 1958 with a successful adaptation by the leading actor Alec Guinness. *The Horse's Mouth* provides an excellent vehicle for the actor's talents and brings to the screen a more full-blown picaresque character than the filmed Captain Macheath portrait by Sir Laurence Olivier in *The Beggar's Opera*, a 1953 production based on the eighteenth-century ballad opera satire. The picaresque Macheath can be considered one of the first important renderings of this type of character in the British film; the highwayman, who is not only a robber but also a con man and amorous rake, is a traditional portrait of the rogue. Gulley Jimson of *The Horse's Mouth*, on the other hand, has many of the dimensions of the modern rogue in literature.

As conceived by Cary in the novel, painter Jimson has become a vagrant who must scrounge for his existence. Not only is he a sponge, but he blithefully pilfers from almost anyone, without any scruples. Furthermore, he threatens a stingy patron who gives him a few pounds a week. Condensed considerably in the movie adaptation is the incident in which Gulley Jimson makes frequent phone calls impersonating various dignitaries:

> "I am the President of the Academy. I understand that Mr. Jimson is now destitute. And I was informed on the best legal advice that you have no right to his pictures. I understand that you conspired with a drunken model to rob him of this valuable property. . . . He is in touch with your accomplice Sara Monday, and he has powerful friends who mean to bring the case to law. . . . Such dangerous blackguards as Jimson oughtn't to be allowed to live. But I'm speaking as a friend. If Jimson doesn't get his rightful due in the next week, he fully intends to burn your house down, and cut your tripes out afterwards." [Joyce Cary, *The Horse's Mouth*, New York: Harper & Brothers edition, 1944, p. 7]

Adapter Alec Guinness renders the essentials of the above speech and as an actor in the film gives the "President" a creaky

In *The Horse's Mouth* Alec Guinness as Gully Jimson is interrupted by the law as he impersonates a patron of the arts in an attempt to raise money for himself.

and crackling voice of an aged sophisticate. For this imitation the actor is shown in a phone booth, pinching his nose to alter the resonance of his voice. This harassment is followed by another in which Jimson taps his Adam's apple rapidly to give a ludicrous vibrato to the falsetto imitation of a dowager called the "Duchess of Blackpool," who wants people to give money for three painting projects: "The Fall," "The Raising of Lazarus," and "The Creation." These phone calls are directed to patron Hickson, who by this time has been harassed so much by Jimson that he has his butler trace the call. Thus, the attempts to con his crotchety patron have put the police on their guard. And Gulley often ends up in jail for his intemperate behavior. In the novel, using the first-person narrative point of view,

Jimson coyly refers to such an action that puts him in jail as a "piece of carelessness" (the novel, p. 109).

While the adaptation by Guinness does not use any voice-over narration to obtain the mental reflections of Gulley Jimson, the adapter-actor uses well the presence of a young man, Harry Barbon, who admires the artist. As in the novel, the movie shows Jimson trying to get rid of the young man he calls Nosy because he hounds his footsteps, wanting to learn his skills. To Nosy the cantankerous painter explains the less noble aspects of art: how it ruins people—not only the artist himself, but all around him. And in this depreciation of art and a self-effacing attack on the romantic notions that develop about the creator lies much of the profundity of the satire in *The Horse's Mouth*. The novel is more direct in its statement on the anarchy of modern art as Gulley tells Barbon:

> "You are a good boy," I said, in spite of myself. "And so I'm telling you something for your own good. All art is bad, but modern art is worst. Just like the influenza. The newer it is, the more dangerous. And modern art is not only a public danger—it's insidious. You never know what may happen when it's got loose. Dickens and all the other noble and wise men who backed him up, parsons and magistrates and judges, were quite right. So were the brave lads who fought against the Impressionists in 1870, and the Post-Impressionists in 1910, and that rat Jimson in 1920. They were all quite right. They knew what modern art can do. Creeping about everywhere, undermining the Church and the State and the Academy and the law and marriage and the Government—smashing up civilization, degenerating the Empire." [From the novel, p. 18]

The movie adaptation concentrates more on the personal tragedies that surround the artist, with the dauntless, persistent Nosy's failure to learn anything from Gulley's constant harping on how becoming an artist will ruin him and his family. Furthermore, the naive Harry Barbon sticks by the cynical creator and witnesses the failure of his twelve-by-fourteen-foot and fourteen-by-twenty-five-foot masterpieces as Gulley's life crumbles. But the tale of Gulley Jimson's fall is not written for tears but for laughter. However, this does not mean that serious elements do not become integral to the final fabric of *The Horse's Mouth*.

Jimson's relationship with two women forms an important part of the artist's life and reveals the dimensions of his character. A benefactor who gives him money as he panhandles, "Cokey" (Miss Coker), evolves as a more interesting character than Gulley's former wife, Sara. Cokey is a picaresque woman—a relatively rare portrait in a literary strain that is heavily populated with male deviants. An aggressive, stocky, ugly woman who manages a bar, she can bounce men who are causing a ruckus out of her pub even if they are a foot taller than she. Of all the artist's friends, mostly men, she is the only one with the stamina to help Gulley in his attempt to get back the pictures he painted, which he believes to be rightfully his. Cokey argues tenaciously with Hickson until she learns that the pictures were legitimately obtained by this patron for Jimson's debts. With equal fury she turns on the artist when she learns the truth. But eventually Miss Coker forgives Gulley and continues to help him in each misfortune—often a result of his obsessions, excesses, and tirades. In many adverse situations throughout the story, both in the novel and in the film, she uses her statement of dignity, "I got my pride," which keeps her going and sets her inner rage in control. For she is, like Jimson, looked upon by society as a grotesque. And it may be this that draws them together; however, she sees the charm emerging from the cynical creator, understands a basic honesty that he possesses even though she does not understand his art or philosophy. Much of the humor in their relationship evolves from a curious battle of the sexes in which they engage; both enjoy playing the game. She even possesses a cynicism that shows how she can pin down the irresponsibility of the men she has known: "No one expects anything of a man except mess and talk" (the novel, p. 93). Carey and adapter Guinness give her a supposed prudery that is really a cover-up for her jealousy of beautiful women. When Cokey views a nude painting of his former wife, Sara, she declares: "It's disgusting." To which, Gulley, in rapture on viewing one of his early works, counters: "It's a work of genius" (from the novel, p. 96, and used in the film). Cokey understands the incorrigible nature of Gulley Jimson more than anyone else. She takes him for the man that he is, not the myth that envelops the artist who has some recognition by a society that really cares very little for him as a person.

Sara Monday, the former Sara Jimson, and model for the paintings that brought some credit and fame to Gulley, is a much different woman. A middle-aged, faded beauty, she has the cunning that surpasses that of her former husband. In both the novel and film versions she cons people with her feigned innocence and sweetness. At one point in the novel we see that Gulley understands the games she plays. He chides her by stating: "You don't believe a word you say, do you Sall?" (the novel, p. 27). Thus, much of the humor is achieved by the games people play. In both the novel and film the deception of Sara is depicted by such sweet utterances as "It's quite like old times" and "And how well you look." With the appearance of complete cooperation Sara willingly signs a statement that Jimson's early works belong to him, knowing that George Hickson has rightful possession of the sketches and paintings. In the last part of the novel and film, Sara and Gulley come to blows in a slapstick sequence as the artist physically tries to repossess one of his paintings that she still has in a trunk. Finally, she seems to give up. In another room she graciously wraps the painting to give to Jimson. When he takes home what he believes is the early work and unwraps it, he finds that he has been gulled. Rolls of toilet paper have been used to mock up a presumably priceless work.

While the irascible Jimson engages in many bouts with his female companions that result in his failure to win, he seems more on top of the world as he meets high society and such would-be patrons as Sir William and Lady Beeder. The movie has Gulley engaging in a direct assault on their genteel status with their secretary Alabaster (in the novel he is a professor of art) when he suggests that he paint "The Raising of Lazarus" on the couple's apartment wall. (He has an obsession to paint when he views large spaces.) He tells Alabaster he will include the patrons, seemingly following the tradition of medieval and Renaissance painters, who included their sponsors in a monumental work. He declares that Lady Beeder will be shown as a nude in one corner and Sir William will be depicted dead drunk in the other corner. Soon after he has met them, he gets raving drunk and wants to go to bed. He indicates that he wants to go to bed with Lady Beeder. While the Beeders are shocked, they hope to get a canvas from him and indulge him in almost all of his eccentric requests. While they are on vacation he takes over their apartment. In his creative fervor he strips the apartment bare of priceless furnishings to pay for paint and models for his colossal work, "The Raising of Lazarus."

In this sequence a reader of the novel or the viewer of the movie can see the satire not only on the wild artist, but also on the gullibility of patrons who end up with a "masterpiece" that doesn't fit their modest expectations. Instead, they are stuck with a monstrous mural that has taken over their home and is a wild work they do not comprehend.

As a film with a picaresque protagonist, *The Horse's Mouth* remains as one of the richest works created. While adapter Alec Guinness could have extracted from Cary's novel more scenes featuring Miss Coker to mine the full quality of that character, the dimension of the protagonist seems full-blown. Guinness has included scenes with Miss Coker and Sara which show the artist in his more relaxed, tender attitudes to show that he cares for people. Furthermore, some of the weaknesses in the adaptation are compensated by the brilliant acting of the role by Guinness. As effective as the actor's work was in that golden age of British comic cinema, the late forties to the mid-fifties, he never produced another character with such depth. Anyone who has witnessed *Kind Hearts and Coronets* (1949), *The Lavender Hill Mob* (1950), *The Man in the White Suit* (1952), and *The Captain's Paradise* (1953) can attest to the delightful comic portraits created by Guinness, but these works pale when compared with the satirical dimensions and the warmth of Gulley Jimson in *The Horse's Mouth*. While audience acceptance of this 1958 work was not as widespread and approving as that of earlier efforts, the critics of the late fifties recognized the contribution he made. Henry Goldman's reflective evaluation in *Film Quarterly* summed up the importance of the film with this view:

> It is difficult to recall a film about creative artists that is not somehow patronizing. If "art" is treated seriously, it is too often attended by solemn proclamations about the divinity of the creative spirit (or perhaps madness). If, however, the treatment is comic, it is all quite silly: artists are a gay and irresponsible bunch not to be taken seri-

ously. With *The Horse's Mouth* Alec Guinness, both as screenwriter and actor, has avoided taking either approach. He had in Joyce Cary's novel wonderful material to begin with. But there is his own comic talent, too, which can be funny and serious at once without being foolish or sentimental. Selecting from Cary to suit his talents, yet preserving somehow the tone of the original, Guinness' screenplay and performance amount to a rare comic achievement that speaks of serious things from behind surface flippancies and outrageous hokum. [Spring 1959, pp. 44–46]

One facet the picaresque character must have, if he is to amuse us without revolting us, is a charm and humanity that make the scoundrel likeable. Also, if the character has any depth, this rebel must have some solid basis for his rejection of standard moral practices and accepted personal relationships. *A Fine Madness*, as a film created in 1966, provides a character that fulfilled at least partially one of these requirements. Samson Shillitoe as portrayed by Sean Connery, better known for his James Bond movies, does display a type of charm that makes the picaresque character acceptable and even fascinating to some viewers. However, the script adapted by Elliott Baker from his own novel does not measure up to Cary's *The Horse's Mouth* as rendered on the screen by Alec Guinness. Comparisons are possible since the basic plot of *A Fine Madness* seems to ape this earlier work, with some deviations. Instead of using the character of a painter in his sixties like Gulley Jimson, Baker employs a character in this thirties who is a poet. While both are at odds with society, Samson Shillitoe's rebellion seems to have little purpose that has any significance beyond his own life. Even his poetic bent seems self-serving; he makes glib statements that do not approach the profound. The artistic fury of Samson does not match the artistic fervor of Gulley. While Gulley's madness seems to possess a personal rage that transcends all his faults and gives him a perceptive, cynical view of the world and his art, Samson seems to be a neurotic without a cause who espouses liberal views that are sophomoric.

One of the best scenes of *A Fine Madness* features an abortive poetry reading by Samson before a fashionable women's club. It is one of those types of comic scenes that most audiences like to see: propriety assaulted. Shillitoe, bored by the proceedings before he is to read his poems, takes repeated drinks of champagne to the point of drunkenness. When he arrives at the lectern to read from his book of poems called *Hellebore* (probably referring to the chemical from the plant to treat insanity), he abandons this effort and turns to the women to lecture them on freedom. He reduces this to sexual freedom by using the simile of the woman as a flower who should open up and bloom; "Open your corsets," he declares. When one woman starts to leave the room, he demands that she sit down. He then begins to tear into all the women by calling them hags. There is a reaction of rage from them as they verbally and physically attack the poet. This riot of proper women may be amusing in a way of superficial comedy, but it is obviously not the stuff that leads to significant satirical statements on society.

Baker's adaptation of his novel unfortunately does not contain universal satirical points on social issues as does *The Horse's Mouth*. Instead, it remains stuck in time, the sixties, as it lampoons the social mores of that decade. (The novel was published in 1964, two years before the movie came out.) While Samson's wife, Rhoda (played by Joanne Woodward), seems to function as the supportive woman in somewhat the same way the colorful Miss Cokey does in the Joyce Cary novel, she seems to be more of a caricature of the brash, low-class, but kind-hearted person who admires the artistic spirit even though she cannot understand it. She remains one of many sexual objects of the incorrigible Samson. When Rhoda manipulates a psychiatrist (played by Patrick O'Neal) to help Samson cure a writing block, jokes on psychiatry reign. In the sixties this was one of the staples of many movies. The faddish humor of the period also focused on sexual intrigues, and so the two are combined. In such an intrigue in *A Fine Madness* the mad poet emerges as a satyr-maniac when he has affairs with a female psychiatrist (enacted by Colleen Dewhurst) and the wife of the O'Neal character, Dr. Oliver West. These complications focusing on sexual comedy become contrived, and the movie degenerates about halfway into what could have been an effective work. In short, the writing is weak when viewed today even though the acting and directing of the film seem competent. *A Fine Madness*, although it deals with a similar type of protagonist as that of *The Horse's*

Mouth, the creative artist as an antisocial person, remains a superficial lampoon.

On a much higher level than *A Fine Madness* is the classical picaresque character that came to the screen in 1963 in the lively, colorful film, *Tom Jones*. Of all the movies that have picaresque leading characters, it probably is the one with the most popular and critical acclaim, although the 1975 *One Flew Over the Cuckoo's Nest* received a great deal of popular recognition. While it may seem ludicrous to make any comparison with the weakly drawn and less sympathetic protagonist in *A Fine Madness*, Tom Jones and Samson Shillitoe nevertheless do have some characteristics in common. Both are depicted as incorrigible libertines. Tom, as a classic portrait of a young rake, cannot resist the charms of just about any woman. This seems to be one of his basic weaknesses as first depicted by Henry Fielding in the 1749 novel. But with his lust exists a devil-may-care desire to poach (a hanging offense at the time) and to carouse to the point of drunkenness, which sometimes leads to a fight. In short, Tom has a wildness of spirit and a temper that get him into the same kind of trouble that the modern Samson Shillitoe portrait often gets embroiled in. However, the similarity ends there, for Tom has a kind of winking innocence even when engaged in his debauchery: a charming, youthful air that provides a comic license in fiction that we find appealing. Samson's debauchery has little fun in it since he seems to be a case of arrested development, merely a man ten years older than Tom, feeding not only his appetites but also his ego.

Henry Fielding's novel employed one of the first, fully developed youth initiation themes during the development of the modern novel in the eighteenth century. Using an epic design, the author ends the work with the protagonist tamed; after many temptations, trials, and failures, Tom Jones learns the values of a more sober life. There is a maturation and regeneration theme as Tom becomes a responsible adult. This last portion is considered by some critics to be the least convincing phase of the novel since Fielding's slant in the earlier portions of the work satirizes the uptight morality of that age and the sentimental novel which espoused the gamut of propriety. It would almost appear that the author wished to please the avid readers of the sentimental novel with a

The famous eating and drinking scene that leads to the bedchamber in *Tom Jones,* starring Albert Finney as Tom and Joyce Redman as Mrs. Waters.

happy and moral ending. However, as it will be seen by those who read the novel, many of Fielding's moral statements are tongue-in-cheek. Narrative reflections on the hero's questionable conduct are full of ironic comic comment.

If the theme of regeneration in *Tom Jones* seems to be slighted in the film adaptation by John Osborne and Tony Richardson, it may be that they wish to comment on the changes in our own age. One of the ways in which the satirical points are revealed by Osborne is in the use of Fielding's narrative reflection on the action of the hero. Here are some examples appearing in the screenplay which are closely reproduced by a voice-over action commentary in the movie:

1. Early in the film Tom finds Molly Seagrim in the woods and yields to her charms; the couple then sink into the foliage as the narrator states, "It shall be our custom to relieve such scenes where taste and decorum and the censor dictate. . . . " (Screenplay by John Osborne, *Tom Jones: A Film Script*, London, Farber and Farber, p. 17.) Here the tongue-in-cheek concept relates closely to our own society, particularly in the handling of sex in the movies, as a more liberal view on depicting sex in the medium evolved in the sixties.

2. Another Fieldingsian comment is employed when Tom gets drunk, "It is widely held that too much wine will dull a man's desire. Indeed it will in a dull man" (from the screenplay, p. 49). Since Tom is approaching Molly with lust, this comic view on drunkenness has, of course, the added sexual connotation.

3. One comment is included in the voice-over narration which satirizes the conventional hero of the novel and film, "Heroes, whatever high ideas we may have of them, are mortal not divine. We are all as God made us and many of us much worse" (from the screenplay, p. 86). This is stated in the movie just before Tom engages in the famous sensuous eating scene with Mrs. Waters as a prelude to a sexual liaison.

Each of the illustrations from the screenplay show a concentration on the more liberal views on sexuality which, at least in some portions of the society, were prominent in the eighteenth century. This stress by the filmmakers also illustrates the growing use of sexual material in the movies in the early sixties. However, Osborne and Richardson do cull many other aspects of eighteenth-century society—the follies of gluttony, suppressive propriety, hypocrisy, sadism, and borishness. In the development of an interesting translation of *Tom Jones*, some of the most penetrating narrative reflections seem to take place during sexual encounters.

John Osborne, one of the leading playwrights of the British theater with such works as *Look Back in Anger* (1957) and *The Entertainer* (1958), can be credited with at least suggesting some of the presentational style or playing the action directly to the camera* existing in the production of *Tom Jones* as a movie. He developed the prelude which reveals the discovery of the abandoned baby Tom in the manner of the silent screen melodrama, with titles instead of spoken dialogue and with a broad acting style. Along with this concept of a period-acting presentation, the author suggested a parallel with humorous etchings by such artists as Hogarth. The screenwriter gave directions for the handling of the prelude to the stag hunt: "The whole of the meet will be shot in a loosish way packing each set-up with the maximum amount of incident and comedy business. The broad satirical comedy of contemporary prints" (from the screenplay, p. 35).

Camera takes by the actors, a type of movie presentationalism, are suggested when Osborne describes the conclusion of the orgiastic hunt in which the stag has been mangled by the dogs. "With a great cry of triumph Western holds up the carcass, streaming with blood, by the antlers. He thrusts it almost into the lens" (from the screenplay, p. 37). Richardson stages this scene in much the same manner, with the added emphasis of a fast zoom to show Western holding the deer. Also, at one point in the screenplay, when Tom is ogling the well-endowed Molly, the directions state, "Tom ogles at camera" (from the screenplay, p. 50), indicating that the author desired camera takes to point up the comedy in a way not employed in the realistic modern comedy film.

Director Tony Richardson does not always follow these descriptions by Osborne, but he adds some significant ones to the film: (1) When Tom and Sophie (the heroine) develop their lasting relationship, she is shown guiding a sailboat as Tom lounges comfortably in the little craft, smoking a clay pipe. A reversal occurs immediately after this shot when we see Tom steering the boat as Sophie reclines and smokes the pipe. She looks at the camera and smiles; (2) After Tom rescues Mrs. Waters, who has been nearly stripped of her clothes by a villain who intended to beat and rape her, he sees the lack of clothing

---

*Presentationalism was the dominant style of production and acting in the theater even into the late nineteenth century. When realism evolved to create a representational style, a more restrained manner of acting developed. Asides to the audience and soliloquies faded as the realistic mode took over.

and seems to blush yet also lust for her. He takes off his hat and places it over the lens of the camera to end the scene; (3) When Tom wakes up in an inn to find that someone has stolen fifty pounds from his breeches, he argues with the landlady vehemently and, in the most blunt presentational device added by Richardson, he turns to the camera and asks, "Did you see her take it?"

Many other devices of the medium are used by Richardson to draw a parallel to the way Henry Fielding used his medium of the novel. The eighteenth-century author made frequent reference to other authors and even set forth long essays (sometimes a whole chapter) on the art of his medium. This is why critics such as Martin C. Battestin in *Virginia Quarterly Review* (Summer 1966, pp. 378–393) and authors Annette Insdorf and Sharon Goodman, "A Whisper and a Wink" in *The English Novel and the Movies*, (Frederick Ungar, 1981, pp. 36–43), find the adaptation of *Tom Jones* one of the most effective novels ever brought to the screen. Osborne and Richardson were wise enough to find the analogical aspects of their medium to assist in the translation of this famous novel. Just as Fielding used a vigorously self-conscious narrative that mocked the sentimental novel of the period, the filmmakers used their medium to make a comment on the follies of our present-day society, even though the work is set in the past. There is a stress in the film *Tom Jones* on sexual liberation as it became more openly examined in the sixties, but coupled with this is the hypocrisy tied to those who profess a decorum that is superior to others. Blifil, the nephew of Allworthy who is also Tom Jones's guardian, proves to be the villain of this story. He appears to have all the virtues without the sins of the flesh that plague Tom, but he is bent on destroying Tom's favorable status with the uncle to secure his own fortune. In order to do this, Blifil informs on Tom whenever possible, indicating that he is doing so in the cause of high morality. In league with the nephew are Tom's tutors, Thwackum and Square, who mouth pieties, but who are as equally hypocritical. Square even gets caught in a liaison with Molly Seagrim after he has tried to get Tom accused of impregnating the sexually active young woman. These three characters' activities add dimension to the satire and contrast strongly with Tom's basic honesty.

The movie version of *Tom Jones* is a drastic condensation of the novel, but it remains one of the best adaptations of the sixties. Furthermore, the movie does not suffer from the fads of the time in the way that *A Fine Madness* does because the filmmakers grasped firmly some of the universals Fielding developed in the examination of the follies of society.

While the adaptation of *Tom Jones* might be said to be a triumph that few people will question, the transcription that takes place with Ken Kesey's 1962 novel, *One Flew Over the Cuckoo's Nest*, is quite another matter. Critics have been divided on the acceptability of the translation to the screen. Some seem to favor the less allegorical statement of the film with its realistic mode (Marsha McCreadie, *Literature/Film Quarterly*, Spring 1977, pp. 125–131), while others find the final statement of the film lacking in the dimension which characterizes the novel (Richard Schickel, *Time*, December 1, 1975). Still other critics find the work a mixture of virtues and faults (Ruth McCormick, *Cineaste*, Fall 1976, pp. 42–43). While I tend to favor this last view, I believe Richard Schickel has touched upon the basic problem which seems to be a popularization of the original source. Here is Schickel's view:

> The movie version of *Cuckoo's Nest* is faithful to the external events of the novel—no complaints there. The trouble is that it betrays no awareness that the events are subject to multiple interpretations. Jack Nicholson plays McMurphy as an unambiguously charming figure, a victim of high spirits, perhaps, but without a dark side or even any gray shadings. He is a fine fellow to spend a couple of hours with, but he has no depth or resonance, and his fate leaves us curiously untouched. Similarly, the zany behaviors of his fellows is amusing, but the depth of their need for McMurphy is not even suggested. Finally, there is a problem of Big Nurse, the chief authority symbol in McMurphy's little world and his main antagonist. In the book, a good deal of tension between them is oddly sexual. In the film, Big Nurse (Louise Fletcher) is merely a prim, quite sexless nag and a symbol only of niggling institutionalism. So nothing of any dramatic power gets going between her and McMurphy. The fault for this lies in a script that would rather ingratiate than abrade. . . .

Much of the loss of depth in the character of the protagonist does seem to lie in the script adapted by Lawrence Hauben and Bo Goldman. The McMurphy of the screen seems to be a blithe adolescent when compared to the hard-nosed craggy, demonic, yet joyous con man of the novel. Also, Nicholson's enactment of the role tiptoes on the edge of being merely an acceptable or even cute statement on machismo. Randle Patrick McMurphy in the novel is a flinty Irishman, raging against the establishment—the embodiment of the free spirit. It is possible that director Milos Forman influenced this popularization of the character to make this scoundrel more appealing to the mass audience of cinema. Director Forman might have chosen Anthony Quinn, a rugged monster of a man, who played an incorrigible with skill and with a comic sense, if one considers the portrait of the protagonist in the 1964 *Zorba the Greek*. But a more youthful image and a more standard image were desired. An interview with Forman in *Filmmakers Newsletter* (December 1975, pp. 28–29) has the following statement by the director:

> In the book the physical description of McMurphy is totally different, and of course your first thoughts are influenced by that vision—a huge man with red hair and a macho kind of personality. Then we also wanted to have a name, a star, because we felt it would be very good for the film since the film is about us, you and me, entering an unknown world. It seemed a good idea to have McMurphy be someone with whom we could identify, someone we knew. Jack Nicholson is that somebody who could enter the unknown world of the mental institution where everyone else was an unknown.

If a person checks the description of McMurphy, one will find that he is a large man and a man with battle scars on his face from fist fights—a grotesque, but a man with a warm, inviting laugh (see the novel, the Signet Book paperback of 1962, p. 16). By using the slight, handsome Nicholson, the director was opting for a type of identity that would mute any possible satire that could come from the character of the picaresque protagonist.

As the screenwriters and director diminished the character of McMurphy, they also cut its mythical dimension which the narrator of the novel, the Indian Chief Bromden, clearly

In *One Flew Over the Cuckoo's Nest* McMurphy (Jack Nicholson) confronts Big Nurse (Louise Fletcher) as he strives for more rights in the mental ward of an army hospital.

establishes by describing this man's superior powers to bring the mentally disturbed inmates out of their cocoons. Randle's fight against the establishment fails, and he is greeted with repeated electric shock treatments and, finally, subjected to a prefrontal lobotomy so that the rebel is reduced to a vegetable. Chief takes action by smothering Randle as he lies in a near coma, and by this act it is suggested that the Indian wishes to preserve the myth. The film does show this active euthanasia, but it seems little more than shooting the horse with a broken leg; Randle McMurphy as a sacrificial god cannot be fully realized in the movie version even when it shows Chief breaking out of the institution after killing his friend and savior.

As a novel, *One Flew Over the Cuckoo's Nest* was one of the typical protests of the time that examined the relationship of the individual with the establishment. Ken Kesey achieved a comic, and I believe satirical, dimension by making the protagonist a picaresque who, while he has a free spirit that is admirable, harbors many faults. While he has a basic charm that makes him more acceptable than the cool, humorless, rigid establishment personified by Big Nurse Ratched, he also has a crudeness and an egocentricity that make him an ambivalent character. Furthermore, his egocentricity leads to a misogyny that is almost intolerable. Women are to be used or abused. As noble as Randle's efforts with his fellow inmates of the asylum sometimes appear, he seems like a case of arrested development and appears to be a grown man still in the gang stage of his relationship with women. In fact, the movie's lighter comic touch seems almost to appeal to the adolescent mind, and some members of the theater audience might easily go along with McMurphy's throttling of Big Nurse, which is a type of triumph of the free spirit over the establishment. But the violence of this act in the movie is direct and simple in a way that might provoke sympathetic laughter for Randle's temporary victory over his adversary. Note the complexity of this act in Kesey's description of the attack:

> Only at the last—after he's smashed through the glass door, her face swinging around, with terror forever ruining any other look she might ever try to use again, screaming when he grabbed for her and ripped her uniform all the way down the front, screaming again when the two nippled circles started from her chest and swelled out and out, bigger than anybody had ever even imagined, warm and pink in the light—only at the last, after the officials realized that the three black boys weren't going to do anything but stand and watch and they would have to beat him off without their help, doctors and supervisors and nurses prying those heavy red fingers out of the white flesh of her throat as if they were her neck bones, jerking him backward off of her with a loud heave of breath, only then did he show any sign that he might be anything other than a sane, willful, dogged man performing a hard duty that finally just had to be done, like it or not. [From the novel, p. 267]

This assault seems like a rape, yet it exposes the sexual characteristics of the hard, dominating woman in a way that humiliates this very proper woman—maybe more of a put-down than the actual throttling. The movie uses only the direct choking of nurse Ratched.

Further development of this incident in the novel gives the scene dimension. A metaphor of a wounded animal being attacked by dogs is used to describe the restraint of Randle. A philosophical detachment regarding this incident gives it profundity. The scene is not merely a straightforward personal drama—the downfall of McMurphy achieves mythical proportions in the eyes of the Indian, Chief Bromden. The unfettered spirit of nature has been crushed. Coming from a race that has seen its environment and its people raped, Bromden sees this act as the sacrifice of some god of nature. Chief does finally break away from the asylum to a possible freedom, but the significance of his escape exists on a simple level. In the movie, so many of the ironic qualities of this satire have been expunged by a direct approach which does not examine the thoughts of Chief Bromden, the narrator of the novel. As a result the movie is a pale imitation of the original vision of novelist Ken Kesey.

The British cinema in the sixties and seventies handled many works that used the eccentric rogue, but the social comment in them merely borders on the satirical without having the sharpness of corrective comedy. Examples of such works are *Alfie* and *Morgan!* in 1966 and *Butley* in 1974. Each of these works uses the rogue protagonist's name for the title. Alfie is a low-class Don Juan, or a Cockney Casanova, who engages in affairs with many women to satisfy his ego. As a character adapted to the screen by playwright Bill Naughton from his own stage play, the protagonist would be insufferable if his self-centered conquest of "birds" did not also feature his mental reflections on his affairs with women. These inward, personal views show a ludicrous inversion of values when he has difficulties, such as one of his conquests backfiring; he rationalizes to defend his own ego. Most of the reflections are delivered directly to the camera in a presentational way that was first introduced by such New Wave French filmmakers as Jean-Luc Godard and François Truffaut. In the title role, Michael Caine delivers one of the best performances of his career; he imparts a disarming charm to a cocky, amoral egotist. In fact, some ambivalence in audience reaction develops toward the character of Alfie so that he may be viewed more sympathetically than he should be. As a result, the comic comment on such a self-centered rogue seems muted.

Morgan!, starring David Warner, presents a different type of rogue: a child-like madman who engages in a number of caprices as he attempts to regain the affections of his former wife who has found him impossible to live with. Morgan cannot stand the thought of the divorce and plans wacky pranks, even to the point of abducting the woman and trying to break up her marriage to a rival by donning a gorilla suit and crashing the wedding party. Furthermore, Morgan has some skill as an artist, although certainly not of the stature of Gulley Jimson; nevertheless, he is a kook whose obsession with painting gorillas has received some notice from faddish London art collectors. While *Morgan!* focuses on the antics of the eccentric artist, the final comic tone is more that of *A Fine Madness* than *The Horse's Mouth*. At best, the directing by Karel Reisz (noted for his 1960 *Saturday Night and Sunday Morning*), plus the acting by David Warner of the title role and by Vanessa Redgrave as his former wife, make the movie an enjoyable dark comedy. Most of the pokes at conventionality prove delightful, but screenwriter David Mercer, adapting his own television play, ends up with a potpourri of comic digs that do not add up to an effective whole.

Butley, adapted by Simon Gray from his own stage play and directed by one of Britain's most important playwrights, Harold Pinter, proves to be one of the most successful of the American Film Theater presentations in 1974.* Alan Bates's enactment of Ben Butley is a *tour de force*, with the overall development of the character displaying one of the most complex picaresque portraits in a movie. Butley is a college teacher who becomes a leech on the educational system. With all kinds of diversions and excuses he avoids tutoring students; he engages in various mechanisms to control, discredit, or mock his colleagues. However, he has an awareness of his own faults and even mocks these

---

*Examples of other works created by this group were such well-known stage plays as Eugene O'Neill's *The Iceman Cometh* (1973), Ionesco's *Rhinoceros* (1974), and John Osborne's *Luther* (1974).

weaknesses. Here is a rogue who smiles and destroys—a relentless sadist who can tear almost anyone apart with his wit and invective. By the end of the film we realize that his ridicule of people and social relationships has become a type of self-destruction; he ends up without his wife and friends. It may be that this portrait becomes too narrow and too individual to make a significant statement on society. Ben Butley does expose some of the desultory and muddled approaches to education plus the sham of intellectuals in higher education, but the attack seems too indirect. We are focused more on a clever but hollow psychological goof-off. However, his fall remains more personal than that of the Evelyn Waugh character, Captain Grimes, in his 1928 novel *Decline and Fall*, which was brought to the screen in 1969. The portrait of Captain Grimes as a con man who takes advantage of the educational system is a simple, direct satire on this type of rogue.

In the same period of many works that concentrated on the rogue, con man, madman, and incorrigible, the United States film industry created such films as *The Life and Times of Judge Roy Bean* (1972), *Dead Heat on a Merry-Go-Round* (1966), and *They Might Be Giants* (1971).

Least successful of the three is John Huston's *The Life and Times of Judge Roy Bean*. While director Huston handled the satirical dimensions of *Wise Blood* in 1979 with adroit shadings, the tone of this 1971 work lapses into fantasy and a puzzling combination of the serious and comic which produces a type of ambiguity confusing to audiences. In an attempt to develop the legend of Roy Bean—a capricious, likeable blackguard who establishes himself as a judge in a remote western town in the late nineteenth century in order to be a king in his own domain—the writer seems to be partly at fault. Playing the title role, Paul Newman, never too distinguished for his comedy portraits, tries to use the best of high spirits and charm to show this self-appointed judge's comic, high-handed way of taking property and lives away from passerby victims who have questionable pasts—all, of course, in the name of law and order. It becomes a way of developing his own kingdom. The basic idea seems to have the potential of satire, but all concerned with this production of *The Life and Times of Judge Roy Bean* must have wandered in the desert of the Old West without a clear-cut goal.

Another production using an original screenplay, developed by director Bernard Girard, *Dead Heat on a Merry-Go-Round*, proves to be a more successful work. James Coburn's portrait of a con man assists in developing this film with the aid of Girard's concept that the criminal society and the establishment both operate with questionable values. It is a cynical notion that has been used in many serious novels and films before *Dead Heat on a Merry-Go-Round*, but it seems more fully developed in this particular comedy. The protagonist, Eli Kotch, is constantly playing games with each type of society or institution he encounters. And these societies and institutions play games with him. From his work with a prison psychotherapist to his crime caper in which he robs a bank during the visit of a Russian Premier, Eli is shown for his slippery and shrewd assault on society. In an indirect way the film does make a statement. While dark comedies with protagonists who were often labeled "anti-heroes" were not clear-cut satirical statements, such films in the late sixties and early seventies represented the maverick in all of us in the adolescent age of rebellion against the establishment. In this case it is the maverick who succeeds in a heist that embarrasses the forces of law and order; he also delights in his amoral, self-centered relationship with all women. Through its title, *Dead Heat on a Merry-Go-Round* may take on another meaning that was not intended. The result of Eli Kotch's victory becomes nihilistic, in much the same way that some of the protest against the establishment became nihilistic. There is no result of the merry-go-round ride; it is circular, without purpose.

They Might Be Giants also is a study of a maverick, but a much different type. It is the case of a madman named Justin Playfair, who believes he is Sherlock Holmes. This eccentric dons the garb of the famous fictional detective created by Sir Arthur Conan Doyle. As played by George C. Scott, the unhinged former judge becomes likeable and seems more sane than a brother who is trying to commit him to a mental institution with the assistance of a city psychiatrist (played by Joanne Woodward). Ironically, the would-be Sherlock Holmes seizes on the name of this woman, Dr. (Mildred) Watson, as an indication of a fortunate encounter through fate. Against her will at first, she is merely fascinated by a "classic paranoia" case; however, she is finally captivated by his sincerity and charm to the extent that she becomes his assistant and sidekick, Dr. Watson to his Mr. Holmes, to fight the evil Moriarty. Tied to the title's allusion to *Don Quixote*, Playfair does attempt some knightly tasks in the fashion of Don Quixote as he flails at the windmills of a regimented metropolis establishment and, as a result, gets into many scrapes. Furthermore, he is pursued by his brother and his brother's hired hands (who become a parallel to the evil of Moriarty). This whimsical piece was adapted by James Goldman from his stage play. While it received little critical acclaim, at its best the work speaks for individualism in a society that has become too mechanized and depersonalized to allow room for the maverick, and, consequently, the free spirit.

While the result of this movie production of *They Might Be Giants* seems somewhat fuzzy, missing its whimsical target, salted and peppered with sentiment and fantasy, it does have one feature of the classic satire that needs to be noted—the use of analogy or fable, a type of fancy of the author's mind, used for ironic or satirical intent. Two works that lean in this direction, *The Magic Christian* (1970) and *The World According to Garp* (1982), seem to be good examples with which to conclude this examination of the picaresque character in literature adapted to the film.

The fable nature of the novel and film versions of Terry Southern's *The Magic Christian* focuses on a "What if . . . ?" or "Once upon a time . . . " premise. This 1960 short novel relates a fanciful tale of a millionaire named Guy Grand, who decides to use his money in a way to "make it hot" for people—to expose their foibles. As a result of his action the novel chronicles over twenty tricks that Grand arranges to show the greed, hypocrisy, pretentiousness, gluttony, and superficiality of humans, to name a few of the vices and follies he exposes. The film changes the locale from the United States to Britain, rearranges many incidents, drops some, and adds others, but the looseness of the plot development still remains, with the adaptation presenting a string of elaborate practical jokes by the picaresque character.

The two most complicated mechanizations by Guy Grand are the cruise on a ship called the *Magic Christian* and the contest of finding money in a large pool filled with manure, urine, and blood from a slaughterhouse. Using extensive public relations and advertisements, the joker lures wealthy, snobbish people to board a ship that is merely a magnificent movie studio set which gives the illusion of taking a cruise to exotic lands. Many mishaps on this mock voyage confront the proprieties of the rich, who expected the essence of plushness and comfort. But all goes wrong as the ship appears to be hijacked by modern-day pirates; assorted grotesques also pop up from hiding to plague the distinguished clients of the ocean cruise. In the movie version this situation is multiplied to include dwarfs, homosexuals, transsexuals, dope fiends, and even Dracula—a bizarre collection of weird creatures who run amok on the ship until there is an order to abandon the vessel because it is thought to be on fire and sinking. Mae West life preservers inflate to gigantic size, turning the fleeing passengers into helpless rolling balls. To the chagrin of these escaping dignitaries, they discover the voyage was a hoax, that no one has moved an inch away from London, that an illusion of a trip has merely been created by using a large movie studio containing a stage version of a cruiser. In this most elaborate sequence of the movie, high society's propriety is punctured. It is the most elaborate practical joke of both the novel and the movie. The adaptation to film seems to be faulty when *The Magic Christian* concludes the drama with the wallowing of people in the ghastly pool of slaughterhouse refuse as the climax. Guy Grand throws thousands of pounds into this venture and into the pool in order to portray the length to which people will go to obtain money. After advertising that a pool of money exists, Grand watches the people gather and dive into the horrible mess to retrieve the money. And, of course, this severe test by the millionaire exposes the greed that exists in people. Evidently the filmmakers believed this concluding practical joke would bring home the point of the movie's dark humor approach to social comment. This portion of the movie is often considered questionable in its taste by television stations which air the film, for when *The Magic Christian* is broadcast, the pool sequence usually is eliminated.

A number of incidents throughout the movie, however, illustrate one of Southern's most telling exposures of human weakness: greed. When Grand opens a cut-rate grocery store, greed combined with gluttony is revealed as people pounce on the bargains. A city official who issues overtime or improper parking tickets is given five hundred pounds by Grand to eat the ticket he has just issued for illegal parking. The protagonist also bribes the Oxford rowing team not only to lose the race, but also to display a lack of sportsmanship by ramming and sinking the boat about to win the race.

Good sportsmanship is also lampooned when the millionaire goes on a hunt for partridge with dignitaries who pride themselves on their decorum for properly stalking, shooting, and killing the game. Grand conceives an elaborate ruse by introducing a military maneuver. Using a walkie-talkie, he informs his cohorts, dressed as a military division with heavy armament, to shoot the flying birds out of the sky with ack-ack guns. One little bird is slaughtered, and a cook armed with a flamethrower fries the fowl on the spot. The hunters are, of course, horrified by this display of bad sportsmanship—at which point Guy Grand informs them he was merely intent on a "clean kill." Added to the movie, this sequence is probably the most innovative scene and remains effective today since the United States has a very strong government lobby group of hunters in the National Rifle Association.

Peter Sellers, as the eccentric millionaire who is bent on exposing the weaknesses in humans, does a fair job of enacting the role of Guy Grand. Given credit for scripting *The Magic Christian* with director Joseph McGrath and novelist Terry Southern, the famous comic actor employs a keen sense of glee as he tricks people. Sellers's protagonist proves to be a different type of picaresque character than found in many novels and their adaptations. Despite the character's obsessions and odd quirks, he always remains on top of each situation. Because he has so much money, he can always buy his way out of any legal punishment that might be directed at him for his continued mischief.

Part of the reason *The Magic Christian* does not develop into a full-fledged satire lies in the disjointed fable: the story that consists of one practical joke after another. And, nothing ever backfires on the millionaire in his machinations. The superiority of this eccentric on the attack makes him not only an unusual picaresque character but, in the end, somewhat of a villain. As a trickster he also seems to be exposing minor foibles. A person could ask what the total effort adds up to—that people are weak or gullible? But they do not seem to be vicious. As a prankster

Guy Grand appears to be archetypal—a sophisticated version of the village mischief-maker of ancient folk tales, a Till Eulenspiegel.

Since the creation in the early seventeenth century of the fanatical, would-be knight-errant Don Quixote by Spanish writer Cervantes, there have been many variations on rogues, con men, madmen, and deviants in literature. Most protagonists have been men. In the age of feminism, it is only fitting that at least one important picaresque woman would appear: Jenny Fields in John Irving's novel *The World According to Garp*. This work, like *The Magic Christian*, has the quality of a fable for our times, with an examination of controversial issues that exist in contemporary society. In a work that punctures sexual stereotypes and sexual roles, Garp, a struggling fictional writer, might be said to be the protagonist. He deviates strongly from the norm of society by becoming the househusband with all the roles generally assigned to the mother. An excellent cook who takes pride in his dishes, he becomes a protector of the offspring and, without complaint, the always-on-call chauffeur for the family. However, Jenny Fields, the assertive, independent woman and mother of Garp, becomes a co-protagonist in the novel. Even more emphasis on her character in the 1982 adaptation to the screen extends this status.

Journalist critic Marilyn French, writing about the movie in *Ms.* magazine, perceptively pinpoints the comic inversion of traditional roles advanced in Irving's novel:

> Since it is androgynous, Garp's world is also a place of sexual equality. If any political, economic, or social inequity existed (none is suggested), it would be offset by the general worldly superiority of the women. For most of the males, even the heroes, are to some degree unsure, ineffectual, silly—laughable; whereas the major female characters, Jenny Fields (a nurse and Garp's mother), and Helen Holm (a professor and Garp's wife) are supremely assured, confident, and competent: they seem as unfamiliar with self-doubt as they are with fear. The women deal with life directly, practically, prudently, decisively, yet with compassion and wisdom. The men deal with life indirectly through imagination (fantasy, delusion, or art), play, or through sports, which sublimate both erotic and

aggressive tendencies. If the men are more appealing, the
women are more admirable. ["The 'Garp' Phenomenon,"
Ms., September 1982, p. 14]

From this passage movie critic French would seem to be
inclined to favor the adaptation, but she also seems to be
disturbed, as many women critics were, with the harsh satirical
treatment given to such liberationists. Anyone reading the book
or viewing the movie should keep in mind that in Irving's
whimsical world he is both embracing feminist tenets in our
contemporary society and ridiculing their excesses. As eccentric
as Jenny Fields is, she is treated sympathetically and respectfully
in the novel and film. But her attitudes are also satirized.

Jenny's character could not be said to have the mad traits of
the romantic, would-be knight errant, Don Quixote, who
wanted to turn back the clock; however, she is a person who tilts
her lance at the windmills of conformity. There is a type of
madness in her character and that of others who defy conventional behavior. For example, two such picaresque women were
created by Nathanael West: Fay Doyle in *Miss Lonelyhearts* and
Faye Greener in *The Day of the Locust*. These satirical portraits
of obsessed women show Doyle as a middle-aged, lonely woman
with manic sexual frustrations and Greener as a seventeen-year-
old amoral creature who is wrapped in the cocoon of her own
ego. Both become destroyers of men, making them dark comedy
variations on the femme fatale. The only way these two obsessed
women relate to Jenny Fields is in their deviations from what
society thinks is a socially accepted approach to the opposite
sex. Jenny has rejected the standard and accepted relationship
with men, for she completely avoids them as sexual partners.

In John Irving's novel Jenny Fields looks about her to view
what she calls "a dirty-minded world . . . where a woman must
be [as the narration interprets her views] either somebody's wife
or somebody's whore—or fast on your way to becoming one or
the other" (from the novel, *The World According to Garp*,
Pocket Books edition, p. 13). She will have no truck with men
except on a business basis. She wants to live her own life without
them—an attitude that puzzles her father and mother. When
Jenny later writes a best-selling autobiography called *A Sexual
Suspect*, she sums up her plight: "I wanted a job and I wanted to

live alone. That made me a sexual suspect. Then I wanted a baby, but I didn't want to share my body or my life to have one. That made me a sexual suspect, too" (from the novel, p. 15).

Her autobiography becomes the bible for feminists, and Jenny Fields becomes a heroine and guru for the movement. As John Irving's fable unfolds, we as readers and viewers of the movie find in Jenny what might seem to be a bundle of contradictions. She loves babies but does not want the burden of a husband; she coolly impregnates herself by having relations with a comatose World War II casualty (a type of rape in reverse that bothered some feminist movie critics); and, she never worries about the social stigma of having an illegitimate child. As a single parent by choice, she takes a job as a nurse for a boy's school to give her son a solid education. The narration in the novel indicates Irving's whimsical comment on traditional morality: "Pride was well loved in the community of the Steering School, but Jenny Fields appeared to be proud of an illegitimate child. Nothing to hang her head about, perhaps; however, she might show a *little* humility" (from the novel, p. 35).

The movie version of *The World According to Garp*, with adaptation by Steve Tesich and direction by George Roy Hill, retains most of the features of the picaresque Jenny Fields. In some ways the movie softens Jenny's relentless determination and rigid, personal moral codes. Nevertheless, Irving's original conception prevails as Jenny continues her defiance of many conventions. And she is shown rearing Garp in a way that does not smother him with motherly attention even when she tries to control all phases of his education and social life. Her magnificent independence ironically serves as a good influence in the long run. Garp becomes a liberated male and, usually, a man who matures in his thinking at an early age. His mother, in her own oddball way, produces a very successful book and gains fame as an author while he remains relatively obscure, a writer appreciated by some critics but not by the public. And, of course, he is a much better writer than she is. The movie might be faulted for its handling of this last aspect. The novel with its looser structure presents diversions—two short stories by author Garp called "The Pension Grillparzer" and "The World According to Bensenhaver." Both have the distinct Irving whimsy that is so admired by the novelist's fans. The movie substitutes two examples of experimental cinema in order to bridge the gap between the media, an animated fantasy of the boy Garp as he imagines his father as a World War II flying ace (executed in a series of moving images as if by a child artist) and a live-action fantasy in surrealistic fashion about a lover who cannot experience emotion, called *The Magic Gloves*. As the film medium's substitute for short stories, this device by the filmmakers proves to be a noble attempt at translation, but it cannot fully bridge the difference between the media to make Garp a credible author.

On the plus side of the movie adaptation is the screenwriter's ability to show some of the contradictory facets of Jenny as she becomes involved with her son Garp and a prostitute. Because she finds any form of sexuality disgusting, Jenny at first treats the woman of the street with prudish objectivity; that is, she keeps aloof from what she detects as a lustful contact being established between the woman and her son. However, she wishes to hear all about this woman's professional views on sex—curious about her views on her relationship with men, wondering if she, as the prostitute, is exploited by the man or she, as the professional, is exploiting the man. Movie adapter Tesich adds an exchange between Garp and his mother as Jenny gives money to her son to do, as she puts it, "Do what you must do, I expect." Garp tells Jenny that she shouldn't give money to the prostitute that openly because she might be detected by the police and arrested. Jenny, in a seeming contradiction, sharply declares that since the woman is using her own body, she should be able to do as she pleases. When it comes to the rights of women, Jenny, ever the female liberationist, takes a strong and sometimes paradoxical stand. This added elaboration from the novel by the screenwriter helps condense and focus on the amazing and complex character of Jenny Fields.

The co-protagonist of *The World According to Garp* takes on a different position in life when her son has a family of his own. At her parents' mansion she establishes a refuge for oppressed women as she becomes the grand dame, a type of mother superior to all the rejects of society or ones who have rejected society. Dark comedy reigns as Jenny gathers a group of women who have mutilated themselves by having their tongues cut out to demonstrate the plight of an abused girl, Ellen James, whose rapists had mutilated her. They cut out her tongue to prevent the girl from revealing their identities. This bizarre cult aggravates and disturbs Garp because he views the extreme nature of the group as merely negative: a cult to hate men. But Jenny, ever the goddess in her domain, is tolerant of all beliefs held by women. She even welcomes a transsexual, Robert Muldoon, a former big league football player who, after an operation, uses the name Roberta. Roberta, still retaining the strength of her former profession, becomes Jenny Fields's bodyguard.

In both the novel and film Roberta becomes one of Garp's best friends. Mentally, this transsexual experiences many of the disappointments that confront women in a world structured by a male-dominated perspective. In a satirical way much is revealed about our society's narrowness—the inability to accept a person's desire to take up a new lifestyle.

As a film, *The World According to Garp* has been underrated. Movie critic Richard Schickel in *Time* magazine rightly has observed that "the world according to novelist John Irving is a dangerous place, the individual's position in it much more fragile than he imagines it to be" (*Time*, August 2, 1982, p. 78). And as most critics realize, it is a difficult world to reproduce on film. It is to the credit of adapter Steve Tesich and director George Roy Hill that such a difficult task has been at least partly realized. This film is not one for the average audience. Irving's novel, however, proved to be a bestseller, so there is an audience for both the book and film. The movie version does reflect the novel faithfully. Even critic Schickel, who is not inclined favorably toward the movie, states that the creators of the film have not tampered with the plot or characters. And most critics, and audiences, find the skill of Glenn Close's portrait of Jenny Fields intriguing. She plays a convincing role of the woman from early twenties to old age—a feat in itself. However, she plays the role in a way that avoids the ludicrous and yet makes a strong comment on the excesses in her attitudes. John Lithgow as Roberta Muldoon handles the role with his comic gift and still makes this unusual transsexual sympathetic. Critics were mixed in their evaluation of Robin Williams's handling of Garp. Some could not see him as divorced from the creature from outer space in the sitcom television series that made him a well-known actor. However, director Hill restrains the comedian to the point that he almost plays the role as a straight part. In short, he is restrained enough so that his Garp doesn't quite seem to be from the planet Ork.

It is possible that *The World According to Garp* will gain favor with time in the way that George Roy Hill's other satirical adaptation to screen, the 1972 *Slaughterhouse-Five*, has now increased in critical acclaim. It may even be a case of the movie transcending the novel as the years go by. While I do not hold as severe a view as *National Review* critic John Simon maintains, I see some pretensions in the novel that seem to work against Irving's satirical intent. In Simon's review of September 3, 1982 (p. 1096), he calls the execution of the work "an intense, cute, rather labored brilliance that obscures all else—both the little that is there and the lot that pretends to be." He claims that the simplifications executed in the film version were beneficial. At times Irving's novel seems unnecessarily convoluted and arch, but I'm sure the novelist's defenders will find this observation a typical detractor's annoyance with his whimsy—an approach that has style and substance integrated by the author's innovation. With the movie adaptation of *The World According to Garp*, use by the filmmakers of a less complicated structure and character development shows some defects evolving. In the Tesich-Hill creation Jenny Fields becomes more believable while Garp becomes less credible and more sentimental. Feminist movie critics Katha Pollitt (in *The Nation*, September 4, 1982, pp. 187–9) and Marilyn French (in *Ms.*, September 1982, pp. 14–16) are quick to seize on this adaptation lapse or distortion, although they do not object to the more favorable portrait of Jenny Fields. These evaluators' mixed reactions to the book and the movie seem to result from Irving's and the filmmakers' exploding sexual stereotypes in a direct assault on both sexes' attitudes. While they believe the male views emerge relatively unscathed, I believe they are mistaken. To me the comic attack is well-balanced in both the novel and the film.

A question does occur regarding both the novel and film. Do we the readers and viewers witness a satirical statement on sexual roles that is substantial, that has depth? Black comedy it surely has, but Irving's novel and the adaptation slip at times into emotional scenes that touch the heart in a way that mutes the satire. It is possible that Irving and the filmmakers have revealed our own ambivalent attitudes toward sexual roles in our society. Maybe time will provide us the ability to reflect more objectively on *The World According to Garp*.

As far as the strength of the picaresque protagonist in film versions of novels is concerned, if they can be rated on a scale, the eccentric artist Gully Jimson of the 1958 *The Horse's Mouth* and the delightful rogue Tom of the 1963 *Tom Jones* will rank among the top of the lot. Time will tell if Jenny Fields will join the top rank of these film deviants of society and if *The World According to Garp* will be an outstanding satire on the changing sexual roles in our culture.

CHAPTER 7

WAYWARD YOUTH AND THE FLOUNDERING FAMILY

WHEN JAMES DEAN CREATED an intense portrait of a disenchanted teenager in *Rebel Without a Cause* in the 1955 film directed by Nicholas Ray, it became clear that movies were showing a relationship between an offspring and his parents that was nearly the opposite of that depicted in many thirties works that focused on the family. The Andy Hardy of the fifties no longer had a kindly, wise, tolerant patriarch like Judge Hardy, who could steer the youngster through his struggles to attain adulthood. James Dean's father, played by Jim Backus, was an effete man who would only knit his eyebrows and wonder where he had gone wrong in raising such a wayward young man.

Rebel Without a Cause reflected cultural change in a decade when youth embraced its own music, rock, and the drift between parent and offspring widened until this manifestation would be called "the generation gap" in the sixties. While this James Dean movie of the fifties was a serious exploration of the theme, the 1967 *The Graduate* became the quintessential satirical treatment a decade later. A rereading of Charles Webb's 1963 novel, *The Graduate*, convinced me that the initiation of youth fiction of the time did attempt to make some significant social statement. The adaptation of this work four years later brought both critical and popular acclaim to a genre that would flourish in the late sixties. Besides *The Graduate*, the most noteworthy youth-oriented movies were *You're a Big Boy Now* (1967) and *Good-*

160

bye, Columbus (1969), with a more obscure example of this type of film, *Portrait of the Artist as a Young Man* (1977), appearing a decade later.

If the novel and film versions of *The Graduate* are examined closely, it will be discovered that the adaptation is generally faithful. Charles Webb's conception became a natural for the medium of cinema. The novel framed its narrative in the dramatic mode: a straightforward, chronological approach with extensive use of dialogue.

Benjamin Braddock, a successful college graduate who is admired by his parents and his parents' friends because they perceive his potential as outstanding, proves to be morose and uncommunicative on the eve of the celebration of his college achievements. Ben will not join in the festivities of his own party; he is a young man of twenty-one who does not know what he will do with his skills, and most frustrating of all for his parents, he doesn't seem to care. As in the serious examination of familial degeneration witnessed in *Rebel Without a Cause*, the son in *The Graduate* becomes the source of his parents' anguish. But in this latter work the blame which the father and mother heap on themselves for not having been successful in raising the son becomes the subject for comedy.

Screenwriters Calder Willingham and Buck Henry follow the novel's pattern of development, starting with a graduation celebration arranged by the proud parents. The film traces the sexual affair of Benjamin with the wife of his father's law partner and concludes with the final revolt of the youth who abducts the daughter of this older woman, Mrs. Robinson—an abduction which Ben executes with a flair, taking the daughter as she is about to be married in an elaborate church wedding. Benjamin Braddock exemplifies the wayward youth because he proves by this act that he will not follow the dictates of his parents and the life-style they espouse. Charles Webb's novel assaults the staid, regimented world of the middle-class, affluent suburbanites as typified by the husbands and wives, the Braddocks and the Robinsons. Fortunately, the film version retains much of this satirical approach.

Both the novel and film versions of *The Graduate* do not etch the characters of these two offspring, Ben, and his girlfriend, Elaine Robinson, with heroic or sentimental facets. They are

Offscreen in this shot Mrs. Robinson (Anne Bancroft) displays a shapely leg to Ben Braddock (Dustin Hoffman) in *The Graduate*.

two young people struggling inadequately to live their own lives. They, like their parents, are comic portraits, for they have mixed emotions about striking out on their own. Ben Braddock's naivete when Mrs. Robinson tries to seduce him after his graduation party and their subsequent meetings in a hotel room create effective humor. His "turned off" attitudes toward a future profession and the well-intended but shallow guidance of his parents give his character dimension. Elaine Robinson seems more a product of her suburban society as she is somewhat easily pushed into a marriage by the career-oriented Cal Smith, who proposes to her in a way which reveals his business mind intruding into personal relations. As Elaine describes it, "He thought we'd make a pretty good team" (from the novel, *The Graduate*, New American Library edition, p. 134). However, the dogged pursuit of Elaine by Ben impresses her and causes her to waver from Cal to Ben in her affections. This indecisive nature produces effective comedy of frustration. Also, she cannot quite break away from the mold that her parents have designed for her, causing more mental stress for Ben.

In both the novel and film versions the attitudes of the fathers of Ben and Elaine produce the most satirical comments on the suburban culture, with the corporate mentality fusing all aspects of love, marriage, and the "good life" in the establishment of a traditional, emotionally desensitized life-style that is safe, secure, and bland. Inculcated with a relentless work ethic, Mr. Braddock is appalled by his son's lack of ambition. In a heart-to-heart talk between father and son, there almost seems to be a parody of the sentimental comedy scene often witnessed in the Andy Hardy films of the thirties. In the novel this encounter goes as follows:

> "And let's be honest about this, Ben. Your mother and I are certainly as much to blame as you are for whatever is happening."
> "No, you aren't."
> "Well we are. We've raised you. We've tried to instill certain values into your thinking."
> "Dad, I'm not blaming you."
> "Well, I'm blaming me then."
> "Well, you shouldn't."
> "Ben," Mr. Braddock said, "something is horribly wrong."
> "Look Dad," Benjamin said. "This is getting kind of melodramatic. ... The graduate comes home. He gets disillusioned. He gets bitter. He sits around home and goes to pot. His parents wring their hands and blame his failings on themselves. I mean—yes." He nodded. "It has kind of a hearts and flowers ring to it." [From the novel, p. 57]

There is a similar but condensed scene in the movie version, with some of the reflection of the above last speech of Ben deleted. In cutting this reflection by the protagonist, some of the character of Ben is diminished. The father, essentially a comic caricature in the novel, remains so in the movie. But the thrust of satire does not fade with his portrait because the comment on the crushing weight of the success drive on the middle-class man in our society becomes well-established by Mr. Braddock's distress with Ben's disengagement from what is expected of him as he slips into an aimless existence.

Elaine's father, Mr. Robinson, also is given a rather narrow character dimension in order to parody the strained, genteel attitudes of the middle-class, middle-aged male when he is faced with a domestic crisis. He learns of the affair his wife is having with Ben, a young man the same age as the Robinson's daughter, and confronts this hapless youth; Ben tries to exert his own manhood by rebutting Mr. Robinson's accusation that his actions were a betrayal of "trust and confidence" on the level of a conspiracy:

> "There was no reason for it, Mr. Robinson."
> "Well," Mr. Robinson said. "I can see why you'd like to say no one's responsible, I can understand how you might like to leave it at that, but Ben, you're a little old to be saying you're not responsible—"
> "I am responsible!"
> "You're responsible for it but there was no reason for it? That's interesting—"
> "There was no personal—no personal—"
> "No personal element involved?" [From the novel, p. 140]

From author Webb's dialogue it is obvious that comedy evolves from a professional mindset that lawyer Robinson cannot shake off when dealing with personal problems. It is a comic technique the master satirist Molière loved to use when ridiculing lawyers and physicians. Ben's attempt to defend himself in this delightful scene in the novel produces some of the best humor:

> "Listen to me," Benjamin said, taking another step forward. "We got—we got into bed with each other. But it was nothing. It was nothing at all. We might—we might as well have been shaking hands."

"Shaking hands," Mr. Robinson said. "Ben, I think you're old enough to know there's a little difference between shaking hands with a woman and—."

"There wasn't!"

"Oh?" Mr. Robinson said, raising his eyebrows. "I always thought when you took off your clothes and got into bed with a woman and had intercourse with her there was a little more involved than—"

"Not in this case!"

"Not in this case," Mr. Robinson said, nodding. "Well. That's not saying much for my wife, is it." [From the novel, p. 141]

This comic struggle for honor and some way to save face creates a type of humorous confusion that exists in both the novel and film. The scene concludes with the indignant husband looking at his watch and declaring that he may be able to sue Ben—if not, he assures the youth that he will see that he is put behind bars if he even looks at his daughter. Once more, there is the mind-set of the bourgeois lawyer who is incapable of making adjustment in dealing with a delicate situation. In his parting shots at Ben, Mr. Robinson does lose his "cool" by calling the youth "scum" and a person with a "filthy mind." He must cover up the fact that his wife is an alcoholic degenerate whose sexual promiscuity promoted the whole affair. While there is some condensation of this scene from the original source, the film provides the same comic comment on the face-saving tactics of the proper male who will not face the truth.

Mrs. Robinson, in both the novel and the film adaptation, also possesses the hypocrisy that often accompanies the values of those who believe they come from the higher class. In her predatory way she establishes a longtime affair with Benjamin, but turns on him when he starts taking an interest in her daughter, Elaine. To his amazement Ben learns from his middle-aged mistress that while he is good enough for the mother, he is not the proper mate for her offspring. Webb and the filmmakers parody middle-class views on the importance of the proper marriage which is arranged by the parents in the twentieth century as rigidly as it was in past ages and cultures.

The translation of *The Graduate* to film works well in establishing this satirical comment; and the parents, played by Anne

Bancroft (Mrs. Robinson), Murray Hamilton (Mr. Robinson), and William Daniels (Mr. Braddock), flesh out their roles with consummate skill under Mike Nichols's direction. Where the film version seems to go astray is in the last fourth of its development. A switch in comic tone and a growing sympathy for Ben cause the satirical points developed on the characters of Ben (played by Dustin Hoffman) and Elaine (enacted by Katharine Ross) to meander out of focus. The director and writers seem to have opted for a direct appeal to the youth market by giving Ben's battle to marry Elaine over the objections of her parents a more serious tone than was intended by novelist Webb. Richard Schickel seems to be one of the few critics to detect this basic flaw. He writes of the protagonist's struggle:

> From anti- or at least non-hero he suddenly starts to emerge as a romantic hero of the unhyphenated variety. Oh, he still fumbles and mumbles and trips all over himself, but the emotional distance from which we previously viewed him—a distance absolutely essential for satire— suddenly disappears. We find ourselves asked to stand shoulder to sympathetic shoulder with him as he attempts to rescue his (young) lady love from living death—marriage to a square. The movie loses its shrewd. Sentiment replaces even-handed toughness, and there is an attempt to force our acknowledgment of Ben's final superiority over environment and elders. [*Life*, January 19, 1968, p. 16]

Schickel's view on a "distance" that is "absolutely necessary for satire" is a bit overstated. But he is on the right track regarding the fading of satire when sentiment is stressed. The moviemakers probably were opting for the youth audience who had become some of the most important consumers of the theatrical film in a decade when small children and parents seemed to be satisfied with television programs—movies were wooing the 18-to-26 age group.

A retrospective view reveals that *The Graduate* has lost some of its social importance and retains most of its value from the strength of the performances by Dustin Hoffman as Ben and Anne Bancroft as Mrs. Robinson. While the middle-aged woman and twenty-year-old man type of love affair had long ago appeared in the novel and the French cinema, such a depiction in the United States movies was a novelty in the late sixties. The picture was a box-office hit, and the majority of the critics found it at least an effective work when compared with many of the film comedies created in this period. However, the nagging view still exists that the film could have been so much better. Pauline Kael writes:

> *The Graduate* only wants to succeed and that's fundamentally what's the matter with it. There is a pause for a laugh after the mention of "Berkeley" that is an unmistakable sign of hunger for success; this kind of movie-making shifts values, shifts focus, shifts emphasis, shifts everything for a sure-fire response. Mike Nichols' "gift" is that he lets the audience direct him; this is demagoguery in the arts. ["Trash, Art, and the Movies," *Harper's Magazine*, February 1969, p. 83]

An adaptation of a novel that does not seem to pander to the audience appeared two years later, and critics compared the work with *The Graduate*. Director Larry Peerce's 1969 execution of Philip Roth's *Goodbye, Columbus* (1959), a literary creation superior to the Webb novel, seems more relaxed and vital today. *Goodbye, Columbus* has weathered well; *The Graduate*, with the virtues of a more slickly conceived production, seems now to be a more superficial rendering of its source. Although Peerce was not noted as a particularly accomplished director, and the quality of his output during his career was erratic,* he was able to get excellent performances from Richard Benjamin (as Neil Klugman) and Ali MacGraw (as Brenda Patimkin), the young lovers in the screen adaptation of Roth's novel. Screenwriter Arnold Schulman transferred a first-person narrative into a third-person drama with deftness and retained a good deal of the novelist's dialogue with a minimum of cutting. Journalist critics were generally favorable in their reactions, with some reservations that the updating of the 1959 novel by

---

*Some critical praise for *One Potato, Two Potato* (1964) and *The Incident* (1967) gave Peerce a favorable reputation, but after a series of flops in the early seventies, his status had slipped and he moved to soap opera with *The Other Side of the Mountain* (1975) and its sequel in 1978.

ten years did not always seem consistent and some objections to the Jewish wedding sequence as being too heavily handled.

Roth's initiation-of-youth novel, *Goodbye, Columbus*, does capture the embryonic stages of disenchantment that would be more widespread in the fiction and films of the sixties. The author employs a basic plot device of a protagonist who, after a stint in the military service, tries to enter the business world but finds library work more to his satisfaction. Neil Klugman is an earlier, more believable version of Benjamin Braddock of *The Graduate*, but he is a more perceptive and mature youth from a lower-middle-class Jewish family who finds the vulgarities of the *nouveau riche* distasteful and yet becomes fascinated by this social stratum's world of affluence. It evolves into a type of attraction-repulsion view as he courts a colorful, independent young woman; he envies the freedom that Brenda's lifestyle allows her. The plot has some of the realistic qualities of the serious treatment that F. Scott Fitzgerald imparts to the short story "Winter Dreams." Like this 1920s tale, *Goodbye, Columbus* shows a young man and woman engaged in an affair that eventually ends—that is not consummated in marriage—not only because of a difference in social status but also because of a difference in emotional development and maturity of the lovers. Brenda's freedom brings no growth of the human spirit because she is vacuous; what passes for independence (and, at times, even depth of character) is a basic insensitivity to every person with whom she comes into contact. Roth's satirical points remain relatively simple: he attacks the lack of substantive values in the concept of upward mobility; he sees those who struggle to transcend a modest background as leading empty lives with a focus on the material possessions they have acquired. Furthermore, the drive that has assisted the family in the climb for wealth and security seems to be directed toward sports by each family member except the mother. Ron Patimkin, the son, plays football for Ohio University; the father dotes on basketball in his backyard; Brenda always agonizes to win in tennis; the little sister, Julie, cheats or asks for special privileges because of her age when she plays basketball or ping-pong. Mrs. Patimkin plays a more deadly game, a social one, by cutting down her daughter Brenda and grasping any control she can from the males of her family.

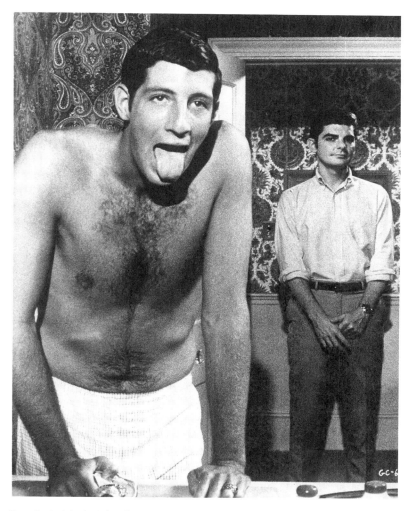

Ron Patimkin (Michael Meyers) is the innocent oaf of the *nouveau riche* Jewish family in *Goodbye, Columbus*. Richard Benjamin as Neil Klugman looks on.

Some mixed reviews on *Goodbye, Columbus* by such movie critics as Robert Hatch of *The Nation* and John Simon of *The New Leader* seem to suggest that Larry Peerce's version of the novel is an overstatement of Roth's dissection of a Jewish culture in which social climbers gain financial success. Both critics see some virtues in the film, especially the acting, so they are not producing wholly negative views of the work. It may be that dramatizing and, especially, visualizing some of the facets of the Patimkin family create a more startling portrait of vulgar ambiance than the novel produces. But the novel does suggest much of that which is visualized in the film. Comic overstatement emerges in the excellent description by Roth when he depicts Neil Klugman witnessing the attack on food by the Patimkins:

> Mr. Patimkin reminded me of my father, except that when he spoke he did not surround each syllable with a wheeze. He was tall, strong, ungrammatical, and a ferocious eater. When he attacked his salad—after drenching it in bottled French dress—the veins swelled under the heavy skin of his forearm. He ate three helpings of salad, Ron had four, Brenda and Julie had two, and only Mrs. Patimkin and I had one each. [From the novel, *Goodbye, Columbus*, Houghton Mifflin Co., p. 21]

The comic nature of the food orgy is condensed effectively by Roth as guest Neil reflects on the ordeal:

> There was not much dinner conversation; eating was heavy and methodical and serious, and it would be just as well to record all that was said in one swoop, rather than indicate the sentences lost in passing of food, the words gurgled into mouthfuls, the syntax chopped and forgotten in heapings, spillings, and gorgings. [From the novel, p. 22]

Magnified to a crowd proportion, a similar example of over-indulgence takes place in the wedding sequence of the novel:

> And the night continued: we ate, we drank, we danced—Rose and Pearl did the Charleston with one another (while their husbands examined woodwork and chande-

liers), and then I did the Charleston with none other than Gloria Feldman, who made coy, hideous faces at me all the time we danced. Near the end of the evening, Brenda, who'd been drinking champagne like her Uncle Leo, did a Rita Hayworth tango with herself, and Julie fell asleep on some ferns she'd whisked off the head table and made into a mattress at the far end of the hall. I felt a numbness creep into my hard palate, and by three o'clock people were dancing in their coats, shoeless ladies were wrapping hunks of wedding cake in napkins for their children's lunch. . . . [From the novel, p. 110]

A lot of the details suggested in this passage were translated into a visual presentation by the film version of *Goodbye, Columbus*. Professionally bent, the husbands are always aware of the fixtures wherever they are, and the wives are left to entertain themselves. Life at the top brings domestic agony—the humble roots cannot be forgotten, and the Jewish mother must be sure the food, the cake, is used in a practical way. Thus, the wedding sequence provides a microcosm for the book's satire and the film's satire. To view this portion of the film, as journalistic critics Hatch and Simon do, as excessive or heavy-handed seems to be to miss the basic point of Roth's satire and his style. He is not as subtle as the critics often suggest. (Evaluators of the late sixties were all too ready to defend the author of the novel and find the filmed version as a distortion.) A more reflective piece by Stephen Farber (*Film Quarterly*, Fall 1969, pp. 34–38) defends Larry Peerce's execution of this portion of the film:

The long wedding scene has been attacked as gross and vulgar and viciously exaggerated, which probably means that it strikes too close to home. On the other hand, maybe this scene *does* look exaggerated to someone who has never attended a Jewish wedding. I found the details witty and observant—the compulsive guzzling of food, fat women and little girls waltzing together, the bridegroom dancing amiably with his maid, the two uncles from the carpet business measuring the length of the dance floor, women waddling off with centerpieces at the end of the evening. The scene is twisted slightly so that it looks larger-than-life and more appalling, but in essence it is

truthful. And when Neil recoils from his ghastly spectacle,
we know that he knows, finally, who he is.

But a hotel tryst of Brenda and Neil provides the final realization for Neil that he cannot become a part of the world of the
petty bourgeoisie—although Roth and the filmmakers never
use such a harsh definition of the world Neil almost joins.
Brenda informs Neil that the sexual intent of their meeting
cannot be consummated because her parents have discovered
her diaphragm in her drawer at home and have written long
letters on their disapproval of her relationship with Neil, which
they now know has been a long sexual one, making Neil unfit to
wed their daughter. Again, narrow values are satirized, since it
would appear that Brenda had left the diaphragm at home to be
discovered and that she wanted Neil to "make an honest
woman" of her by marrying her. But the dialogue of the novel
and the large segment reproduced by screenwriter Arnold
Schulman provide the reader or the viewer with a kind of
ambiguous situation often found in real life. Neil breaks off his
tryst and his whole relationship with Brenda by leaving the
hotel. Roth does not give us the clear-cut mental reactions of
the protagonist as he leaves the hotel after questioning Brenda
about why she left the diaphragm where it might be found by
her mother. Instead, he employs a mental reaction from his
protagonist that remains a series of questions: "What was it
inside me that had turned pursuit and clutching into love, and
then turned it inside out again? . . . If she had been slightly *not*
Brenda . . . but then would I have loved her?" (from the novel,
pp. 135–136). The film remains even more an enigma at the
parting of ways as it shows Neil leaving the hotel, entirely in
pantomime—only suggesting his perplexity at the resolution of
their once promising relationship.

The filmmakers, therefore, have not compromised themselves with the ending as the creators of *The Graduate* have
done. There is certainly great difficulty in translating the brilliant narrative style of Philip Roth into the visual medium, but
their humble efforts have borne some fruit over the years. The
rating of this work as a film satire is apt to grow. Also, Peerce
and Schulman have retained the symbolic concept of the title.
Ron Patimkin listens over and over to a public relations record

that extols the virtues of good old Ohio State. Roth describes it
this way:

> There was goose flesh on Ron's veiny arms as the Voice
> continued. "We offer ourselves to you then, world, and
> come at you in search of Life. And to you Ohio State, to
> you Columbus, we say thank you, thank you and goodbye.
> We will miss you, in the fall, in the winter, in the spring,
> and some day we shall return. . . . " [From the novel,
> p. 105]

Ron, the jock, is an innocent and an oaf who will inherit his
father's kitchen and bathroom sink business; he will live in his
past glory as a football player, a sentimental man easily adapting
to his family's lifestyle—the opposite of Neil Klugman, the
cynical outsider who must move on to another world.

While the filmmakers of *Goodbye, Columbus* do not distort
the ending of Roth's conception by catering to audiences' taste
in the manner of the creators of *The Graduate*, two other
initiation films of the period, *Lord Love a Duck* (1966) and
You're a Big Boy Now (1967), show directors and writers taking
two minor novels and pandering to the attitudes of the youth in
the late sixties. There are some good dark comedy moments in
these films, but the total works make few statements of any
significance and do not stand the test of time.

From Al Hine's second-rate novel *Lord Love a Duck*, adapters Larry H. Johnson and George Axelrod employed an initiation of youth tale that focuses more on a high school girl named
Barbara Ann Greene rather than a boy—one of the few novels
of the period that depict a female protagonist. She is a naive
youth who is mesmerized by a wacky boy genius named Alan
Musgrave, a manic character who is only a couple of years older
than she. He is, in many ways, a co-protagonist or what might
be thought of by some as an antagonist. The title used by the
author is derived from Alan's continued reference to a bird. The
movie dialogue uses a more specific designation when Alan
directly and sarcastically states, "Mollymauk. A bird thought to
be extinct but isn't. That's me." In the film he also draws Barbara
a picture of the bird. At times in the movie, when he is excited

by some trick he has played on a person, he flaps his arms to imitate this strange bird.

In the novel author Hine often refers to this antagonist as "Gooney Bird" rather than Alan. Co-scenarist and director of the film, George Axelrod, seems to shift the emphasis from Barbara Ann because of the stronger humor that results from Alan's attack on middle-class values. Barbara Ann is portrayed as an attractive girl with a cheerleader-type mind—to her, one must be popular, and her goal is to be a movie star. The love in her shallow life, Bob Bernard, proves to be as square as Alan is eccentric. Much of the novel and movie's best humor evolves from Alan's manipulation of the lives of this young couple and his frequent jabs at the superficial values these two and their parents posses. The novel reveals the thoughts of Alan, who envisions himself as a "wily bird" soaring over people and juggling their destinies. His power to control all persons he meets is colorfully stated as he thinks: "The world on a string like a live and quivering yo-yo" (from the novel, *Lord Love a Duck*, Atheneum, 1961, p. 177).

Barbara Ann and Bob symbolize the plastic caricatures that some young lovers become in a culture that stresses popularity and propriety; these two have all the bland, blond good looks of the Mattel dolls, Barbie and Ken. When they marry, the author explains in the novel that they want a house with a kitchen that has metal which looks like wood and plastic which looks like metal and they want all the rooms wired for music (from the novel, p. 272).

As in the novel the movie shows this couple accepting "Gooney" into their life because he provides some color to enliven their uneventful existence, not merely because he serves as a court jester. However, they value his advice as if he were also the court counselor. Eventually, Alan controls their life completely and seduces Barbara Ann. Black comedy develops when Alan decides to murder Bob in a way that will look like an accident so that Barbara Ann will be free to pursue a movie career under the Svengali-like influence of Alan.

The mothers of Barbara Ann and Bob also help to create black humor. Contrasting social situations, used to an extent in *Goodbye, Columbus*, are devices used by the novelist and film-makers to develop comedy. Mrs. Greene, a divorcee, comes from a lower class and is employed as a waitress although her interest in men indicates that she could easily become a prostitute; the movie makes her even cruder, brasher, and more common than the novel. Mrs. Bernard, on the other hand, prides herself on her background derived from sturdy pioneers and influential founding fathers. When she hears that her son might marry the daughter of a divorced woman, she is horrified and muses on her view that it would all be very proper if the father were dead (from the novel, p. 169). In the movie George Axelrod gives Mrs. Bernard an even more scatterbrained propriety, with a matronly toughness regarding divorce: "In our family we don't divorce our men—we bury them."

Director George Axelrod had the background as an excellent writer of stage plays, with the 1953 *Seven Year Itch* and the 1955 *Will Success Spoil Rock Hunter?* to his credit, and it has been reported that he was a superior stage director on Broadway. One only has to see such works as *Bus Stop* (1956), *Breakfast at Tiffany's* (1961), and *The Manchurian Candidate* (1962) to realize his talents as a screenwriter. But *Lord Love a Duck* may not have been his meat, or he may have been pandering, as Mike Nichols did, to the youth audience of the sixties with this 1966 production. There are, however, strong comic moments, especially in the acting of Ruth Gordon as Mrs. Bernard and Roddy McDowall as Alan Musgrave, but Axelrod's lampoon of beach parties seems self-indulgent to the point that the gyrations of dancing youth seem to be savored rather than satirized. The climactic slapstick pursuit by Alan of Bob in another attempt to kill him is a weak and strained attempt to gain humor; Alan pursues his prey during an outdoor high school graduation, using a tractor with a scooploader. Poor Bob, in the wheelchair to which he has been confined since a previous "accident" arranged by Alan, tries to avoid the "Mollymauck." Such madcap humor strains credibility.

The novel and the film depict Barbara Ann as thoroughly corrupted at the end of the tale when she obtains movie star status in beach party films. However, the novel suggests an even stronger state of degeneracy of the pure, model, American high school girl—that she will employ her sexuality (schooled by Alan) to further her career. In the final critical analysis of both the novel and the film, the tale proves to be a type of surface social criticism tied to the fads of time. It does not add up to a firm bite of satire.

In the 1967 movie version of David Benedictus's *You're a Big Boy Now*, a 1964 British novel, the filmmaker switched the locale of the film from England to the United States. It was twenty-seven-year-old Francis Ford Coppola's first major commercial film effort. He scripted and directed the film, using some well-known veteran actors: Geraldine Page, Julie Harris, and Rip Torn. Of initiation theme movies adapted from novels, this work proves to be the most freely translated production. Coppola does retain much of the character of Bernard Chanticleer, the naive protagonist who seems to be the archetypal, youthful klutz from literature throughout the ages; and, the parents of Bernard are on the opposite end of the self-blaming ("Where have we gone wrong?") husband and wife of *The Graduate*. The Chanticleers relentlessly dominate their offspring to make sure he knows they are right and he is wrong.

Movie critics complained that director Coppola's handling of *You're a Big Boy Now* was self-conscious and immature even though some admitted that the work is lively and has some effective acting. Maybe some of the blame could be leveled at the source—the novel is replete with clever asides by the author, many of them self-conscious and lacking in wit. Sometimes this flip aside and observation is embarrassingly weak. Early in the novel the author declares: "Let's take a closer look at Bernard. . . . He lives by love (Bully for Bernard) but loves at random wherever his love will stick" (from the novel, *You're a Big Boy Now*, E. P. Dutton and Co., 1964, p. 15). This type of self-conscious cleverness may have influenced the young Coppola to create the movie and may have influenced his style. Literal movement in this film sometimes seems to have the characteristics of a California film school graduate who has not forgotten his class projects—who has decided that not only do such images change, but the characters in the film should be highly mobile. *Life* critic Richard Schickel sarcastically states this manifestation: "Sometimes people run around for no reason at all—they just run, run to demonstrate what free spirits some of the younger characters would be if the world were not so much with them" (*Life*, March 24, 1967, p. 6).

Schickel and his fellow critics were often reacting to a type of "with it" youth-oriented film that had quite a few visual excesses plus some poorly motivated chases exhibiting some of the crude slapstick of a Mack Sennett chase of the teens decade. Coppola's examination of a young man's struggle to be an adult might be characterized as an effort with more style than substance. Points from the novel become submerged in technique as the director assures us he can handle his medium. Consequently, the film becomes a somewhat faddish lampoon of youthful attitudes of the period. The author's attempt at satire seems to be lost when the movie changes the ending by having the protagonist get the right girl after all—an exemplary woman (there are none in Benedictus's version) named Amy, played by Karen Black. At the end of the novel the author leaves the young man's love life still unfulfilled. No woman has saved him, and love does not conquer all; he continues bumbling his way along, without learning anything from a self-serving actress who merely likes to have him around because he dotes on her, giving her more adulation than she deserves. When he is rejected by Barbara Darling, he has nowhere to go. Obviously, Coppola cops out.

The director's interpretation of Barbara Darling, however, does work effectively in *You're a Big Boy Now*. Actress Elizabeth Hartman as the kookie temptress remains one of the most interesting portraits in the film, and her enactment of the role was surprising to critics since she had previously played fragile young ladies such as her effort in the 1965 *Patch of Blue*. Coppola also retains a faithful portrait of the cynical con man, Raef Delgado, whose function as a male advisor to the greening of Bernard goes astray. This would-be poet tries to guide the young man in sexual conquests only to end up taking Barbara Darling from him.

Certainly, Benedictus's *You're a Big Boy Now* and Hine's *Lord Love a Duck* remain second-class satirical novels, but the filmmakers' shaping the material into the movie medium might have been much better off if they had used a more tender, less showy touch. A decade later Joseph Strick would have a different problem when he tackled the precursor of youth initiation novels of the twentieth century, James Joyce's *A Portrait of the Artist as a Young Man*. This director chose a famous novel which almost any filmmaker would find difficult to transpose to the screen. And it appears that Strick had neither the grasp of this type of novel nor the flair to pull off the project.

Some evaluators may feel that Joyce's first novel, written in 1916, is a basically serious work with some ironic touches, but it is possible to discover enough satirical elements in *A Portrait of the Artist as a Young Man* to include it as a type of narrative that has strong social comment. Joyce shows a type of detachment in his approach to his subject that sometimes submerges the attack below a seemingly serious surface story about the struggles of Stephen Dedalus. However, there are definite assaults on the church, the family, and the nation, and many of the characters not imbued with the broad comic facets that are often associated with satire. If one carefully considers the remarks directed toward the institution of the church, particularly the portraits of the priests, satirical intent by Joyce becomes more apparent. In the first part of the novel the reader may observe the reaction of Stephen's father, Simon, when he complains that priests become advocates of a political stand. He repeats a friend's complaint to a priest in an argument with Stephen's aunt, Dante Riordan: "I'll pay you your dues, father, when you cease turning the house of God into a Pollingbooth" (from the novel, *A Portrait of the Artist as a Young Man*, Viking Press, 1970 edition, p.31). Simon also declares in this long, heated, Christmas dinner conversation, "We are an unfortunate priest-ridden race . . . " (from the novel, p. 37). This conversation, witnessed by Stephen as a child, reveals a comic tone of invective early in the novel and depicts his eventual separation from the influence of the church when he reaches manhood. Remarks by the boy's father take on a black comedy twist at one point of the argument with Aunt Dante when Simon pronounces a piece of turkey which he has just carved as the pope's nose and, with a wink at Stephen, he pops it into his mouth.

As Stephen grows into a precocious teenager with writing gifts and a strong interest in great literary figures of the past, he finds himself confronted by his Jesuit teachers and his school chums who judge writers by their political and ethical views. Tennyson is declared a more effective author than Byron because the latter is "a heretic and immoral" (from the novel, p. 81). Such bias eventually causes Stephen to rebel against his teachers and religion. However, before he takes that step, there is a period when the young man develops strong religious feelings—to the point that he considers studying for the priesthood. Profound satirical roots are obvious in the writing of Joyce when an elaborate sermon on the pitfalls of sexual lust steers the potential artist into a period of religious fervor. Joyce shows the young man's naiveté in a comic way. Since he has had a number of sexual encounters and is influenced by the power of the priest's sermon on lust, he is thrown into an excess of penitent piety. He also comes to the realization that he has foolishly switched into a type of fanatic that he previously disliked. Such immature sensitivity and rapid inversion of views have a comic basis which James Joyce blends with the serious elements in *A Portrait of the Artist as a Young Man.*

The disenchantment of Stephen Dedalus eventually leads to his rejection of his nation and his family. In a discussion toward the end of the novel he says, "Ireland is the old sow that eats her farrow" (p. 203). When Stephen's mother complains about his skepticism at the very end of the novel, Joyce has switched his narrative to an even more direct, diary, stream-of-consciousness technique: "Said I have a queer mind and have read too much. Not true. Have read little and understand less" (p. 248). His rejection of standard values leads to a conflict with his mother that is unbearable. The young man breaks away from his roots and declares that he will not serve anyone—that his defense in the world "will be silence, exile, and cunning" (p. 247).

Given the wealth of material that *A Portrait of the Artist as a Young Man* affords, a director, remembering his own youthful rebellion, might tackle such a work with an eagerness that would produce a vital work. Not so with director Joseph Strick. He employs nearly every important detail listed above; yet the screen version of this famous novel generally lacks the luster to keep the viewer interested. Strick and his adapter, Judith Rascoe, were probably faced with the same problem that John Huston had with his 1979 production of Flannery O'Connor's *Wise Blood*: the interpretation of a work that employs a mixture of the serious and comic. Added to this difficulty, and probably more of a problem, is the ambiguity of the writer's approach to satire so that evaluators may, by inclination or by design, stress the serious or the comic side of the work. Strick seems to have tried to strike a middle-ground interpretation and come out with a dull, defused work. He is less successful than John Huston in the handling of this type of less direct, more subtle twentieth-century satire.

Director Strick is most successful in his creation of the Christmas dinner argument on the role of the church in society (already detailed above). There is a fidelity to the original work, and he gets the most out of the comedy, especially T. P. McKenna's enactment of the father as he comments on the church. His sarcastic remarks needle Aunt Dante to such an extent that her defense of the church becomes strident—a satirical portrait of a fanatic. However, the hellfire and brimstone speech of Sir John Gielgud as the priest does not seem to have any comic dimensions. This priest's concept of the avoidance of and repentance from "impure habits" appears so excessive that some risible aspects using overstatement would have added much to the production. Strick shows Stephen's overreaction to the sermon with surrealistic devices that reflect his guilt. Blood comes from his scalp, dung falls from above onto his face, bugs crawl on him and, finally, his head literally cracks apart and open. Even with this cinematic device it is not clear whether the viewer should take Stephen's plight seriously or humorously. The confession to the priest that follows does not have the humorous treatment needed. The fanaticism of the priest in the novel regarding sex has the ring of comic overstatement; however, Strick does not seem to capture this fully in the film. Steering the middle ground of interpretation, he seems to come up with an interpretation that has no point of view—the results are bland.

Since there is a surface fidelity in Strick's version of *A Portrait of the Artist as a Young Man*, an evaluator might also make the conjecture that he has an overly serious devotion in this adaptation of an important literary work. In his 1967 version of Joyce's *Ulysses*, Strick faired somewhat better in his attempt, but this screen translation is merely a *Ulysses* sampler.* Leading actors Milo O'Shea as Bloom and Barbara Jefford as Molly

---

*Part of the reason for this rather skimpy version could be attributed to Strick's financial problems in launching his project. He wanted to do either an epic version of the novel or a two-part version of the work.

Bloom assisted in giving various shades of the serious and comic that existed in this novel so that the work is at least a respectable art theater film and provides interesting fare for a college film society. In the final analysis of his ability, however, there is a strong indication that Joseph Strick's early work as an experimental documentarian with *Muscle Beach* (1948) and *The Savage Eye* (1959) is his real province. One has only to view *The Balcony* (1967), an adaptation of Jean Genet's play, and *Tropic of Cancer* (1969), a film version of Henry Miller's novel, as well as the already mentioned James Joyce works to realize that this director has a taste for cynical views of society. Unfortunately, he has difficulty giving life to these literary works on the screen. British critic David Thomson sums up Strick's weaknesses well:

> The truth is that Strick impresses as a wintry, disenchanted personality, much more suited to the cynicism of *The Savage Eye* and the brutal pragmatism of *Tropic of Cancer* than to the lyrical exuberance of a Joyce or Genet.... Strick has fought strident battles over freedom from censorship, freedom to bring art to the people, freedom of speech; but his work is tightlipped, grindingly unfluent and unable to shed the approach to life's variety of the tabloid press. [*A Biographical Dictionary of Film*, 2nd Edition, William Morrow and Co., 1981, p. 587]

Thomson does not label Strick as a phony, but sees him as an artist with goals that he cannot fulfill with his medium.

A broader yet still bleak vision of family problems that does not concentrate on the initiation of youth evolved in the sixties. Two films adapted from what have been labeled absurdist stage plays provide good examples of the degenerating family: *One Way Pendulum* (1965) and *Oh Dad, Poor Dad, Mamma's Hung You in the Closet and I'm Feelin' So Sad* (1967). N. F. Simpson wrote the drama *One Way Pendulum* in 1960 and focused his story on the trivial pursuits and debilitating obsessions of an eccentric British family. Each member of the Groomkirby family seems to make very little contact with the others. Simpson seems to be carrying on with one of the favorite themes of French absurdist Eugène Ionesco or Irish writer Samuel Beckett—the barrenness of complete lack of communication between people.

One of the keys to the satire of *One Way Pendulum* lies in the obsession with travel of Aunt Mildred, who is confined to a wheelchair. A neighbor, Robert Barnes, comments in a way that indicates he is a spokesman for the playwright:

> "She's got this bug about transport. Wants us all moving about. Don't you, Aunt Mildred? Plenty of destinations—so we can feel as if we're getting somewhere. She's probably right. Nothing like a good old destination for giving you a sense of purpose. Till you get there, of course. Then you have to start looking round for another one. That's why you need plenty of them. Can't have too many, can you, Aunt Mildred?" (*No reply*) "Too wrapped up in her brochure." [From the play, *One Way Pendulum*, Faber and Faber, Ltd., rpt. 1972, p. 19]

There seems to be a need for some pursuit for each member of the family, but as Barnes points out, it is aimless and any effort by the individual lacks significance. These obsessions keep the immediate family, relatives, and neighbors in a state of limbo. As indicated in the quote above, sometimes even the most superficial type of contact with another person is impossible. Other examples of strange fixations are the father's curious hobby of attempting to reproduce a life-size model of a British court of law in his own house and the son's bizarre attempt to teach talking weight machines to sing. And in the manner of the absurdist drama, the father and son have some success in their meaningless endeavors. There is a madness in these obsessions that outstrips that found in the odd hobbies of another eccentric family in the comic drama, the Sycamore family in the George S. Kaufman and Moss Hart 1936 play, *You Can't Take It With You*. But this 1960 play, *One Way Pendulum*, is filled with dark humor that focuses not only on the obsessions of the family, but on the concept of procedures of the court and the perversion of justice. Simpson seems to expand his theme to say that not just the family is out of joint, but the world is out of joint. Such a dislocation evolves when the father, Arthur Groomkirby, gets his court room constructed; a dream-like or surrealistic trial develops in which the son, Kirby Groomkirby, is revealed to be the mass murderer of forty-four people. The defense counselor points out that Kirby's skill and attention to his weighing machines have usually kept him from coming into conflict with the law, as if he were a model citizen except for the forty-four indiscretions. This lawyer stresses the fact that the young man told his victims a joke before he killed them so they would die laughing, and he thoughtfully mourned the victims' death by wearing black (from the play, p. 90). The judge renders a strange verdict as he addresses the accused:

> "And so it has gone on: victim after victim, until even you could not have expected the authorities to overlook it any longer. . . . I have been influenced by one consideration, and it is this: that in sentencing a man for one crime, we may be putting him beyond the reach of the law in respect to those other crimes of which he might otherwise have become guilty. The law, however, is not to be cheated in this way. I shall therefore discharge you." (pp. 91–92)

Much of this "Alice in Wonderland" type of humor was appreciated by the British in 1960, and the N. F.. Simpson drama was a hit on the London stage. However, his work has only a limited appeal in the United States, where his plays receive off-Broadway and college campus productions.

The 1965 movie version has a screenplay created by the author, who opened up the action of the play slightly to include not only the rooms in the Groomkirby house but also the backyard, the office where the father is employed, and the streets of the city. British director Peter Yates, most noted for his American production of *Bullitt* (1968), places *One Way Pendulum* too much in a realistic world that seems to work against the basically theatrical world of this absurdist drama. Occasionally, Yates uses the movie device of "he thinks" when the father envisions himself in judicial robes and a wig as he walks down the street, but the director needs more of such interjections to divorce the film drama from the world as we know it. Even with effective acting Yates has paced the movie version of the Simpson play too slowly; he also does not utilize the comic shadings of overstatement in many of the characters and seems to be most effective when British understatement in the trial scene best reveals the humor of non sequiturs in the situation. He and his actors get the best out of Simpson's puns in this last sequence of the drama. Nevertheless, the overall production is lacking in the spark that might have produced an effective satirical work for the screen.

Oh Dad, Poor Dad, Mamma's Hung You in the Closet and I'm Feelin' So Sad, as a movie version of the 1960 Arthur Kopit play, proves to be a much livelier production than *One Way Pendulum*, but in the translation from stage to screen the British work loses some validity of interpretation. The basic flaw is tied to the attempt to add material to the original play which does not follow in the same tone as Kopit's type of humor. Evidently, unfavorable 1965 previews of the movie indicated to the producers that off-Broadway dark comedy would not sell to a mass audience. The role of Jonathan Winters as the father who is dead (appearing in the film only in a home movie created in the past to reveal the wife's problem with a philandering husband) was expanded so that Dad could comment on the action of the drama. British director Alexander Mackendrick, noted for his 1949 *Tight Little Island*, was hired to rework the film with a story frame and periodic inserted portions in the work. An added running commentary by Winters as an angel who observes the struggles of his son with a domineering mother contrasts sharply with the dark humor of Kopit. For example, the author's portrait of Madame Rosepettle as the bitch mother and black widow spider who humiliates her suitors and whips her son into sniveling obedience becomes the subject of a series of lighthearted jokes. An attempt to suggest some of the predatory beast imagery of this woman goes awry with the self-conscious aside by Winters when he tells the audience how he met his wife. He says that he met her walking through the park. "I took a thorn out of her paw" he wisecracks. Also, when Dad, as the ever-present angel, observes his naive son unable to understand the intentions of a youthful seductress who announces herself as a birthday present, he urges the boy, "Unwrap it!" It is a remark that, of course, the son cannot hear and is solely for the audience. While a few viewers of *Oh Dad, Poor Dad* during the sixties might have liked such asides to the audience better than the humor that remains from the original play,* the tone of this type of clever

---

*Even *New York Times* critic Bosley Crowther favored Winters's humor, but Hollis Alpert of *Saturday Review* and Judith Crist of *New York World Journal Tribune* objected to the blatant clash of these added comedy inserts in the screen version.

remark works against the grain of the author's satirical humor. It moves toward a light lampoon instead of satire.

Arthur Kopit's drama shows a type of family that exists in absurdist plays in which the members are almost as mad as the Groomkirby clan of *One Way Pendulum*. Madame Rosepettle transports the body of her husband in a casket wherever she goes; she keeps such pets as a piranha that feeds on Siamese cats, and she keeps Venus flytraps that try to attack humans. In the absurdist tradition the fish and the flytraps utter sounds that are animal-like snarls or growls and, finally, human-like cries for help when the rebellious son, Jonathan, destroys them.

While director Richard Quine, who successfully directed *Bell, Book and Candle* and *Operation Mad Ball* in the fifties, attempts to use some of the surrealistic aspects of the original work by at least employing the snarling Venus flytraps, he avoids many devices from the original work that helped divorce the play from reality and set forth a comic tone identified with the absurdist drama. Furthermore, adapter Ian Bernard mutates the monologues of Madame Rosepettle, a role played by Rosalind Russell in the film, by softening her tirades. Here, in the play, is her savage rejection of one of her suitors, Commodore Roseabove, when he says that he feels sorry for her son:

> "And I feel sorrier for you! For you are *nothing*! While my son is mine. His skin is the color of fresh snow, and his mind is pure. For he is safe, Mr. Roseabove, and it is I who have saved him. Saved him from the world beyond that door. The world of you. The world of his father. A world waiting to devour those who trust in it; those who love. A world vicious under the hypocrisy of kindness, ruthless under the falseness of a smile. Well, go on, Mr. Rose-above. Leave my room and enter your world again—your sex-driven, dirt-washed waste of cannibals eating each other up while they pretend they're kissing. Go, Mr. Rose-above, enter your world of darkness. My son shall have only light!" [From the play *Oh Dad, Poor Dad*, New York: Hill and Wang, 1960, pp. 71–72]

This bitch goddess, Madame Rosepettle, becomes the fanatic, satirical version of Diana hurling her barbs at all males and smothering her son to the point of his becoming a case of arrested development. The movie version cuts this rejection scene and reverses the whole situation. Instead, Madame Rosepettle gets the Commodore, enacted with skill by Hugh Griffith, to marry her so that she will have another conquest of this older man whom she is sure she can outlive. Much of the severity of her portrait has been muted by cutting her most vicious remarks and by the performance of Rosalind Russell, which places more emphasis on the spirit of play than on the spirit of invective. A similar switch in tone is created when the movie dramatizes one of the mother's longest monologues—an account of how she found sex with her husband, Albert Edward Robinson Rosepettle III, disgusting and the way her philandering husband's lust led to his heart attack and death. This tale of the past is innovatively presented as a home movie which develops the incidents of this story in comically exaggerated pantomime with a voice over narration by the indignant wife. Well suited to the medium, this dramatization of the monologue, nevertheless, switches to a lighter tone which does not fit that of the original work.

Probably one of the few scenes from the play that seems to retain the flavor of the original work in the movie is the well-written seduction scene with Jonathan, enacted by Robert Morse, and Rosalie, played by Barbara Harris. It is close to the dark comedy of the play, for Jonathan becomes so distressed by the advances of Rosalie that he kills her. Not only is this odd-ball conclusion of the scene retained from the original, but the acting of Ms. Harris, who created the role in the New York Phoenix Theatre in 1962, proves to be completely in tune with the original work. She may have been drawing from her past performance and less from Richard Quine's interpretation, a view of the play that leaves much to be desired. As in so many of the satires that Hollywood attempted to bring to the screen, it would appear that filmmakers tried to make an adapted work more palatable by molding the material in a way that made it lighter and less offensive to the mass audience of the movies. It seems more likely that Richard Quine was less at fault for this change than the producers, Ray Stark and Stanley Rubin.

While Jonathan in *Oh Dad, Poor Dad* employs a son who has been reduced to a social misfit by his mother, a girl offspring in the movie, *A Day in the Death of Joe Egg* (1972), depicts a spastic girl of ten who, through no person's fault, has been incapacitated by an illness so that she is little more than a vegetable. Her parents' and friends' reaction to this tragedy hardly seems to be a fit subject for satire; nevertheless, Peter Nicholas' original conception of this situation in the 1967 play and his screen adaptation in 1972 reveal startling explorations with satirical comment on dispassionate physicians, modish clergymen, and liberal, well-meaning friends as they give their advice to soothe the many anxieties that parents have with a disabled child.

Dramatist Nicholas uses a technique of showing the parents, Brian (also called Bri) and Sheila, engaged in a game-playing series of dark humor skits and remarks as they pretend that their daughter is aware of all occurrences about her, and he makes subtle distinctions among the attitudes of the parents' friends. This game-playing extends to vaudeville type skits, with Brian parodying the diagnosis of a Viennese physician and the recommendation to use a faith-healing session conducted by a faddish vicar to solve the problem. As the wife joins in the playacting, the playwright clearly indicates that the husband engages in a comedy routine similar to that which would appear on stage:

> (*For this sketch, BRI uses a music-hall German accent.*)
> BRI: Vell, mattam, zis baby off yours has now been
>   soroughly tested and ve need ze bets razzer
>   battly so it's better you take her home. I sink
>   I can promise she von't be any trouble. Keep
>   her vell sedated you'll hartly know she's zere.
> SHEILA: But, Doctor—
> (*He is making for the door, turns reluctantly.*)
> BRI: Ja?
> SHEILA: Can't you tell me the results?

After the doctor tells of all the elaborate tests he has given the child, he starts to leave again and Sheila insists on a diagnosis:

> SHEILA: What can she *do*?
> BRI: Do? She can't do nozzing at all.
> SHEILA: Will she ever?
> BRI: Mattam, let me try and tell you vot your
>   daughter iss like. Do you know vit I mean ven
>   I say your daughter vos a wegetable? [From the
>   play, *Joe Egg*, Grove Press, 1967, pp. 36–36]

There is, naturally, an agony in this playacting or game-playing beneath the humor that reveals dark comedy used as an escape valve for the parents. But the lampoon of the doctor shows a bitter frustration with and an attack on the dispassionate medical establishment with whom they have had many dealings throughout the years.

A similar sketch develops which shows Sheila, still playing herself, encountering a clergyman with a strange mind—a vicar who has absorbed all the clichés, fads, and nostrums of the modern-day church. It is Brian, again depicting a professional man who claims he has helped children in the past, who says "Now for those poor innocents I did the Laying On Of Hands bit" (from the play, p. 41).

Asked if any success came from this faith-healing session, the vicar replies that one boy made such rapid recovery that he became the runner-up in the South West Area Tap-Dancing Championships (p. 42). With capricious inspiration the vicar, as imitated by Brian, jumps into a song and dance routine.

This music hall turn technique on the stage was used by many of the young, nonestablishment playwrights in the late fifties and sixties. For example, the device appears in John Osborne's 1957 *The Entertainer*, Shelagh Delaney's 1959 *A Taste of Honey*, and Brendan Behan's 1959 *The Hostage*. The anti-war satire, *Oh! What a Lovely War*, produced by Joan Littlewood in 1963, shows an even more extensive use of the music hall sketch to explore a theme. In each of these works such routines were comedy sketches that attacked institutions and professionals who maintain establishment values to the distress of the average person.

Movie director Peter Medak retains the skits from the play *Joe Egg*, but places them in a more realistic environment than the home—the actual locations of the hospital and a church. By using direct cuts to these locations some abstraction via cinema techniques stylizes the comedy in a different way from the stage version where the actors themselves make the switches. Furthermore, Alan Bates, playing the part of Brian for the movie, provides the broad strokes of a music hall comedian to lampoon the physician and the vicar so that the satirical intent of the author is transferred to the movie version of the play. As the husband, Bates develops a performance that nearly equals his creation of a degenerate college professor in *Butley*, two years later in 1974. Janet Suzman also does a credible job of portraying the wife, Sheila.

The third satirical stab of the movie *A Day in the Death of Joe Egg* concentrates on the reactions of the bleeding-heart liberal Freddie, a friend of the family. Handling the role with the necessary prissiness and overly serious concern, Peter Bowles portrays this character as a person who merely has a Sunday supplement knowledge of the problem. When he gives advice, he becomes the butt of Brian's and Sheila's invective because it appears a simple matter of putting Joe in an institution and concentrating on having another child who will provide them all the joys of a normal parent and offspring relationship.

Faithfully following the play, the movie version avoids the upbeat ending. Brian finds the strain of this odd marital relationship too great; he flees from his wife and child. With a hanging ending, it appears that Sheila will remain to nurse her offspring. Consequently, the grim nature of what might be called a dark comedy moves the work in a serious direction—a characteristic of such diverse works in the twentieth century as *Animal Farm* and *Wise Blood*. It now proves to be one of the best family satires that has been filmed. This relentless pursuit of the serious social comment causes the film version of *A Day in the Death of Joe Egg* to be, like these two works, less laughable than many film adaptations that came out in the two decades when the movie medium grappled with satire and dark comedy.

However, more laughable popular films that depicted the generation gap and floundering family that did not have stories derived from novels or plays were created in the 1960s and 1970s. Three works that displayed the best of this sub-genre were *Alice's Restaurant* (1969), *Joe* (1970), and *Taking Off* (1971).

Surrogate parents for what might be called a "family" of drifters provide a focus for *Alice's Restaurant*, a film that explores the counterculture commune during the late sixties youth rebellion. Based on the song "The Alice's Restaurant Massacree" by Arlo Guthrie, the work was scripted by Venable Herndon and Arthur Penn—with Penn directing one of his most off-beat films after his successful and controversial work, *Bonnie and Clyde* (1967). The surrogate mother, Alice (Pat Quinn), and father, Ray (James Broderick), as older members of the flower children commune, establish the "family" in an abandoned church. The struggles of this counterculture group become essentially a parody of the standard family interaction—a relationship that would be restored to its conventional status in such popular works as the 1980 *Ordinary People*. Humor develops in this late sixties film as the group strives to be different. For example, a hippie wedding ceremony with an abundance of wild music and powerful drugs contrasts sharply with what we know to be the sedate, standard wedding rites. However, as gay and as joyful as this seemingly carefree existence seems to be, there reigns an undercurrent of disillusionment and eventual disenchantment. The family degenerates as each "child" leaves the commune and substitute parents, Alice and Ray. A key statement is made by one of the members who is afflicted with a drug problem: "Where the hell are we?" Consequently, a strong social comment evolves: the attempt to develop a more open and free family life-style does not work.

Another negative view of family life appeared a year later than *Alice's Restaurant*—the 1970 *Joe*, with an original screenplay by Norman Wexler and direction by John G. Avildsen. The working title of the film was *The Gap*, in some ways a more suitable title because it indicated that the story focused on the disparity between the attitudes held by parents and those held by their offspring in the sixties and early seventies. Evidently the filmmakers found the portrait of Joe, a disgruntled bigot, mushrooming into the dominant figure of their tale.

The acting talent of Peter Boyle might also have contributed to the growth of the character. Joe is a hard-hat, "Love America or Leave It" type of personality who has some of the comic facets of television's Archie Bunker from the series *All in the Family*. This is especially true of his inconsistencies of thought and action. But Joe is a more dangerous creature than the TV prototype; he believes society's offenders, by his definition, "niggers and hippies," should be eradicated. And this hatred of those he believes are corrupting his world eventually leads to drastic action. The movie evolves into a sour attempt to satirize a complete inversion of a Manson clan killing of establishment figures. Long before this shocking event develops in the final scene, Joe joins another middle-aged reactionary, an adman called Bill Compton, in an experimental examination of the counterculture whose life-style they dislike. The traditional philandering of the male is parodied when they drunkenly seduce two young girls, but remain steadfast in their view that their own offspring should remain virgins until married. They become confused with the sexual freedom this other world affords—to the point that a jealousy of this free life-style creates even greater hate. For these two middle-aged men, the American dream has been shattered. With vigilante justice they use their own rifles to slaughter an entire hippie commune of which one member is Bill Compton's daughter. This bizarre ending seems forced, and a viewing of this part of the movie today appears merely sensational.

A much lighter, more consistent, and well-developed generation gap comedy was created by Milos Forman, a Czech director, in his first American film, *Taking Off* (1971). Written by the team of John Guare, Jean-Claude Carriere, and Forman, the work effortlessly explores the attitude gulf between parents and a daughter.

As a title, *Taking Off* refers to the actions of a daughter who frequently runs away from home only to come back again—a phenomenon quite a few parents struggled to comprehend in the rock-youth and drug-oriented culture of the late sixties and early seventies. In this particular story the parents find the actions of their Jeannie bewildering as she seeks refuge with some of her rebellious peer group in the Greenwich Village area of New York City. Seeking her, the father, accompanied by another middle-aged father, go from bar to bar. Since they have had a drink at each bar, they come home thoroughly plastered. When the father, played by Buck Henry, discovers that his daughter has returned on her own volition and is high on some drug, he staggers toward her in an outrage and tries to strike her.

Forman and his writers expose even further the hypocrisy of the parents when they strike up an acquaintance with another couple during a meeting of an organization called the Society for Parents of Fugitive Children. The two couples experiment with a marijuana high in a group session under the supervision of a qualified drug abuse specialist. After this exploration of pot, which is designed to make them realize what the younger generation experiences, they go home and continue the evening with a great deal of drinking (their own drug abuse) and finally become childishly enthralled in a game of four-way strip poker. The wandering daughter once more returns and is shocked by seeing her naked father drunkenly singing an operatic aria to his guests. Again, the point is brought home that these parents who consider the orgies of their offspring to be immoral don't fully realize the parallelism of their own vices with those of their daughter. Furthermore, the daughter's hypocrisy is exposed because she expects proper behavior from her parents, but views her own hedonistic life-style as the innocent pleasures of youth.

Most viewers found *Taking Off* a delightful offering and a significant contribution to the American cinema. Thus, Forman's first film in the United States had many of the understated thrusts of comedy that he exhibited in his Czech films, *The Fireman's Ball* (1967) and *Loves of a Blonde* (1971). He seemed to be dissecting the previous works in his own country. Even the ending of this work has a satirical thrust as the father, Larry Tyne, tries to get to know the rock singer who has captured the affections of his daughter. At a very formal dinner in the middle-class house of the Tynes, he asks the young, bearded, long-haired man if he is skilled in his profession. The young man, Jamie, shyly reveals that he does protest songs and that he has made $290,000 before takes. Naturally, the father, whose god is money, is impressed by financial success and wants to learn more about Jamie's music. *Taking Off* ends with Buck Henry as the father trying to render a spirited version of "A Stranger in Paradise" to introduce his musical preference to Jamie as the young couple sit listening and very bored. The attitude gulf will not be bridged as much as Larry Tyne tries. As a result, the whimsical satire of this movie makes the work one of the best of the times among the original films dealing with family generation-gap problems.

By the end of the decade of the seventies there was an amazing reversal of the film's depiction of the wayward youth and floundering family genre. Influenced by conservative trends in the country, the United States switched to something akin to "making up" rather than "taking off." Through commonplace trials and tribulations family members reached some understanding of each other. Even journalistic critics saw this drastic change. Late in the year of 1980, *New York Times* reviewer Vincent Canby observed the predominance of conservative subjects and themes. He noted that filmmakers were merely following the trend of times, just as in the late sixties and early seventies these creators had presented such works as *Easy Rider, Catch-22, M*A*S*H, Five Easy Pieces, A Clockwork Orange*, and *The Conformist* to fit the taste of that age. Among the movies that illustrated the trend of the first year of the decade of the eighties was *Ordinary People*—a work with a title which might be considered symbolic of that trend—a favorable investigation of the middle-class family. Of this change Canby perceptively wrote:

> Moviegoers have been on a decidedly conservative kick for some time, not, certainly, for ideological reasons, but because these conservative movies satisfy mostly unexpressed needs of social and political order, for efficacy of individual struggle to make life better, for the possibility of salvation. ["When Movies Are Political Harbingers," *New York Times*, December 14, 1980, Sec. II, p. 21, col. 1]

In this reflective article Canby detects emotional emptiness in the lives of the characters in *Ordinary People* even though the picture uses an upbeat ending. However, it is obvious from his previous *Times* exploration of the picture (September 19, 1980, p. 6) that the movie was a serious treatment with no satirical intent. *Ordinary People* presents a struggle of parents with a son who is mentally ill. Two previously produced films, released in 1979, indicate the movie industry's obsession with ordinary people and with commonplace problems of the backbone of our society. *Kramer vs. Kramer* examines the difficulties of a father left to raise his son and the agony of divorce. On a more genteel and humorous key, family life is depicted in *Breaking Away*. The title has none of the connotation of the 1971 *Taking Off*; instead, it refers to the son's exhilaration when he gains a lead over the pack in a bicycle race. As in *Kramer vs. Kramer*, a father-son relationship is explored. Minor, non-destructive difficulties within the family become the focus of the film, and the success of the son in the climactic bicycle race has all the earmarks of the "local boy makes good" magazine story that silent screen comedian Harold Lloyd was burlesquing in his features *Safety Last* (1923) and *The Freshman* (1925) over five decades earlier.

Just as so many of the sentimental dramas of the twenties have faded with changing emotional tastes even with sentimental treatments, so will much of the late seventies and eighties work become dated. It is my belief that such social statements on the family afforded by *Goodbye, Columbus* in 1969 and *A Day in the Death of Joe Egg* in 1972 will live on. Sentimental film dramas are more temporal—clearly stuck in a narrow world of attitudes that soon become outdated. Only the most jaundiced form of nostalgia in a person's taste can prompt one to perceive the exploits of the family in the television series *Father Knows Best* as significant humor when the series is viewed today. Satire, on the other hand, shuns sentiment and, when it grasps the object of its attack, has a life of its own that does not fade with the passing years.

CHAPTER 8

FABLE, FANTASY, PARODY, AND OUTRAGEOUS LAMPOONS

WHEN *FRITZ THE CAT* APPEARED in 1972 as the first feature-length X-rated cartoon, Hollywood had come a long way from the world of Walt Disney—a world inhabited by people-like animals that uttered no expletives stronger than "Gee whiz" and creatures that were as sexless as silly putty. Not so in the fable that Ralph Bakshi created, drawing from material underground cartoonist Robert Crumb developed in the sixties. Here, mirroring the conflicting attitudes of the times, Fritz the cat struggles to express himself with dogs, pigs, crows, cows, lizards, and rabbits, with an aardvark thrown in for variety; and he engages in many activities as he tries to be "with it," a part of the "swinging" world.

When black comedy or satire employs many of the characteristics of fable, myth, fantasy, and parody, the final product, even in the mass media, reflects the universality of these tales. Even before Aesop's stories of Ancient Greece, the fable existed with what is thought to be animalistic analogies of human foibles—tales to teach a moral or even to exist as veiled attacks on political tyrants. Aesop's creation of the story, "The Frogs Who Chose a King," for example, has been thought to represent dissatisfaction with the ruler Peisistratus. But more of the fables attributed to this semilegendary writer seem to use animals to reflect virtues and faults of humans.

The movie *Fritz the Cat* is a fable for our time—providing us with situations which are abstracted from reality in loosely knit tales that intrigue us. We are fascinated by the antics of creatures with human faults and are delighted by this analogical approach. Witness the popularity of such newspaper cartoon strips as *Garfield* and *Bloom County*. In the eighties we followed the life and times of Garfield, the cat, and Opus, the penguin. Garfield, a creature that exhibits many negative facets of our natures—sloth, gluttony, and self-serving cunning—is different from Opus. Opus is an animalistic equivalent of the comic character created by actor-director-writer Woody Allen. He is the loser: a creature with all the physical, mental, and psychological traits that prevent him from realizing his dreams of success. This comically pathetic soul is a character of reaction, while Garfield and Fritz are creatures of action, and, of course, their bold movements to express themselves often boomerang.

The feline hero in the movie *Fritz the Cat* seems well removed from his alley cat lineage (although his sexual habits still remain), depicting a character who is the essence of the would-be liberal of the late sixties and early seventies—a person who agonizes over the plight of blacks and the excesses of the police and the F.B.I. This feline wants to experience the full range of the joys of life and to "relate" to the common folk and the poor. Before he becomes a drop-out from New York University, Fritz affects skills as a folk singer to impress women and the faddish pseudo-intellectuals of the moment. Animator-director Bakshi therefore focuses on a character who remains, in fact, strictly a middle-class WASP, grasping at straws of "being with it"—a creature who surely must have become a yuppie when he turned thirty-three, comfortable in his public relations job because by the late 1970s it was acceptable to be well-heeled and part of the establishment. However, Bakshi, working in the Robert Crumb mold, lampoons the total range of affectations and foibles of the society during this period.

Police, anarchists, and blacks become the target for filmmaker Bakshi as he humorously attacks these factions of society. Police excesses of the time are the target of this *Fritz the Cat* creator. The defenders of law and order are depicted as anthropomorphic pigs with limited intelligence—creatures who derive sadistic kicks from raiding relatively harmless, youthful pot parties. Furthermore, when a serious problem does develop, such as a street riot, the police overreact to the point that the

Fritz becomes disgusted as two others at a wild party take over his seduction in a bathtub in the first X-rated feature cartoon, *Fritz the Cat.*

destruction they wreak is far more immoral than that created by the initial disturbance. Wild-eyed rebels against the establishment are viewed by Bakshi as being just as sadistic as the police. These extremists are shown to have enough hate left over in their warped minds to harass and torture their own like-minded kin. In a decade when it was fashionable to romanticize the plight of blacks, this filmmaker shows many blacks to be self-serving, unreasonably hostile, and often unconcerned about the status of their race. However, the excesses of Fritz and his kind receive the most comic knocks. Of the many journalistic critics who reviewed the film, Judith Crist in *New York Magazine* (April 17, 1972—also see *Film Facts*, Vol. 15, p. 152) realized more than other evaluators that the main target was "the muddle-headed radical chicks and slicks of the sixties."

In this first feature-length X-rated cartoon Fritz's desire to experience the range of the sexual revolution is lampooned. Group sex is delightfully ridiculed as this feline climbs into a bathtub with three dog-girls. To his chagrin a hawk, lizard, and aardvark join him for an orgy that is broken up by the police-pigs. In the final scene of the film Fritz fares much better as four of his girlfriends weep over what they think is his deathbed wish. He urges them to climb into his hospital bed. This horny cat becomes revitalized, even though bandaged from head to toe, as he bounces about and up and down on the bed with his eager quartet in blissful, trampoline sex. More closely allied to satire is the protagonist's attempt to make connection with oppressed blacks. Usually he finds rejection because of his fawning, cliché-ridden overtures as he tries to impress these crow-creatures that he can empathize with the pain felt by their ostracized race. One crow, Duke, becomes his friend because he thinks Fritz brings him luck as he plays pool. But this would-be, radical sympathizer gives a speech urging the black crows to revolt against their oppression. The whole of Harlem becomes a scene of discord as the law moves in, resulting in a police riot, with many blacks, including Duke, killed. This dark comedy reversal of good intentions remains one of the best touches of filmmaker Bakshi's work, as a poke is taken at the pseudo liberals of the sixties.

Not as experimental as the 1968 *Yellow Submarine*, a feature-length cartoon depicting the famous Beatles rock group in a fantasy wonderland, *Fritz the Cat* abstracts real social conditions. While this 1972 work does not have the psychedelic brilliance of the Beatles film, it does exhibit strong visual deviations from reality that make significant comments. When Duke, the unskilled, pool-playing black, gets shot by the police, he views his blood draining away in a "he-thinks" vision as pool balls bounce into a hole one through fifteen, with the last balls going more slowly as he dies. Another innovative "he-thinks" image, a huge pink girl, appears to Fritz as he rejects the academic grind for a life of pleasure; then, he is shown dashing down a tunnel of female breasts—a surrealistic vision which is repeated when Fritz lusts after a "big mother," black prostitute. Such comic moments are the province of the cartoon world, providing the viewer a dimension of humor that cannot be achieved in the live-action black comedy or satire motion picture.

Another fable for our times about the big city, *Shinbone Alley* (1971), a feature-length, animated version of the 1957 Broadway musical, with a book by Joe Darion and Mel Brooks and music by George Kleinsinger, seems to derive some of its inspiration from *Yellow Submarine*. This is particularly evident in the same kind of mixture of artistic styles—pop and op designs—used during the songs. But there is also some homage paid to cartoonist George Herriman, who is noted for his Krazy Kat newspaper comic strip and his illustrations for the collected works of Don Marquis under the title *archy and mehitabel*, the basis for *Shinbone Alley*. These original tales about a strange relationship between a poetic cockroach and a nymphomaniac alley cat present a more universal comment on our society than the youthful attitudes of the counterculture of the late sixties and early seventies do in the films *Yellow Submarine* and *Fritz the Cat*. Marquis had, at least, a pop profundity that spans generations.

Drawing from the whimsical efforts of Marquis and some of the stage musical alterations, *Shinbone Alley* focuses effectively on two picaresque characters, Archy and Mehitabel. They reflect the attitudes of lowlife characters in the big city as they dream of glory and claim to be from a higher state of being in a previous existence. Archy claims to be the result of the "transmigration" of a human poet who composed in free verse, whose life was so unbearable that he committed suicide; and Mehitabel boasts of a past as another human, Cleopatra. Both characters in the original work, of which much is fortunately retained in the stage and screen adaptation, reveal many black comedy facets, which may seem surprising to some viewers since Marquis started writing this fable as early as 1916. Perversely, Archy is in love with a feline that goes from one cat to another. After an affair with a has-been actor who rejects her, she declares, "To think I gave that bum the best three days of my life" (from the motion picture, *Shinbone Alley*). Archy, like his former human self, remains philosophically fixed on suicide as he views a moth trying to destroy himself in a flame. Poor Archy reflects on his desire for a more vibrant existence when the moth tells that he (the moth) wants a lively, brief life. Archy says, "i wish there was something i wanted so badly as he wanted to fry himself" (from Don Marquis, *the lives and times of archy and mehitabel*, Doubleday and Company, Inc., p. 96).* Fortunately such reflections, plus the loose morality of Mehitabel, are retained in the movie version. A fair adaptation of Mehitabel's song is set to music. An example from Marquis's work shows her view of life:

> i have had my ups and downs
> but wotthehell wotthehell
> yesterday sceptres and crowns
> fried oysters and velvet gowns
> and today i herd with bums
> but wotthehell wotthehell
> . . .
> my youth i shall never forget
> but there s a dance in the old dame yet
> toujours gai toujours gai
> [From *the lives and times . . .* , pp. 25–26]

Mehitabel reveals a fascinating picaresque portrait of a very lively, sexual woman, the personification of a charmer on the skids. Animation director John D. Wilson errs by depicting Mehitabel as too young and too sexy. The poetic, philosophical cockroach looks like a four-armed, two-legged version of Jiminy Cricket from *Pinocchio* (1940). While these depictions smack too much of Disney Studio artwork, the voice contributions by Eddie Bracken as Archy and Carol Channing as Mehitabel produce quite a different image if one just listens to these two splendid voice-track interpretations. Wilson probably was reluctant to design the total work in a way that reflected the George Herriman illustrations for Don Marquis's poetry in the original work. *Shinbone Alley* pays homage to this more primitive, and more apt, artistic style of Herriman in the "archy declares war" sequence as translated from the original book. Use of the early, rugged cartoon style in this portion of the film invests the motion picture with the vigor and bite of the original Marquis creation. Archy revolts against the oppression of

---

*The absence of capital letters in Archy's poetry is, according to the author, the result of the cockroach's laboriously jumping from key to key on a typewriter and his inability at the same time to reach the shift to capitalize.

humans who are bent on exterminating insects. As he urges all his "crawlers and creepers" to strike back at humans, we witness a brilliant satire on revolutionaries which outstrips the lampoon of the Yippie extremists in Bakshi's *Fritz the Cat*. Archy's declaration of war closely adheres to Marquis's parody of Dadaist or surrealistic poetry in the original work. The cockroach urges his kin:

> out of equatorial
> swamps and fever jungles
> come o mosquitoes
> a billion billion strong
> and sting a billion baldheads
> till they butt against each other
> and break like egg shells
> [From *the lives and times* . . . , p. 115]

Animator Wilson cleverly illustrates these images as voice-over Archy is enacted by Eddie Bracken and Kleinsinger's score punctuates the rabble-rousing speech. Even wilder surrealistic images are developed by animation when Archy cries angrily:

> little little creatures
> out of all your billions
> make great dragons
> that lie along the sky
> and war with the sunset
> and eat up the moon
> draw all the poison
> from the evil stars
> and spit it on the earth
> [From *the lives and times* . . . , p. 116]

In this portion of *Shinbone Alley*, three quarters through the film, the animators show the potential of what might have been. The original Herriman drawings fit well the tough street humor of Marquis's adventures of Archy and Mehitabel.

Along with *Yellow Submarine*, *Fritz the Cat* and *Shinbone Alley* prove to be some of the best adult feature-length cartoons created. All three make some comment on society and are more successful than such later efforts as *Watership Down* (1978) and

Heavy Metal (1981). If, of course, we look into the past, we may see that the British pioneer effort, the feature-length animated adaptation of George Orwell's *Animal Farm* created in 1955 can be added to make a quartet of superior adult cartoon films which are in content a far cry from the Disney feature in this unique film genre, the animated cartoon.

Earlier film animation works in the fifties and sixties indicate a type of film that employed the fable. Defectors from the Disney Studios who objected to the prevailing, literal picture-book style of this company formed the United Productions of America company to engage in more experimental projects, such as *Gerald McBoing-Boing* (1951), and a series of Mr. Magoo cartoons. These artists also created an excellent cartoon version of James Thurber's short story "The Unicorn in the Garden," employing the distinctive cartoon style of this famous American humorist. This work retains the sophisticated comedy of the *New Yorker* magazine and exemplifies the Thurber collection entitled *Fables for Our Time*, published by Harper and Row. As a film, *The Unicorn in the Garden*, a 1954 release, tells the whimsical tale of a meek husband who feeds a lily to a unicorn in his garden and tells his wife about the phenomenon. When the wife sternly rebukes him, declaring that the unicorn is a mythical beast, he sadly goes back to the garden to find the unicorn gone. In the rebuke she called him a "boobie," and he contemplates his revenge. Since the wife has called a psychiatrist and the police to take him away, the husband shrewdly retracts his report of such a happening before the police. Screaming at the husband to admit what he previously told her, the wife is taken away and confined to a mental institution. In Thurber's fable (following the tradition of Aesop), there is a concluding moral for this tale. "MORAL: Don't count your boobies until they are hatched."

This brief, one-reel film skillfully reproduces the lumpy and fluid bodies in the same style of cartoonist Thurber's way of caricaturing people to illustrate his own writings. With *The Unicorn in the Garden* a new depth in humor, focusing on the battle of the sexes, came to the popular medium of the cinema. This created a breakthrough for dark, sophisticated comic comment in the movies. Similar, significant social humor would be

The creators of *Yellow Submarine* employ innovative, surrealistic scenes such as this cartoon depiction of the Beatles bouncing about in a sea of holes with Jeremy, the Nowhere Man.

realized in the feature-length cartoons *Animal Farm* in 1955 and *Yellow Submarine* in 1968, both of which are fables.

Since *Animal Farm* has already been examined under the broader social context of "corrupt and crumbling institutions," the most important feature-length cartoon of the sixties, *Yellow Submarine*, now needs to be explored because it does reflect some of the counterculture movement of that decade. Resembling some of the characteristics of a mod vision of *Alice in Wonderland*, this work was developed from a story created by Lee Minoff and based on the song "Yellow Submarine" by John Lennon and Paul McCartney. Instead of Alice in a strange underground world, this cartoon features the Beatles' odyssey to Pepperland, a kingdom under the sea, where the quartet try to save this previously happy country from the domination of the Blue Meanies. The inhabitants of this land have been turned into pale, blue statues, and the countryside has been drained of its brilliant colors by these villains. Through song, especially "All You Need Is Love," the Beatles convert the Blue Meanies and restore harmony and color to Pepperland.

This seemingly slight fable has, of course, some overtones of opposition to authority expressed by the counterculture of the late sixties—youth striving for a freer existence and a fuller expression of their emotions. Significantly, the Blue Meanies look like fat, blue rats with Mickey Mouse ears—probably a lampoon of all authority figures who seem to embrace a life-style of controlled emotions and a negative view of those who do not believe as they do. While there are some allusions to a police state, fascism or communism, such a focus becomes blurred. Lee Minoff's story concentrates on a more personal note: a burlesque of those who would restrict a more open and natural expression of emotions. Significantly, the objects of this lampoon are animals while the Beatles have cartoon human forms. Pedantry and dilettantism also come under attack as they become linked to authority. A hedgehog called Jeremy, the Nowhere Man, becomes an object of comic attack, laughing at human pretension as expressed in trivial educational pursuits and vain artistic endeavors. It is possible that Minoff's lampoons become too complex even if there is some focus on the establishment figures in society.

It is also possible that some of the brilliant style in this animated feature smothers the substance; social comment becomes buried in an orgy of design and color. Art director Heinz Edelmann and his battery of animators use styles that vary from pop and op art to impressionism and surrealism, with something akin to rococo designs from India. A person might conclude that the creators have mixed styles rather than the development of one, unified art form for *Yellow Submarine*. But Edelmann is dealing with a story that reveals many of the attitudes of the late sixties when the songs of the Beatles became quite eclectic, embracing many kinds of music and expressing attitudes more universal than those presented in early rock music. Particularly impressive is the art work for "Lucy in the Sky with Diamonds" which, if reduced to an acronym, becomes LSD—a common hallucinogen of the age. Art director Edelmann borrows directly from live-motion picture photography via the rotoscope technique by overlaying photographed images with a kaleidoscope of color. This portion of the film reveals the freedom of expression desired and the need for new, vital experiences. "Eleanor Rigby," on the other hand, using similar techniques, expresses the theme "all the lonely people": many humans live pointless, routine lives and are crushed by their inability to free themselves from this common life-style.

Put simply, *Yellow Submarine* advocates the freer aspects of the counterculture and the views of the youth of the period. Four years later *Fritz the Cat* would lampoon some of these attitudes as well as take pokes at the establishment. The conclusion of *Yellow Submarine* strikes a note that reveals the Pollyannaish viewpoint of the creators. The song "All You Need Is Love" brings a reconciliation between the people of Pepperland, the Beatles, and the Blue Meanies. All conflicts are resolved too simplistically as opposing factions end up singing together in the finale. But, there is something ironic in the resolution. Eventually, the Beatles' music received wider acceptance with older people who might be considered establishment—partly through a more eclectic musical idiom and a sophisticated style that could be appreciated by intellectuals. Youth found a less complicated and, in some sense, more rebellious music, for their own—another counterculture idiom called punk rock.

Less well-known than the Beatles, but certainly a significant rock group, The Who has a 1975 live-action fantasy dramatization called *Tommy*. *Tommy* was among the first of the rock operas. The work reveals some of the excesses of the search for kicks and thrills. As Vincent Canby of the *New York Times* opined, it is a humorous view of "a world inhabited by people too jaded to react to anything but overdoses" (March 20, 1975, p. 48, col. 1). As interpreted by director Ken Russell, this black comedy lampoons the role of parents, the quackery of counselors, conventional religion, and lust for possessions plus even perverts and hop heads. While some critics complain that this extravagant excursion lacks taste, its outrageous vigor somehow exposes a period in the past that wallowed in sensations.

Director Ken Russell, noted for such diverse films as *Women in Love* (1969), *The Devils* (1971), *Mahler* (1974), and *Altered States* (1979), has often been criticized for being too lavish and self-indulgent, but he is often an innovator with a flair that works. In *Tommy* he employs his own brand of pop surrealism to advantage. Particularly effective in making a point in the Acid Queen sequence with Tina Turner is the use of red filters, wide-angle lenses, and a Dali-like iron maiden to symbolize the crushing encasement for the drug addict. Equally inventive in lampooning medium-madness is Ann-Margret's orgasmic bath in soapsuds, beans, and chocolate syrup, which gush from the TV screen that she has drunkenly smashed with a champagne bottle. In the tradition of black comedy, the rock mass and religious gullibility are mocked by having the screen's greatest sex symbol transformed into Saint Marilyn (Monroe), healer of the sick, maimed, and blind.

Irreverence slices both directions in exposing the attitudes of the parents and the offspring. Tommy's psychosomatic blindness and deafness spring from childhood trauma when the boy discovers his mother's infidelity with the man who would become his stepfather. When Tommy, played by The Who lead singer Roger Daltrey, is able to rise above this affliction, despite the many cruelties of society that are heaped upon him, he becomes a mod Christ figure. Social relations are lampooned: Tommy as a rock star and evangelist for his followers, the adoration of his fans, and the exploitation of the star by the parents. In this fantasy, the fans become a mob, killing Tommy's parents, although he escapes. The wishfulfillment resolution reveals a weakness similar to that expressed by *Yellow Submarine*, and attempts at satire are muted—but the dark comedy elements prevail in this colorful, vital rendition of a rock opera, a type of pop literature of the late sixties. The dream mode of a spiritual death and resurrection on a comic level in *Tommy* makes it a "one of a kind" find for this period.

Another type of dream-mode story, dreams of glory, was attempted in 1947 by Hollywood in the adaptation of the James Thurber short story "The Secret Life of Walter Mitty." Starring Danny Kaye, the film suffered a transformation even more damaging than that in the previously discussed *Inspector General* (released in 1949), a work which was nearly drained of any satirical content that existed in the original Russian satirical classic play. *The Secret Life of Walter Mitty* illustrates the way Hollywood studios designed a starring vehicle with little regard for the original intent of the author. It is understandable that

Ann-Margret, Roger Daltrey (*center*, playing the title role), and Oliver
Reed in *Tommy.*

the daydreams of Walter, a mouse of a man who has an active
imagination that places him in many heroic roles, would have to
be extended and altered somewhat from the concise short story
of only a few pages in length. However, the screenplay by Ken
Englund and Everett Freeman totally distorts the character of
Walter Mitty by changing the antagonist who promotes his
daydreams of glory—a domineering wife. Instead, the adapters
provide the hapless protagonist with a mildly disapproving
mother. By this alteration the writers have eliminated the comic
battle of the sexes, a satirical theme in many of Thurber's stories.
As if this were not enough tampering, the creators of the film
design another basic plotline which is a spoof of the spy story—a
genre that will soon be explored. There is so little of the Thurbian humor left in *The Secret Life of Walter Mitty* that only brief
glimpses of the author's whimsy blossom before us as we view a
couple of dream sequences. For example, Walter imagines

himself a brilliant surgeon who is so clever that he can fix a faulty anesthetizer with a fountain pen in order to continue an operation never performed by anyone else.

We need only turn to the short story's concluding scene to see Mitty imagining that he is bravely facing a firing squad after, in real life, he has been thoroughly put in his place by his ever-complaining wife. It is a case where simplicity makes a stronger comment than the elaborate, overly plotted movie adaptation. Thurber writes:

> Then, with that faint, fleeting smile playing about his lips, he faced the firing squad: erect and motionless, proud and disdainful, Walter Mitty the Undefeated, inscrutable to the last. [From the short story in *The Thurber Carnival*, Random House, Modern Library Edition, 1957, p. 51]

It is possible that animators for the United Productions of America could have created a one- or two-reel rendition of this story in the Thurbian style of their 1954 *The Unicorn in the Garden*, and their faithfulness to the original would have provided us with the whimsy of Thurber that is submerged in the manic humor of this Danny Kaye vehicle called *The Secret Life of Walter Mitty*.

As has been previously stated, Hollywood had a habit of draining satire from such works as those starring Danny Kaye in *The Inspector General* (1949) and Bing Crosby in *A Connecticut Yankee in King Arthur's Court* (1949) because these popular entertainers were thought to need light fare, squeezed of the social comment that distinguished their two prototypes, a nineteenth-century play and a novel. A classic satire from the eighteenth century, Jonathan Swift's *Gulliver's Travels*, received a Walt Disney treatment by animators Max and Dave Fleischer in a 1939 version of the work that was strictly children's fare. In 1977 a combination of live action and animation starring Richard Harris indicated that the British could do a bit better. However, the 1977 version of *Gulliver's Travels* has a distillation effect on the satirical intent because of its use of animated Lilliputians who have a cuteness similar to that displayed in the Fleischer feature-length cartoon. But, unlike the earlier version, it retains some political and anti-war comments in the translation from novel to film. As Gulliver, Richard Harris makes a credible lead, a live actor playing opposite diminutive cartoon characters in the land of Lilliput. These six-inch high humans are, as Swift intended, as petty as they are small—the author's reflections on the society he witnessed in the eighteenth century. Part of the sting of the satire is deadened through the cartoon depiction of the comic villains: the leading general and admiral of Lilliput. Their lust for power and plotting against the peacemaker, Gulliver, do not have the invective that Swift intended. Consequently, the cartoon and live action 1977 *Gulliver's Travels* becomes a soft version of the classic.

Another British production created nine years earlier than the attempted adaptation of Swiftian satire also dealt with classical material and almost achieved the level of parody. In 1968 *Bedazzled*, scripted by and starring the comedy team of Peter Cook and Dudley Moore, produced an enjoyable updating of the Faust legend that has become a cult film. This modern Faust exists many IQ points below the intellectual of the original myth. Stanley Moon is a weak-minded and weak-willed fry cook in a small London cafe who is easily manipulated by a sleazy con man named George Spiggot, a mod Mephistopheles. The Devil, a role played by Peter Cook, has the power to grant seven wishes to the lovesick Stanley, who has been captivated by the minimal charms of a waitress named Margaret, but all the wishes for sexual conquest, wealth, and power go sour. Stanley Moon, a role enacted by Dudley Moore, encounters the seven deadly sins in a curious parody of the medieval morality play in which he meets such characters as Lillian Lust, played by the screen sex symbol Raquel Welch. Some of the cleverness of the personification of the other six sins—vanity, anger, envy, gluttony, avarice, and sloth—goes awry at times, but the efforts of these writers remain spirited and irreverent. *Bedazzled* proves to be one of the best fantasy comic films to lampoon traditional religious views.

Bedazzled employs black humor directed at an order of nuns who have taken a vow of silence when it shows the struggles of the sisters to maintain their way of life. This occurs when the disillusioned fry cook Moon realizes all his attempts to bed Margaret have been jaded by manipulation and deceit. At his request of the modern-day Beelzebub, Spiggot, he is trans-

formed into a nun; he meets Margaret in this restrictive order
of the nunnery where she also is a sister. The repressive nature
of the cloistered nuns contains an undercurrent of strong pas-
sions. When Stanley and Margaret fall in love, he finds to his
chagrin that their love must remain pure, but the situation oddly
creates a joke on lesbianism—a gag seldom considered laughable because female homosexuality generally has not been considered humorous in our culture, whereas male homosexuality
has often been the subject of comedy. But the forced inversion
of roles inflicted on Stanley and his frustration over this "pure"
affair abstract the subject and place it on an unusual plane,
especially in a cloistered nunnery with a vow of silence. Ridicule
of traditional religious beliefs reaches the highest point in the
film when George Spiggot, the Devil, tries to enter heaven as a
fallen angel who wants to regain his previous status. He is tired
of working so hard as the Evil One and wants a rest. George is
rejected by God in a way that makes him almost as petty and
fussy as Mephistopheles. God, a booming, overbearing voice off
screen, will not forget or forgive the Garden of Eden incident
and declares that George has returned Stanley's soul to him in
the spirit of pride and as a self-serving way of getting back into
heaven, not as an act from a pure heart. Snarling his disgust with
God, this spiteful creature vows to botch up the Superior Being's creation with even greater messes. Greater pollution will
come about as he, the Devil, creates a deluge of Tasty Freezes,
Whimpy Burgers, frozen food, concrete runways, highways, etc.
"I'll make it so noisy and disgusting that even you will be
ashamed of yourself. No wonder you have so few friends. You
are unbelievable" (from the movie *Bedazzled*). These final remarks by the malicious, modern-day Evil One show the extent
of this burlesque on religious stereotypes that have become
moldy enough to deserve lampooning. But, of course, the taboo
on depicting God in a negative light causes those who are
offended by it to label it "bad taste"—a frequent objection
leveled at black comedy, a type of humor that punctures all the
taboos. Similar objections were advanced when the Monty Python British humorists produced *Life of Brian* in 1979, a comic
view of a man named Brian whose life parallels that of Jesus
Christ. It remains as one of the tightly structured burlesques
created by this group.

More standard lampoons of literary and film genre flourished in the late sixties and early seventies. Most deserve the designation of burlesque rather than the more subtle literary classification of parody. Feature-length films executing take-offs on the spy, Western, horror, heist, detective, and adventure genres enjoyed a popularity for over ten years. Even directorial styles and subjects were spoofed in such works as Mel Brooks's 1977 *High Anxiety* (Alfred Hitchcock) and Woody Allen's 1982 *A Midsummer Night's Sex Comedy* (Ingmar Bergman). But by far the strongest landmarks of the outrageous spoofs were the spy and Western take-offs. The popularity of the James Bond spy thrillers by novelist Ian Fleming, *Dr. No* and *From Russia With Love*, which were brought to the screen in 1963 spawned two lampoons in 1966: a humorous version of female James Bond in *Modesty Blaise* and James Coburn's comic version of a male Bond in *Our Man Flint*. Since this genre came close to a burlesque of the superhuman spy, the take-offs merely stretched the implausible a bit farther with a few works which made a social statement on the times. One spy spoof, *The President's Analyst* (1967), with direction and an original screenplay by Theodore J. Flicker, focuses on a variety of cultural phenomena of the period.

Many major institutions of society, especially government and business, receive knocks in *The President's Analyst*, a work that reflects many of the concerns of a decade that produced telling changes in attitudes. Organizations of government with slightly disguised acronyms for the FBI and CIA provide some of the most effective comic attacks. The moral majority mentality of the "FBR" and the casual, academic, Machiavellian posture of the "CEA" create an interesting comment on two organizations that some people in real life still see as bent on manipulating not only our country but other nations. Director-screenwriter Theodore Flicker also lampoons AT&T, an organization which the psychiatrist, Dr. Sidney Schaefer, observes is an object of hate not only to his patients, but even to its own stockholders. This nationwide phone and communications corporation is shown trying to take over the minds of all its consumers in order to control everyone by small computers implanted in the brains of individuals. The excesses of "Flower Children," the counterculture of the sixties and early seventies, are spoofed, and the paradoxical attitudes of the "liberal" in *The President's Analyst* are portrayed as those of a typical American family which owns not only a complete musical sound system but also guns to protect the family as its members try to live the gracious life in suburbia. Lighter moments feature the comic intrigue of one spy versus another spy, with a vital undercurrent of meaningful comment. This conflict results in an absurd world where all sense, all reason for the activity, seems to be circular, vain, and completely devoid of a moral code for all countries engaged in spying on each other. Creator Flicker's grasp of this inversion of values that existed in the popular spy film and in our culture in the late sixties does not quite approach satire, but *The President's Analyst* is loaded with dark humor that still is laughable today. Director Flicker guides James Coburn as the analyst, Dr. Sidney Schaefer, who is caught in the middle of the intrigue in one of the star's best comedies. The *In Like Flint* spoof, also starring Coburn but as the Bond-type spy, was created the same year as this film. However, it now appears to be pale, fluffy fare while *The President's Analyst* still exhibits the vitality found in some of the best comedies of the sixties.

Burlesques of movie genres sometimes announce the demise of a moviegoer's fad that has gone sour, but the spy film limps on. Not so with the Western movie. *Cat Ballou* (1965), *Support Your Local Sheriff* (1969), and, finally, *Blazing Saddles* (1974) became the death knell for the genre in the seventies. All the clichés of this type of motion picture were lampooned. As entertaining as these films are, they burlesque an already established mythical world which many viewers realize is false. So it becomes difficult to produce anything of significance that relates to our society. Fortunately, in 1970 one film emerged as an example of a higher comic level than these light spoofs—a film based on the novel *Little Big Man*. While this film generally received favorable reviews, critics seemed not to stress the features that had been adapted from the novel. Director Arthur Penn and screenwriter Calder Willingham combined the early nineteenth-century American tall tale in epic form with a revisionist view of the Old West.

Using a deviation from the standard historical myths, this film provides the viewer with a comic inversion of values as two civilizations, that of the white man and that of the Native

American, are portrayed respectively as unprincipled and principled cultures. Thomas Berger's 1964 novel, *Little Big Man*, thereby presents a new view of the Western movement of pioneers in the United States. Previously held views were often clouded with the myths created by both popular fiction and the cinema. However, the most important contribution of this film was as a satirical retrospective view of the United States as a nation contrasted with the Indian nations. More simplistic than Berger's view of the many ironies in this conflict, the movie version shows the savagery of the white man contrasting with the humanity of the Native American, in almost direct opposition to the tale told by most Western films that deal with the subject.

Symbolic irony that reflects the total work is advanced by the novelist in *Little Big Man*'s climactic sequence which describes the destruction of Custer and his troops at Little Big Horn as the Indians engulf and annihilate the white man. The best strategy seems to be on the side of the Native American instead of the military as the so-called "savages" fight like their adversary. Berger has his protagonist and storyteller, Jack Crabb, reflect on this battle:

> Most fought on foot, with no frenzied displays of courage, and taking every advantage of cover. . . . They took quite as much toll upon us when in hiding with them arrow-volleys swishing through the sky, and had their rifle sharpshooters too, though there wasn't near as many guns on the Indian side as some people think; they simply used well the few they had, most of them not repeaters, either. [From the novel, Thomas Berger, *Little Big Man*, Fawcett Publications, 1964, p. 411]

As the soldiers are being slaughtered, Colonel Custer's mind snaps and he gives conflicting and impossible orders to his men. He launches into what Jack Crabb calls lecturing to the blue sky on how novelist James Fenimore Cooper was wrong in his depiction of the native. The Indian "forfeits his claim to the appellation of the *noble* red man," he declares and concludes pedantically: "We see him as he is, and, so far as all knowledge goes, as he ever has been, a *savage* in every sense of the word" (from the novel, p. 418). So the myth is blackwashed when the famous leader is shown babbling in the face of defeat. All glory of his noble last stand is wiped away in Berger's revisionist, satirical tall tale as told by Jack Crabb, who claims to be the sole white survivor of the Little Big Horn battle.

Further ironies are produced in the drawing of characters in the novel. Berger parallels and contrasts Custer with Chief Old Lodge Skins, the leader of the Cheyenne. While this chief has many ingrained character facets that make him humorous, he is sympathetically drawn. He possesses all the humanity that is lacking in Custer. Custer embodies the philosophy of fanatic, negative white supremacy; contrasted with these negative views are the concepts of Old Lodge Skins who provides the members of his tribe with tempered words of moral guidance that are as outreaching, just, and practical as Custer's harsh orders are narrow, restrictive, and self-serving. However, Berger's portrait of this Indian leader clearly avoids Cooper's nineteenth-century romanticized myth of the noble red man. Old Lodge Skin's character remains on an earthy level as he speaks of sex and trivial matters—and he is not infallible in his judgment.

Screenwriter Calder Willingham and director Arthur Penn tend to simplify the characterizations painted by novelist Berger. Of necessity they could not dramatize many of the incidents that show the range of the chief's character. Many events were telescopes in this lengthy tale that ranges through time and space in epic proportions. In fact, this is one way of looking at both the book and the film: as the odyssey of protagonist Crabb which becomes a parody of Old West epics like the labored, dull *How the West Was Won* (1963).

The revisionist perspective of *Little Big Man* debunks the heroics of the Old West myths through other humorous examinations besides the contrast between the white man and Native American leaders. An example is the supposed idyllic existence of the Indian that can be seen in the loosely adapted poem of Longfellow, the 1952 film *Hiawatha*. This film shows the "noble savage" in a splendid wilderness environment. Outdoor living in *Little Big Man* focuses on the absences of creature comforts, squabbles between braves and squaws, and many struggles for food that put a strain on Chief Old Lodge Skins to keep his tribe from one agony after another. Even the white man fights for survival if he becomes, as Jack Crab claims, a gunfighter. Wild

Bill Hickok exhibits the paranoia of a man who has become the target for all young men who want to show they can outdraw a gunslinger with a reputation. Jack, who tries to become the fastest gun in the West, fearfully withdraws from his pursuit when he sees old Wild Bill bloodily gunning down an adversary. Even the seemingly colorful life of the dance hall woman is revealed as boring. In the movie version of the story, Mrs. Pendrake—who previously tries to keep up the appearance of a religious, faithful wife, although she is actually having affairs— becomes a prostitute in the dance hall and discovers that sex night after night becomes tedious and uninteresting to her even though she is a nymphomaniac. The role is effectively enacted by Faye Dunaway in the film.

Berger's version of the Old West also shows the attack of Indians on settlers (in the novel, p. 116), an encounter from which Crabb escapes because he sees no reason why he, as one person with one gun, should try to hold off fifty attackers. And later, as he travels by coach, another rout of the whites by the Indians seems to burlesque John Ford's film *Stagecoach* (1939). Dustin Hoffman, playing the role of Jack Crabb, even jumps on one of the lead horses after the coach driver is killed in order to control the vehicle, burlesquing the same heroic effort of John Wayne in the thirties film. Thus the movie more directly than the novel (see pp. 195–97) lampoons the images of impossible feats accomplished in the standard Western movie of the past.

In creating the film *Little Big Man*, director Penn and adapter Willingham drew a direct parallel between the rape and near extinction of the Native American civilization and what some people call the U.S. military's attempted genocide in Vietnam. However, the average audience member viewing the film in 1970 probably didn't see such a relationship. Penn's didactic purpose to reveal this parallel in the adaptation of Berger's novel was expressed in an interview by Joe Medjack and printed in the film magazine *Take One* (vol. II, September–October 1968, p. 9). Critics, unlike average film-goers, were quick to latch onto this information and were divided in their views on how the intent of this film influenced the final product. Viewed today, without the controversy of the period, *Little Big Man* remains an effective interpretation of the novel's satirical, revisionist view of the Old West. The

Adopted as a member of the tribe, Jack Crabb (Dustin Hoffman) becomes a full-fledged brave as he fights with a member of the U.S. Cavalry in *Little Big Man*.

performances in the movie still seem fresh, and the comedy still communicates in a way that makes a significant statement on one of our most popular myths. The casting of Chief Dan George as Old Lodge Skins was probably the filmmakers' best stroke of luck. This Native American proves to be a natural actor and an asset to the overall movie. At times he even steals scenes from Dustin Hoffman. Particularly effective acting is achieved as Chief Dan George explains the relationship of his "human beings," the Indian race, to the land and to each other, plus his prophetic dreams. These mystical visions are usually serious but occasionally take on an earthy, humorous tone. Recounting a dream about Jack having four "wives" at once, he marvels on the situation and is puzzled. Chief Dan George skillfully understates the line, "It was a great copulation." This warm, gentle portrayal of Old Lodge Skins contrasts well with the hard, cool portrait of Custer by Richard Mulligan, a role that director Penn guides in order to produce a valid interpretation of the novel.

Dustin Hoffman enacts the role of Jack Crabb by achieving in the true sense of the word the "little" man of this tall tale. Unlike some fabricators engaged in elevating their own image, he comes out as a comic loser in most situations even though his overall perception is superior to that of the other white men in the story. He is the anti-heroic, comic little man, like the little tramp played by Charles Chaplin in *The Gold Rush* (1925) in which Chaplin struggles with oversized brutes in the Yukon. Hoffman gives an even more controlled performance in *Little Big Man* than he did in *The Graduate*. Because of this skilled underplaying of the role, Jack Crabb's revised view of the incidents in the Old West seems less mythical than the standard views and closer to the truth. Consequently, comedy on a satirical level reveals a truth and possesses a profundity that develops in the best film satires.

Another, less satisfactory spoof of the Western myth has been created by erratic filmmaker Robert Altman, who loosely adapted Arthur Kopit's play *Indians*, a 1969 Broadway production. Premiered in London, July 1968, the presentation of the drama prompted a television interview in which Kopit revealed that his study of nineteenth-century Indian genocide in the United States was inspired by contemporary events in Vietnam (as reported by Martin Esslin from London in the *New York Times*, July 21, 1968, II, p. 12, col. 1).

Kopit's final version of the play as presented in the United States in 1969 focuses on a contrast between the circus world of Buffalo Bill's Wild West Show and a nineteenth-century commission studying the grievances of Native Americans. With a neo-Brechtian narrative structure and staging devices, the drama explores the white man's exploitation of the heroic myth of the Old West and his manipulations to avoid facing the real abuses experienced by the Native Americans. Although Buffalo Bill revels in his own past and elaborates on his exploits, building them to mythical proportions, he is shown trying ineffectively to mediate for Indian rights. Although curiously sympathizing with their plight, he tries to prove his superiority to Indians because he cannot understand their inability to accept white people's ways. Some portion of Buffalo Bill's complex character remains in screenwriters Alan Rudolph and Robert Altman's adaptation. Playing the role of pioneer Bill Cody turned showman, Paul Newman expresses his rambling view on facing reality, while boosting his own ego in the climactic portion of the movie. He speaks to his vision of Chief Sitting Bull in this monologue:

> "God meant for me to be white. . . . You see, in a hundred years I'm still goin' to be Buffalo Bill, and you're goin' to be the Indian. Look at you. You want to stay the same. Well, that's goin' backwards. . . . I'm curious, Chief, my friends are curious, my women are curious. And they pay me for it. I give them what they expect. That makes you more make believe than me. The difference between an Indian and a white man in all situations is that an Indian is red! And an Indian is red for a good reason. So they can tell us apart!" [He repeats this line two more times. Looking at his own portrait on the wall and rambling on about Custer, he says with a flourish the final line of the monologue.] "Carve our names and celebrate the event!" [From the movie *Buffalo Bill and the Indians, or Sitting Bull's History Lesson*]

This speech by Newman comes close to the stage playwright's vision, but the filmmakers obscure the basic concept of the drama by cutting out views expressed by Native Americans themselves and views expressed by the commission investigating the wrongs of whites against them.

Some of the more negative features of Bill Cody may be seen in the stage drama. In a stylized way the slaughter of buffalo by Bill is depicted and shows the accomplished hunter bragging about killing one hundred without missing one shot. Much is made of how this pioneer helped to reduce the herds to near extinction, thereby cutting off a basic food supply for the Indian. In the ending of the stage work, Bill capitulates to the established line of the whites in a disoriented way which indicates his suppressed guilt; but his muddled, desultory speech is not as extreme as that of the insane Custer in *Little Big Man*. Nevertheless, the speech has similar polemics:

> "The excuse that the Indian way of life is vastly different from ours, and that what seem like atrocities to us do not to them, does not hold water, I'm afraid! For the truth is, the Indian never had any real title to the soil of this country. We had that title. By *right of discovery!* They *had* to be vanquished by us! It was, in fact, our *moral obligation!*" [From the play by Arthur Kopit, *Indians*, Hill & Wang, 1969, pp. 90–91]

His jumbled utterance continues as he tries to justify his own role in the near extermination of the buffalo and to rationalize the broken Indian treaties. He concludes with a shaky statement, "I just want to say that anyone who thinks we have done something wrong is *wrong!*" (from the play, p. 92). Fumbling with a sack of Indian-made trinkets, he starts hawking them (as he did in his Wild West Show) as he states, " . . . to help them [the Indians] help themselves." He is emotionally drained and trembling as the vision of Chief Joseph utters the famous surrender statement:

> "Hear me, my chiefs. I am tired. My heart is sick and sad. From where the sun now stands, I will fight no more, forever." [From the play, p. 94]

If one compares this ending with the ending of the movie, it is obvious that Altman is more interested in the show business theme of the original play and the building of the Buffalo Bill myth. Without these critical elements that have been quoted from the play, the violence against a race, which inspired the author's efforts, has been nearly erased. As a result, Altman's vision of *Indians* obscures the intent of the original. The Buffalo Bill part of his title shows the loose translation in operation. A critical retrospective view of the film might leave one puzzled when the last part of the movie title is considered, . . . *And the Indians, Or Sitting Bull's History Lesson.* One can only speculate that the filmmaker is most interested in the illusion and reality part of the play (the resolution of the movie features the crude reenactment of a hand-to-hand fight between Buffalo Bill and Sitting Bull). It appears that Bill Cody is as much trapped by history as Sitting bull, but the satirical point is too fuzzy to communicate effectively.

The majority of the media burlesques of the seventies made no significant social statements—especially the works engendered by Mel Brooks. His *Blazing Saddles* and *Young Frankenstein* in 1974 followed a pattern employed by a number of spoofs on movie genre—a design set in the twenties by the one- and two-reel films. That same year a British group of filmmakers, whose television programs still exist as reruns on that medium, created *Monty Python and the Holy Grail*. In these three films of that year, the Western, the horror film, and the medieval crusade adventure were lampooned. Retrospective analysis after a second viewing of such works reveals creations that are designed for laughs. While these films do contain some dark humor, the content is slight. As lampoons of traditional genre they really do not question the values espoused by the medium, nor do they set forth a revisionist view of history or the art they mock. Gene Wilder and Marty Feldman, two comedians who had worked with Mel Brooks, respectively created their own burlesques of two film genres—the detective and the adventure film—with *The Adventure of Sherlock Holmes' Smarter Brother* (1975) and *The Last Remake of Beau Geste* (1977). As comic stars in their own works, Wilder as Holmes's brother and Feldman as a soldier in the Foreign Legion spawned a type of take-off that had a short life.

A sub-genre burlesque film using soft-core and hard-core sexual scenes appeared in the seventies. Three examples with high level production values were *Flesh Gordon* (1974), *Alice in Wonderland* (1976), and *Young Lady Chatterley* (1977). Best of the three, the lampoon of the popular comic strip hero Flash Gordon, turns to fleshy relationships involving the hero, Princess Aura (Ming's daughter), and Dale Arden. Superior animation produces a reptilian monster the size of King Kong that strips a woman more explicitly than the predecessor does Fay Wray. Producer William Osco backed this burlesque with enough money that it had the potential to be one of the best X-rated works of its kind, but the acting leaves much to be desired. Osco had better actors for his take-off *Alice in Wonderland*. However, this 1976 production suffers from a poor script, derivative flat songs (the work could be called a musical), and lethargic direction. Understandably, the movie was not the popular success of *Flesh Gordon*. Recently a triple-X-rated version of that production of *Alice in Wonderland* has appeared on the porno video tape market. Explicit sexual scenes do not improve this labored spoof.

While Bill Osco's two films are clearly in the realm of the fantasy burlesque, the creators of *Young Lady Chatterley* seem to be confused as to whether they wish to handle D. H. Lawrence's *Lady Chatterley's Lover* seriously or humorously. Cynthia Chatterley, a grandniece of Lady Chatterley, relives the sexual life of her grandaunt by having an affair with a crude, earthy gardener on the estate she has inherited. Encounters with this modern version of Lawrence's gamekeeper are manipulated to the point of the romantic—the opposite of the novelist's realistic treatment of sexuality. This, of course, does not move toward parody; instead, it creates a type of fiction closer to the Harlequin novels of wish fulfillment.

Depicting the initiation of a young woman into a deeper sexual relationship, the film employs a theme used by the makers of the X-rated *Alice in Wonderland* in which sex is taken seriously. In *Young Lady Chatterley*, on the other hand, flings by servants and one by Cynthia herself, when she picks up a hitchhiker, are played for laughs. A final orgy during an elaborate costume party reaches slapstick proportions. Guests and servants end up disrobing, throwing cakes and pies, and licking the desserts from each other's body. The net result is a confused picture—simply a sexploitation effort by a director named Alan Roberts—with no socially redeeming values. As stated earlier, film creators seem to have a great deal of trouble laughing at our sexual foibles.

One other attempt to spoof a genre which I have labeled the "outrageous lampoon" illustrates how such burlesques become too broad and improbable. In 1980 a lampoon of the airplane disaster film zooms in on four works from the original *Airport* in 1970 to *The Concorde, Airport '79*. Called *Airplane!*, this outrageous spoof heralds the death of a decade of disaster films which were on the wane. A battery of farcical situations, preposterous puns, and slapstick comedy impressed a number of critics and audiences who were tired of the genre. Dark comedy reigns in this poke at the disaster movie; the fear of death becomes the means of achieving humor as the passengers on the airliner are needlessly alarmed by a scatterbrained flight attendant who crudely announces troubles with the plane. A little boy is shown the elaborate mechanisms in the pilot's cabin by the captain, who usually is a pillar of strength during the threat of a catastrophe. Instead, the leader makes overtures to the child, which show his perverted tendencies. However, such insensitive and self-serving acts by figures of authority are merely gags in a long string of jokes; no clear-cut satirical intent emerges. *Airplane!* and the sequel in 1982 reveal little of sociological importance unless a film historian wishes to examine audience taste in this period.

If a socio-historian examined the humorous films and specifically the outrageous spoofs of the sixties and seventies, he or she might find an increase of physical abuse to achieve humor over these two previous decades. But slapstick or physical comedy has been a staple of broad, farcical humor from the Greek and Roman theater to the present-day theater and movies. Often toned in such a way that the spirit of play predominates over the spirit of invective, the laughter that results is more for the pure fun of it all. To find works that explore the violence that exists in society it is necessary to turn to two near-future fantasies, *Little Murders* and *A Clockwork Orange*, movie adaptations created in 1971.

Noted as a widely syndicated cartoonist in the sixties, Jules Feiffer developed *Little Murders* as a stage drama. While its April 25, 1967, Broadway opening proved unsuccessful (only seven performances), the play became a hit three weeks later in London. In a 1969 American revival off-Broadway, the work ran for four hundred performances. The 1971 movie version directed by Alan Arkin was not a popular success but received praise from most critics. Feiffer's strange world of *Little Murders* satirically predicts a nightmare of the future as a complete breakdown in moral values ends up with mass paranoic brutality. Pervasive violence in society reduces the Newquist family, a parody of the average American family, not merely from protecting their property with huge metal screens on the windows of their apartments, but to joyfully killing people on the street for sport. Feiffer's satirical creation reflects on the increase of crime—robbery, mugging, gang fights, and murder—in urban portions of our society. In the film these crimes have created a mass hysteria which degrades even law-abiding citizens, making them insensitive so that they either ignore the violence or retaliate with a violence that is equally immoral. The understated reaction or emotional blandness of responses by the Newquist family develops much of the best humor in this piece. Feiffer's fable seems to stray from the theme of a plagued, degenerate society faced with ubiquitous violence. The author explores a variety of relationships in the family and between young lovers in a changing society. There is, however, some indirect connection of this theme with the degeneration of the family, the confused attitudes towards traditional values, and the more modern pragmatic views of a community under stress.

In *Little Murders* the playwright employs the initiation of an outsider, Alfred Chamberlain, into the family group. Alfred, an object of marriage for the daughter Patsy, describes himself as an "apathist" who has withdrawn from contact with people after his disenchantment with political activism. His character provides a comic antithesis in an age of violence. The play describes via exposition (the film dramatizes the street scene) his non-resistance when he is mugged by a street gang. He explains to the Newquist family his reaction to the beating when the daughter brings him to meet her father, mother, and brother.

> "There are lots of little people who like to start fights with big people. They hit me for a couple of minutes, they see I'm not going to fall down, they get tired and go away." [From the play, *Little Murders*, Random House, 1968, p. 22]

Asked by the father, Carol, about the agony of such frequent maulings, Alfred says he ignores the pain.

> "I daydream all through it. About my work. I imagine myself standing there, in the same spot, clicking off roll after roll of film, humming to myself with pleasure. . . . Muggers tend to get very depressed when you hum all the while they're hitting you." [From the play, pp. 23–24]

Alfred presents the comic other side of the coin in a society gone berserk, like sharks gnawing on each other in a frenzy of destruction. He remains passive until he regains his sensitivity toward others and becomes able to express his emotional responses in a love affair with Patsy. At the moment of direct personal contact, Patsy is shot and killed by a sniper outside the window of the apartment. The incident cuts deeply into Alfred's fragile constitution, totally reversing his character. He joins the family, the father Carol and the son Kenny, in shooting people in the street below the Newquists' apartment. He has been brutalized by a mad world. The dark humor of the play and the movie's ending evolves as Alfred, Carol, and Kenny joke, laugh, and clown with each other over their ability to kill people who are casually walking along the street. With matriarchal pride the mother Marjorie serves dinner and contentedly remarks, "It's so nice to have my family laughing again. You know, for awhile I was really worried." (From the play, p. 104. An almost identical line ends the film.)

Feiffer, whose cartoon series often employs monologues in a mod-Chekhovian way, uses a number of speeches in *Little Murders* that touch on the central theme of indifference to, absorption in, or advocation of violence. He explores our sexual misalliances and our religious and psychological hang-ups as well as the inefficiency of law enforcement. He touches briefly on the homosexual hang-ups of the son, Kenny, but concentrates more effectively on the mismatch of the aggressive daughter, Patsy, with the passive Alfred. Religion fused with psychology enters into a monologue by the mod preacher, Reverend Dupas, who turns the wedding between Alfred and Patsy into a shambles by using all his relative, existential, moral concepts to question each aspect of the rite as spelled out by the State of New York. In the movie this speech is delivered by Donald Sutherland in a cameo appearance. On the other hand, a comic view of traditional values comes from an aptly named judge, Judge Stern (played by Lou Jacobi in the film), who delivers a tirade when Alfred wants to be married without the word "God" mentioned in the ceremony. Alfred and Patsy in the movie and in the play are subjected to a lengthy oration from which one excerpt will illustrate the comedy:

> "What was God to my father? I'll tell you—sit down, I'm not finished!—I'll tell you what God was to my father! God got my father up those six and a half flights of stairs,

not counting the stoop, every night. God got my mother,
worn gray from lying to her children about a better tomor-
row she didn't believe in, up each morning with enough of
the failing strength that finally deserted her last year in
Miami Beach at the age of ninety-one, to face another day
of hopelessness and despair." [From the play, p. 54]

Consequently, both faddish and traditional values are ridiculed. So, it would seem that Feiffer, as a satirist, shoots with a
scattergun, much as he does in his cartoon strips. However, a
monologue by a police inspector named Lieutenant Practice,
enacted in the movie by director Alan Arkin, zeroes in on the
theme of violence in the community. The family has reported
Patsy's murder. Confronted with a deluge of unsolved murders,
the law officer, driven to hysteria and incompetence, explains
his plight:

"What is the effect of three hundred and forty-five unsolved homicide cases? The effect is loss of faith in law-
enforcement personnel. This is our motive. The pattern is
complete. We are involved here in a far-reaching conspiracy to undermine respect for our basic beliefs and most
sacred institutions. Who is behind this conspiracy? Once
again ask the question: Who has the most to gain? People
in high places. Their names would astound you. People in
low places. Concealing their activities beneath a cloak of
poverty. . . . We are readying mass arrests." (*Rises to leave*)
"I'm going to try my best to see that you people get every
possible break. If there is any information you wish to
volunteer at this time it will be held in strictest confidence." (*Waits for a response. There is none. Crosses to the
door and opens it.*) "I strongly advise against any of you
trying to leave town." [From the play, p. 98]

Alan Arkin and his adapter, playwright Jules Feiffer, have
preserved most of these monologues, with some judicious cutting to conform with the film medium—a medium that does not
always reveal kindly the brilliance of long speeches that are
sometimes the staple of the stage play. Adept handling by
Donald Sutherland, Lou Jacobi, and Alan Arkin makes these
long speeches an integral part of the film. Elliott Gould as
Alfred and a good portion of the cast produce polished perform-

ances that result from their enactment of these roles on the stage (Vincent Gardenia as Carol, Elizabeth Wilson as Marjorie, and Jon Korkes as Kenny).

The excerpts from the play presented above illustrate some of the humor that continues in the translation of the work into a film. The mother, the rest of the family, plus Alfred, the judge, preacher, and police lieutenant represent comic characterizations which are deviations from the norm; their personality facets are revealed in their reactions and emotional relationships. Some of the characters have become anesthetized to violence (the mother expects to get shot at when she goes shopping), or they eventually retaliate (the family become snipers) as if this terror from the streets should become the latest form of recreation. As in many satirical works the overall humor is achieved by a sharp inversion of values. Director Arkin may have erred in taking an abstract work from the stage and giving it a more realistic tone, a complaint by journalistic critics Stanley Kauffmann for *The New Republic* and Gary Arnold for the *Washington Post*. However, the acting performances and the humorous details extracted from the screenplay make this work one of the best satirical films on violence in our society, next to Stanley Kubrick's *A Clockwork Orange*.

While Arkin takes a stylized art work and moves it toward realism, Stanley Kubrick stylizes even more the material he has taken from the source novel by Anthony Burgess, a 1963 work which shows a near-future society with a moral breakdown similar to that depicted in *Little Murders*. *A Clockwork Orange* reveals a community plagued with youthful gangs who mug people for pleasure and profit. Eventually the psychological reason for assaults on people works like a perverse therapy on such youths as the protagonist Alex, who refers to these actions as "ultraviolence." Pleasure combined with a sense of power motivates the gangs. Novelist Burgess goes farther than Feiffer by presenting established law and order with a moral dilemma. Feebly ineffective in correcting the violence in society, scientists develop an elaborate conditioning experiment which they try on Alex. It disarms him to the point that he becomes violently ill when he is sexually tempted or when someone threatens to harm him. To Burgess such a drastic solution turns into society's own violence directed on the individual, robbing one of free will.

In the novel this dilemma is directly stated by a prison minister who witnesses a staged demonstration on the psychologically conditioned offender who grovels before an actor that has been instructed to abuse him physically. The minister objects by saying, "He ceases to be a wrong-doer. He ceases also to be a creature capable of moral-choice" (from the novel, *A Clockwork Orange*, W. W. Norton and Co., 1963, p. 128).

This fable for the future uses the protagonist Alex in a much different way than Alfred is used in *Little Murders*. Alfred's mind is twisted by pressures much different from those tormenting Alex's mind. Feiffer offers no explanation for the breakdown of order in the world, and he offers no solution. Burgess suggests that simplistic cures for a warped society can be destructive—even as some social critics now suggest that the "warehousing" of criminals is ineffective as a cure for the ills of our society.

With this complex theme, it is little wonder that the adaptation and direction of *A Clockwork Orange* in 1971 by Stanley Kubrick created controversy. Just as *Bonnie and Clyde* sparked battle among film critics regarding the worth of the work in 1967 and 1968, so did *A Clockwork Orange* produce a similar disputation in 1971 and 1972. Both films were the object of condemnations and counter-defenses; most of the debate focused on the use of violence and the social significance of the movies. Writing on *A Clockwork Orange* for *The New Yorker*, Pauline Kael accused director Kubrick of "catering" to the "post-assassinations and post-Manson mood" (January 1, 1972, p. 51). Vincent Canby of the *New York Times* took an opposite view by declaring that the movie aptly expressed the fears of society in a "real and important" way rather than using violence for a thrill or in the purely melodramatic manner of the exploitation films (December 20, 1971, p. 44, col. 1). Evidently Canby's impression of *A Clockwork Orange* prevailed since journalistic critics from the New York Critics Association gave it the best film award for 1971.

Noted for his *Dr. Strangelove or: How I Learned to Stop Worrying and Love the Bomb* (1964) and *2001: A Space Odyssey* (1968), filmmaker Kubrick has managed to capture many of the complexities of the novel despite some variations which disturbed the critics. His version of *A Clockwork Orange* becomes more disturbing than Burgess's dystopia when he depicts a

In *A Clockwork Orange*, Alex (Malcolm McDowell) displays an enigmatic smile as he lifts a glass of a drug beverage dispensed in a near-future bar.

number of brutalities immediately after the British street gangs are viewed at a "milkbar" spiked with drugs, drinking a potion which would ready Alex and his gang for what he terms "a bit of old ultraviolence" (from the screenplay, *A Clockwork Orange*, New York: Abelard-Schuman, Ltd., 1972, p. [2]*). There is a direct cut from the bar to four scenes depicting the brutal activities of the band of four, Alex (the leader), Pete, George, and Dim. First, they are shown beating up a drunken tramp who states the condition of the degenerate culture: "It's a stinking world because there's no law and order anymore. It's a stinking world because it lets the young get onto the old, like you done" (from the screenplay, p. [7]). When the movie screenplay is compared with the novel, it can be seen that such exposition in the film is more direct and probably, for some people's taste, a

---

*Since the publishers of the screenplay have not provided pagination, I have assigned page numbers starting with a photograph of the film's credits.

bit too blatant. However, adapter and director Kubrick means to be blunt. Another direct cut from the beating of the old derelict shows Alex's group attacking a rival gang—a war fought to the ironic, contrapuntal underscore of Rossini's *Thieving Magpie* Overture. When the police arrive on the scene, the four escape by stealing a car and in a wild drive force others cars off the road. Some of the automobiles end up crashing. In the fourth scene, after the car has been used as a tool for violence, Alex's gang force their way into the house of a writer named Alexander, brutally beating him up and raping his wife.

Novelist Burgess weaves his tale using a first-person account of Alex in the more casual fashion of his medium. After the milkbar scene the narration turns to the young punks beating up a person Alex classifies as a "schoolmaster type" whom the group accuses of taking pornographic books home to read. They tear up his books, hit him, and tear off his clothes, but, unlike the old tramp beaten in the movie, the victim is allowed to stagger away (from the novel, pp. [5–7]). Of course, both beating incidents are brutal, but Kubrick pushes his form of photo-graphic and stylized cruelty into a concise, direct narrative to show the havoc that results from a dour, nightmare reign of young outcasts in a mad future world. Kubrick's opening scene draws first of all on the dress of the young hoods, which Burgess describes as tight-fitting attire. But the filmmaker adds coffee tables in the bar in the form of plastic molds of naked women, bent over backwards on hands and feet, exposing vulgarly their sexual organs. Sexuality and violence are more clearly linked in the film as part of the perversion and degeneration of a culture. Contrasting images by Kubrick in these first five scenes portray some parts of the city with garish, pop-art decor, while other parts are depicted as remains of an older, decayed civilization—symbolically showing buildings in ruins or, as depicted in later scenes, buildings scarred with graffiti.

Critics and audiences have been so confounded by Kubrick's vision of a violent society that they have not known how to receive the film. The work remains an enigma to some, or it appears to others to be an outright exploitation of violence in the cinema—an accusation by Pauline Kael which I believe is a misreading of his film. A key to interpretation may best be grasped by noting how Kubrick uses contrapuntal and contrasting music in his films. His 1964 *Dr. Strangelove* used the heroic music of "When Johnny Comes Marching Home Again" and the romantic "We'll Meet Again" as ironic comments on the action. The first song underscores the unwanted heroic attempt of the crew of the crippled B-52 to bomb Russia, and the second underscores the final image of atomic holocaust and the annihilation of the human race. Such ironic comment indicates the filmmaker's comic and satirical toning of the work. As indicated above, *A Clockwork Orange* employs Rossini's *Thieving Magpie* Overture to underscore the gang war in the third scene of the movie. The composition's lyrical beauty contrasts sharply with the chaos of head and stomach bashings visualized on the screen. Throughout the film Kubrick uses Beethoven's Ninth Symphony in a similar way; the visions which this classical piece of music evoke in the perverted Alex's mind are not in syncopation with the noble intent of the music; instead, the music brings visions of people engaged in sex and torture orgies. When Alex and his gang beat up the writer Alexander and rape his wife, Alex sings the joyful "Singing in the Rain," kicking the husband in the stomach rhythmically at the end of phrases of the song. While Kubrick might be accused of heavy-handed irony or humor with such contrasting music to underscore the action, it seems to show a satirical interpretation of the satirical novel.

Another key to the satirical intent of the film is Kubrick's translation of the first-person narrative of Alex from the novel to the screen. The voice-over image narration by actor Malcolm McDowell, who portrays Alex, uses comic invective remarks directed at authority; and Alex even jokes about his own plight before he becomes the victim of the Ludovico Treatment by scientists. One revelation by the protagonist, after he is arrested for murder, reveals both of these aspects as he reflects in the colorful future language of English and Nadsat devised by Burgess:

> "This is the real weepy and like tragic part of the story beginning, O my brothers and only friends. After a trial with judges and a jury, and some very hard words spoken against your friend and humble narrator, he was sentenced to 14 years in Staja No. 84F, among smelly perverts and hardened prestoopnicks, the shock sending my dadda

beating his bruised and krovvy rookers against unfair Bog in his Heaven, and my mum boohoohooing in her mother's grief, at her only child and son of her bosom like letting everybody down [—] real horrorshow. [From the screenplay, pp. 134–135]

Humor is achieved in such reflections by Alex's put-down of law officials and his parents, but also by a comic abstraction with tongue in cheek when he describes his difficulties as adding up to the "weepy and like tragic part of the story." Alex, a picaresque, comic portrait (as negative as many features of the young man are), is a person with perception, imagination, and self-realization. Not only his words, but also his actions give depth to the character and illustrate the humorous nature of this con man. He bilks his own gang, his mother and father, law officials, a preacher in prison, and, finally in the resolution of the story, the government as it restores him to his normal, despicable self. Also, the portion of the story which shows Alex conditioned against violence and sex, a type of "the worm turns" situation, has both comic and serious qualities.

The sheer power—the drive—of Kubrick's version of *A Clockwork Orange* makes this work one of the best film satires of the sixties and seventies. Inversion of values, a focus of most satires, provides a type of cool, almost abstract satire that has sometimes confused both audience and critic. But Kubrick has given us a film that is as socially significant as his earlier *Dr. Strangelove*. This 1971 film has a serious tone that makes it, like the movie *A Day in the Death of Joe Egg*, less laughable than many satires because of the handling of contrasting comic and serious matters. The skill of execution by the director of *A Clockwork Orange* makes this film more memorable and gives it more impact on audiences than *Little Murders*. However, both works explore violence in our culture, as does *Little Big Man*, making these three films the most important works that are tied to the approach of myth, fantasy, and fable. Using the satirical fable in two cartoon features, *Fritz the Cat* and *Shinbone Alley*, animators have created works that seem to rank on a lower level than the above-mentioned movies, but these two films need to be given credit for giving us insight into our world.

CHAPTER 9

THE SATIRICAL TRADITION CONTINUES

WHILE THE ASSAULT ON SOCIETY by the humorist may seem to
have waned in the eighties, at least to the casual observer, satire
has suffered only a temporary setback. When one considers the
nature and direction of such works as *Arthur* (1981), *My
Favorite Year* (1982), *Tootsie* (1982), and *The Woman in Red*
(1984)—films that reflect on the mores of the community with a
softer, gentler way of revealing the foibles of our culture—it would
appear that a more personal, genteel film comedy of past decades
has reappeared on the contemporary scene. However, below the
surface of a more polite and warmer comic genre lurk the possi-
bilities of future satirical films. *Arthur* and *My Favorite Year* reflect
some of the characteristics of the fruitful, sophisticated comedy of
the thirties, a mode that spawned *Twentieth Century*, *Nothing
Sacred*, and *Topper*. These three films revealed a complex relationship between the sexes that undercut the sentimental notions
expressed in many of the family comedies of that same period. On
a similar level, *Tootsie* and *The Woman in Red* now show the
emerging, assertive role of women in our society.

Even some of the youth-oriented humorous works, *The Last
Starfighter* (1984) and *Back to the Future* (1985) for example,
have some of the dash of the thirties Frank Capra films. And as
in his works, elements of sentiment and satire become paradoxi-
cally blended. Leavened with the clever line that occasionally
reaches the level of witty observation on our culture, the overall
concoction has, nevertheless, a sponginess that does not exist in

a Capra film. As a fantasy dealing with alternative worlds, *Back to the Future* does not achieve the comic social statement of Capra's 1946 film *It's a Wonderful Life*, a work that handles similar material. Shades of a Preston Sturges film exist in *Arthur* and *Tootsie*, but these works do not provide us with as strong a comic view on the battle of the sexes as *The Lady Eve* (1941) or *The Palm Beach Story* (1942). However, the ability of a person to see reminiscences of these master filmmakers' works indicates that comedy in the United States has not reached the low ebb of the fifties.

To keep a clear perspective it should be noted that many sappy comedies, mostly youth-oriented films with crude food fight and peeping-tom scenes, have marred the eighties scene. These "animal house" or "seduce the camp counselor" movies are the modern equivalent of the "beach party" pictures of the sixties. The 1978 *National Lampoon's Animal House*, a slapstick depiction of college life that shows youths more interested in partying than studying, started much of the trend, and various situations at high school reunions, summer camps, and vacation spots were exploited. The 1973 *American Graffiti* by George Lucus has sometimes been credited with starting the genre, but, as thin as this work is, it does reflect honestly the mores of high school youth of the early sixties. *Porky's* (1981) and *Police Academy* (1984) have more of the "animal house" raunchy, tasteless humor with all the contrived, farcical situations that characterize the genre. This genre will fade when the repeated, stale gags become tiresome even for the audience at which they have been aimed.

As sappy film comedy the "animal house" type of film does, at least, show how the trends of the sixties and seventies changed the taste in film humor. The release of language and sex taboos illustrates that we have come a long way from the propriety demanded by censors from the twenties into the fifties. Vulgarity can be an important part of black humor and satire. Satirical masters of the past—Aristophanes, Rabelais, Wycherley, Swift, and Voltaire—employed scatology with a purpose. As much as censors and prudes objected, these satirists used a wide range of vulgar situations to ridicule society. The sixties and seventies film broke more effectively from British and American Victorian propriety—allowing a wider range of sexual material that was eventually accepted by the audience.

Through this examination of the dark comedies and satirical literature adapted to film, it has been noted how journalistic critics' reactions (and less so, academicians' reflective appraisals) have put to question the filmmakers' "good taste" in the final creation for a cinema audience. The "animal house" genre and the "outrageous lampoons" of literary and film genres are the more likely candidates for the label of bad taste because of the handling of the material and the intent of the creators, who often merely want to exploit the vulgar. Mel Brooks's mass farting sequence when ranch hands eat beans in *Blazing Saddles* and the urination sequence in the 1981 *History of the World—Part I* provide examples of lapses into a regressive humor, much on the level of adolescents reflecting on their toilet-training period. In dark comedy and satirical films, the purpose of a scene provides the answer to what is good taste. In *Lysistrata* Aristophanes shows the women revolting against the senseless wars that are favored by the men. They attack the male establishment with pots of excrement. In an antiwar statement the Greek playwright literally and figuratively attacks the dominating old men with urine and feces. Brooks provides his audience only a juvenile snicker without any purpose. Therefore, it remains a questionable practice to equate the serious satirist's use of vulgarity with that of the exploiter of obscenity. In the sixties, *New York Times* critic Bosley Crowther accused Stanley Kubrick's *Dr. Strangelove* and Tony Richardson's *The Loved One* (film versions of the adapted novels) of using bad taste. In the seventies, when he re-examined *Dr. Strangelove*, he recanted; but, his immediate reaction was typical of many critics in those two decades who seemed to reflect at least part of the sentiment of the general public.

A polite society bent on the preservation of what proper folk call good taste has often been repressive in periods when the stress seems to be placed on decency and propriety. Unfortunately, the dramas and novels that too often evolve abound in exemplary characters so that only a genteel poking of fun at minor character flaws is evident. Serious matters, such as cultural decay, are avoided since the establishment wishes to maintain the status quo or even turn the clock back to those mythical "better" days. In such an age only a mild, genteel, sentimental comedy will exist. Preceding our age was the English Victorian society of the late nineteenth century, replete with polite, tea-cup, domestic comedies which on the stage eventually gave way to the witty, socially significant comedies of Oscar Wilde and George Bernard Shaw. So, change will come about from age to age with the emergence of humor that is vital and alive and that reflects on some of the problems in our society.

We have slowly been conditioned to cinematic dark humor and satire in the twentieth century. An investigation of Alfred Hitchcock's entrance into the medium of television and a look at his 1955 movie, *The Trouble with Harry*, will not only show a creator promoting a taste for black comedy but also will help with the definition and classification of various types of dark humor. Even during the reactionary political and social period of the fifties American audiences were conditioned to a type of dark comedy that manifested itself in some episodes of *Alfred Hitchcock Presents* and *The Alfred Hitchcock Hour*, a popular anthology series that ran from the fall of 1955 to the spring of 1962, with many repeat broadcasts on television since then. Quite a few of the serious programs ended with a dark comedy comment from the master of ceremonies, Hitchcock himself. For example, a jilted lover kills his former fiancée, Helen, in "Arthur," a program first telecast September 27, 1959. Hitch-cock announces at the end of the program that Arthur, a chicken farmer, had a grinding machine which prepared a special mix-ture on which the chickens thrived; one of the ingredients was Helen. In another, earlier work (May 13, 1958), "Lamb to the Slaughter," a wife kills her husband with a frozen leg of lamb and invites the policemen investigating the death to a lamb dinner. The law officers are baffled by the case because they cannot find the murder weapon. Such dark humor in murder mystery dramas slowly but surely introduced the American pub-lic to a type of off-beat comedy to which they were not accus-tomed, and, at least for some members of the audience, helped form a taste for bizarre comic murder situations.

Just as Hitchcock was about to launch his television series, he produced a feature-length movie, *The Trouble with Harry*, a work that indicated he had a strong affection for dark comedy. It is also a work that shows the use of dark comedy as entertainment

An eighties revival of Hitchcock's 1955 *The Trouble with Harry* was more readily accepted. Shown here, a body discovered by a boy at play becomes shifted about in the dark comedy fashion of the sixties film, *The Wrong Box*.

without a clear-cut social statement—thereby showing how we can distinguish such treatment by filmmakers from the satirical approach.

The film version of *The Trouble with Harry* was derived from the British novelist Jack Trevor's story of a dead man's body being shifted around by those who try to get rid of it in much the same way Robert Lewis Stevenson handled the dark comedy of people trying to get rid of a body in *The Wrong Box*, an 1889 novel and the 1966 adaptation to film which has been explored in the second chapter of this investigation. Although Hitchcock produced many intrigue films, he achieved only limited success with the full-fledged comic treatment of his 1941 *Mr. and Mrs. Smith* and *The Trouble with Harry*. This later film has been called by some critics the filmmaker's most British movie, probably because of its droll humor, laid-back pace, and the extensive use of comic understatement. Dark humor reigns in the film but remains lighthearted with oblique social commentary that does not add up to a satirical statement.

Well loaded with misconceptions, this farce shows three people who try to get rid of the body because they think they might be responsible for the death of a man named Harry Warp. A warmhearted codger named Captain Albert Wiles believes he shot Harry accidentally when he was hunting rabbits; the feisty young wife of Harry, Jennifer Rodgers, considers herself the killer because she struck him over the head with a milk bottle; and finally, a middle-aged spinster, Miss Graveley, believes she dispatched him with her hiking boot when, dazed from the blow delivered by Jennifer, Harry attacked this elderly woman. All three people feel few qualms about the supposed demise of Harry Warp. The inverted moral sensitivities of this trio and their manipulations to hide the body from the law officer of a small community in the hills of Vermont provide the dark humor for this piece. All of their struggles take place in a tranquil hamlet during beautiful autumn days—contrasting sharply with the usual iconic dark and stormy night of so many comic murder stories. Also, the conclusion reveals that Harry, whom everyone considers a self-serving cad whose death would be a benefit to humankind, died of natural causes. Therefore, the environment, the reactions of the leading characters, and the farcical intrigues of the plot serve to lighten the dark comedy. If Hitchcock is revealing in this work his frequent theme of murder in the hearts of common people (as in *Shadow of a Doubt* in 1943 and *Strangers on a Train* in 1951), he has lightened the dark nature of the comedy to the extent that the point has confused a good portion of the audiences in America.

Significantly, *The Trouble with Harry* played more successfully in England and France in the fifties. Re-released in the early eighties, this work does not measure up to his more "typical" intrigue film of 1954, *Rear Window*, a work also re-released at the same time. But it is not clearly the case of audiences still not ready to accept dark comedy; it is simply not one of Hitchcock's best films. Merely giving the work a faster pace, as Bryan Forbes did with similar material in the 1966 *The Wrong Box*, might have solved part of the problem. But inherent in the script is the lack of social comment; greed in people is satirized in *The Wrong Box* while the inverted values of the participants in moving a body around in *The Trouble with Harry* provide only whimsical comedy.

Two of the most successful dark comedy works that have been examined are Kubrick's *Dr. Strangelove or: How I Stopped Worrying and Learned to Love the Bomb* and *A Clockwork Orange*. They provide a sharp contrast with *The Trouble with Harry*. Displaying dark comedy, these two works are far from the light entertainment of Hitchcock. They have the profundity of satire for our times, grappling firmly with the problem of violence which plagues our society. Kubrick's films were actually box-office successes as well as critical successes—even with the grimness of the filmmaker's approach to comedy. It is possible that he achieved the right blend of dark comedy and satire, which seems to be the trend of twentieth-century works with the most significance. Classical satires had some of this same blend but did not reach the nihilistic proportions of modern satires. Traditional motivation for the literary efforts of Aristophanes, Molière, Swift, Voltaire, and Shaw was corrective: some hope of reform, even remote hope, seems to be present. European determinism, tied to novelist Zola's naturalism, brought new directions to literary circles, a cynical view which saw no possibility of correcting the evils of society.

Even in America, a country noted for its optimistic spirit, the literary giant Mark Twain produced satires that reflected this spirit. The time traveler, the Yankee, in Twain's *A Connecticut Yankee in King Arthur's Court*, finds the conditions of Camelot the opposite of the romantic conception and brings about a reformation with negative results. The utopia established by the Yankee eventually degenerates because of the incorrectable human flaws. Twain seems to be the precursor of a nihilistic tone that would eventually become a trend in the next century. This 1889 work and the posthumously published *Letters from the Earth* revealed a cynicism about human nature that would flourish in the twentieth century. American novelist Nathanael West would draw from the French surrealistic poets and novelists and produce an even bleaker satirical attitude concerning the ills of society. A literary movement of no hope, no correction of faults, and no possible reformation developed. French novelists and playwrights would create a type of movement that would be labeled absurdist literature. Important figures such as André Gide, Jean-Paul Sartre, Eugène Ionesco, and Jean Genet would show us a world beyond redemption. Irony, satire, and black comedy reign in such works.

There are many American and British novelists and playwrights who seem to be influenced by the absurdist movement. Of the movie adaptations discussed, Joseph Heller's *Catch-22* could be cited as a work that embraces the absurdist world. The "catch-22" central concept not only reveals the absurdity of the military system, but has become a part of our vocabulary that embraces our own indignation directed at impossible bureaucracy in government and business. Protagonist Yossarian finds himself trapped in an insolvable, incorrectable maze from which there is no hope, no escape. A private absurd world evolves with grim humor in the 1972 *A Day in the Death of Joe Egg*, adapted by Peter Nicholas from his play *Joe Egg*, showing parents caught in an impossible situation as they try to communicate with a handicapped child who is little more than a vegetable. Another example of a broader scope is the 1975 *The Day of the Locust* by filmmaker John Schlesinger, who adapts Nathanael West's devastating view of the crowd gone mad in the promised land of California gone sour. As in the *Dr. Strangelove* and *A Clockwork Orange* of Kubrick, the world has crumbled; the degeneration of society has become irreversible. So, it would appear, there was a wealth of dark comedy and satire adaptations which fit into the absurdist mold—a twentieth-century variation on the corrective satire of the past.

The cynical climate of the sixties and seventies provided an audience for films that went so far as to tell us we might as well abandon hope. Since then a type of wish fulfillment has mitigated the trend. However, I believe that satire with a pessimistic thrust is merely in a state of retrenchment—that it appears to be evolving again or will be at least a part of the scene. In the sixties, hopeful solutions were depicted along with the apocalyptic view. The grim yet comic *Dr. Strangelove* served a function. As the absurdist maintains, it is necessary to laugh at an insane world with no solution in order to keep one's own sanity. Also created in 1964, Sidney Lumet's *Fail-Safe* presented a serious view on the possible annihilation of the world. Both proved to be effective movies using the same subject; however, it is possible that a person might prefer one treatment over the other. *Fail-Safe* provides us with wish fulfillment: the view that sanity will prevail when two nations come to the final hour of a conflict that could end in nuclear holocaust. *Dr. Strangelove* suggests that insanity will determine the fate of man. Here are two sides of the coin—different treatments that existed in 1964 and will continue to be possible treatments for the cinema. It should be realized that even Kubrick's film, the absurdist's approach, has a therapeutic quality that is sometimes overlooked. We can laugh at our most painful nightmares. Besides, it shows us that we personally have attitudes which are sane, ones that recognize the dangers when others seem to ignore the threat to civilization for political or jingoistic reasons. Logically, it seems to follow that *Dr. Strangelove* more forcefully makes us question the motives of our leaders. *Fail-Safe* provides us with wish fulfillment—that our leaders will make a proper judgment when faced with doomsday. Consequently, a question could be asked: Is it possible that even the absurdist's view of society might influence us toward change, thereby serving the same function as the traditional, older form of satire?

As a complicated literary mode, comedy provides another social function. The films that I have explored may promote an acceptance of change and the acceptance of faults. Therefore, another therapeutic or even constructive quality may exist in satire. This is particularly evident in the theme on strained family relationships in the sixties and seventies movies. *The Graduate* and *Goodbye, Columbus* delineate the struggles of young men breaking away from some of the values of their parents and a success-oriented culture. *Taking Off* indicates ironically different yet, in some ways, analogous life-styles of the parents and offspring. All three films chart the stormy course of the much discussed generation gap of the sixties: each shows need for a change from the past when the family was a more cohesive unit in our society. Of course, even that premise could be questioned because the gap has always existed; nevertheless, the recognition of the struggles between parent and offspring via a comic treatment does create a favorable climate for some adjustment, though not necessarily a reconciliation. The wish fulfillment approach of the genteel comedy, a mode often used in domestic situation comedies on television, too often relies on an improbable restoration of the old order. Satire realistically comes to grips with the problem of change. *The Graduate*, *Goodbye, Columbus*, and *Taking Off* have resolutions which indicate that you cannot go back.

Novels, plays, and films that employ the picaresque character have often been interpreted as a way of making a statement on the stuffiness, rigidity, and unimaginative characteristics of the average person in our society; however, satire also demands that society make adjustment to the individual. Of course, the deviant who might be a rogue, con man, or even a madman, must have some positive qualities along with his negative attributes. Sentimental comedy, which often supports the status quo, will reject the eccentric or find such a person a laughable nuisance. On the other hand, the protagonists of *Tom Jones* and *The Horse's Mouth* not only expose the hypocrisy, blandness, and pretense of people, but they also provide a framework for society's acceptance of the individualist—the free spirit who marches to the beat of a different drummer.

Film adaptations of satirical literature serve another function when a society is under stress—a condition that seems to be moderated only periodically. If the correction of the ills in the country appear a remote possibility, a comic attack may at least benefit us psychologically by releasing us from our frustrations. Observe the political cartoonist as he or she creates caricatures of our leaders with unflattering etchings and commentary that expose their gaffes or questionable positions on issues. We realize that we are presently helpless to change leadership or to institute any new direction in policy, but we are grateful for the barbs of the political cartoonist that reinforce our views. Of course, literature and the film work in a less direct and more complicated way, but they also serve the function of relieving some of our frustration.

Some political satire directed at leaders evolved in the sixties and seventies. The mild-mannered President Muffley in *Dr. Strangelove* who "muffs" negotiations with the leader of Russia, Premier Dimitri Kissoff, could be screenwriter Terry Southern's caricature of the indecisive, cold war leader of the fifties, President Dwight Eisenhower. In league with giant corporation officials, President "Bobby" in *Being There*, a 1979 film, seems as effete as Muffley since he is guided and controlled by big business executives. A caricature of Richard Nixon as a megalomaniac is treated only briefly in the 1980 *Where the Buffalo Roam*. Business and military leaders take the brunt of the attack in the sixties and seventies cinema. *Winter Kills* and *Being There* depict tycoons as Machiavellian or smooth, relentless manipulators. Thomas Kegan of the former film is a tyrant who will stop at nothing to gain international political control; Benjamin Rand of the latter work operates as a power broker with the purse strings. A wide range of military caricatures exists in the motion pictures of the sixties and seventies. Officers in *Catch-22* range from megalomaniacs to effete bunglers, in *Dr. Strangelove* from hawks to madmen, and in *How I Won the War* from jingoists to myopic, unrealistic strategists. Obviously, in the literature and film satires of this period, elected political leaders of democracies are viewed as being at the mercy of more powerful leaders. I believe the creators of these narratives appealed to our frustrations and thereby assisted in giving us some release.

Therefore, the dark comedy and satirical films of two decades have provided our society with three important assets: correction, adjustment, and release. These three aspects, focused by the artist on group and individual concerns, show humor functioning much in the same way it has in the past. The fable, a type of tale that comes from antiquity, the ancient Greeks and even earlier civilizations, obviously still provides a corrective function in society. George Orwell's *Animal Farm* draws from this tradition and is one of the more fascinating and socially significant works with a clear-cut link to the fable. However, even works set in modern times and in the future have the flavor, tone, and content of the fable adapted to contemporary conditions in the world of today. Much like a folk fable, *Being There* shows a jaded society living by code phrases and know-it-all pretensions, being duped by a mentally handicapped man who is perceived as not just sincere but even profound. A naive, young lieutenant, espousing the virtues of a king and country code in *How I Won the War* provides us with another shade from the folk tale about the rogue simpleton who brings havoc into society by his manipulations of a group of people who prove to be simpler than he is. Such fantasies as *A Clockwork Orange*, set in the near future, have some characteristics of the fable. Alex in this twentieth century tale is, of course, more the rogue and less the simpleton of the medieval folk story. But, as in the traditional tales, society looks foolish in its attempt to deal with this type of person.

It is probably more difficult to discover a traditional mode or social function in the adapted satires of West's *The Day of the Locust* and O'Connor's *Wise Blood*, seventies films that expose cultural decay. These works are grimmer creations than most of the movies that have been examined, and they seem to be American examples of the cynicism that can be viewed in the adaptation of the German novel by Günter Grass, *The Tin Drum* (1979). Also, these American works seem closer to the Luis Buñuel attacks on the social order in his *Exterminating Angel* (1962), *The Discreet Charm of the Bourgeoisie* (1972), and *That Obscure Object of Desire* (1977). But these satires have for their subject the political and social class conflicts that are distinctively European nihilism. *Wise Blood* and *The Day of the Locust* have firm roots in American regionalism, depicting in nihilistic tones the disillusioned common man and a mass culture degenerating because it has no valid goals. Along with the screen adaptations of *Dr. Strangelove* and *A Clockwork Orange*, these works by O'Connor and West are probably the most fatalistic satires that have been created by American filmmakers. *Wise Blood* and *The Day of the Locust*, if they lack the corrective function, certainly do provide us with adjustment and release through the use of a grim comic tone and grim comment on the American dream gone sour.

Also, the negative and surrealistic conception of a world full of self-serving, amoral military leaders who have no concern for the men under their command in Joseph Hellers's *Catch-22* is captured in Mike Nichols and Buck Henry's movie version. The bureaucratic "catch-22" system leaves the individual only a treadmill to oblivion—with either physical or mental destruction—a grim destiny from which there is no escape.

The legacy of dark comedy and satire from the sixties and seventies does live on in the eighties. Two examples from the first half of the decade show the way in which this important mode of cinema survives. Picaresque characters and social commentary reign in films that have received critical acclaim, works such as *Reuben, Reuben* (1983) and *Prizzi's Honor* (1985). If satirical dimensions in these films have not been achieved, the works do at least display enough significant critical views of our culture in the dark comedy mode to indicate strongly that the legacy has been preserved and has an audience.

Reuben, Reuben received a valid adaptation by Julius J. Epstein from the 1964 novel by Peter De Vries, a leading writer in the dark comedy movement of the decade. The protagonist of this story, Gowan McGland, a has-been poet, provides the reader and the movie audience with a delightfully funny yet pathetic portrait of the creative genius who is at odds with society. It is a film which ranks among the top works that convey an anti-sentimental view of the artist, on the same level as the 1958 film, *The Horse's Mouth*, with its portrait of a picaresque painter, Gulley Jimson.

Epstein's literate script and Tom Conti's enactment of a rogue poet reveal much about the warped values in our culture as Gowan McGland encounters an inhibited and repressive society that recoils with distaste at the wide-ranging wit and eloquent, caustic observations that spring from this scruffy hedonist. The *bon mot* flows freely and without restraint from this protagonist's lips. On the teacup circuit, this lascivious genius, a poet with a fading reputation, welcomes the attention of middle-aged, sexually deprived women who detect his thinly disguised satyriasis. In the film Gowan observes an eager woman who has just removed her bra in his bedroom, and he cannot resist a poetic observation: "Released from their support, her breasts drooped like hanged men." However, his caustic observations also are self-directed. Forced to place an elaborate orthopedic collar about his neck for his painful, acute arthritis, he refers to his apparatus as an object "upon which my head reposes much like that of John the Baptist's on a platter." He therefore uses his humor not only as a put-down of others, but also as a way of laughing at his afflictions and his role as a poet. "My whole body cried out against regular employment," he declares; and, when his wife wishes to write his biography, he asks, "Who is interested in a poet who is still alive?"

Gowan McGland, a rake and alcoholic with many of the amoral attributes of the Welsh poet Dylan Thomas and Irish playwright Brendan Behan, claims his lineage to be one-fourth Scotch, one-half Welsh, and one-fourth Irish. With his many negative facets there are positive ones to provide a fully realized and fascinating character. McGland is pitted against the ordered stuffy world of suburbanites, a frequent target in the novels of Peter De Vries. Considerably condensed from the novel, *Reuben, Reuben* has an effective scene in which two husbands of the women with whom the poet is having an affair extol the virtues of speed reading. McGland counters with the observation that he wishes to savor slowly the words of great writers. The enthusiasm for a course that can get a rapid reader through *War and Peace* without a struggle is appalling to the poet. The movie version shows McGland indicating to the dentist husband named Haxley that he wants him "to read *Tender Is the Night* as slowly as possible." The movie version of *Reuben, Reuben* also reinforces De Vries's lampoon of a suburban culture that bull-dozes groves of birch to erect a housing addition on a denuded landscape called Birch Hill. Screenwriter Epstein retains some of the dark comedy of the poet losing a tooth unnecessarily through the manipulations of Haxley, who finds out that his wife has been sleeping with McGland. The operation is actually a guarantee that McGland will eventually require false teeth. Epstein changes the death of the poet to a much blacker demise. In the middle of an attempted suicide by hanging, McGland decides to go on writing poems, but a friendly dog jumps up to the chair on which he is standing, toppling it, just as he has talked himself out of the intended hanging. His last words are "Oh, Shit!"—far from the eloquence that had been the charm and downfall of Gowan McGland. In the novel he simply hanged himself. This improvement, I believe, is in the spirit of the De Vries novel.

Tom Conti received an Academy Award nomination for his role as McGland in *Reuben, Reuben*. Critics rated the film high on their list. Richard Corliss sums up the range of the actor's performance when he writes:

> This delightful English actor (TV's *The Norman Conquests*) uses all his honed tools—the dimples, the fluty voice, the hermit-crab walk, the little-boy eyes—to steal every scene just by being in it. Petty and poetic, desperate and delightful, Conti's Gowan is the funniest portrayal of a down-on-his-art genius since Alec Guinness's Gulley Jimson in *The Horse's Mouth*. It is certainly reason enough for a grownup to go back to the movies again. [*Time*, January 2, 1984, p. 91]

Also skilled in the role of Charley Partanna, a hit man for the Prizzi Mafia family, is Jack Nicholson in *Prizzi's Honor*—a picaresque character portrayal that is almost the diametrical opposite of Tom Conti's portrayal. All the comic paranoia of Richard Condon's novel is captured by the understated direction of John Huston and the skilled adaptation of Condon and Janet Roach. This film received even higher critical praise than *Reuben, Reuben* and was nominated by the Academy of Motion Picture Arts and Sciences for eight awards.

Consequently, all three of these creative aspects, acting, directing, and scripting, may establish *Prizzi's Honor* as a superior dark comedy film of the eighties. The conclusion is as black, if not blacker, than the resolution of *Reuben, Reuben*. In a grim farce complication, Charley Partanna meets the woman of his dreams, Irene, only to find out after he has married her that she is a hit woman for the Prizzi family. Ironically, after carrying out murder contracts for the Mafia, they end up stalking each other. Charley must kill his own wife to prove his fidelity to the family; she must kill him for her own survival. This convoluted plot reveals the struggle to maintain values that are both traditional and warped. On one hand the Mafia believes in old country church-oriented values tied to husband, wife, and children relationships, but, when confronted with a loss of power or money, they hasten to invert all values, and the killings are viewed merely as good business practice. Condon's novel provides more insight than the movie into his comic inversion of values as the third person, omnipotent narrator reveals the rationalizations of both the husband and wife as they stalk each other for the kill. At the end of the novel Charley's thoughts are related:

> He opened the trunk of the car and dumped the body into it, thinking that at least he and Irene had never been married. Marriage was a sacrament performed in a Catholic church under the eyes of God, and no justice of the peace named Joseph Tierney Masters in a honkytonk town like Tijuana could perform a real marriage. Only a priest could do that and there had never been time to get that done. [From the novel, *Prizzi's Honor*, Berkley Publishing Group (paperback edition), 1985, p. 324]

After dealing with the perverse course of the individual's value codes when position and wealth are at stake in the earlier novel, *Winter Kills*, Richard Condon repeats (in *Prizzi's Honor*), with even more strength, a satirical story of moral degeneration in our society. Anyone not familiar with the novel would not miss the thought revelations of the printed medium. Under the effective direction of John Huston the film speaks for itself, and the thoughts of Charley and Irene are often revealed indirectly by the pantomimed actions of these characters. The cinema version has retained the naive courtship of the sophisticated, shrewd Irene by the middle-aged, crude Charley and the comic struggles of the married couple to execute an elaborate kidnapping while they attempt to continue traditional husband and wife attitudes. Also retained are the manipulations of both Charley and Irene to survive under the duress of conflicting loyalties as they attempt to circumvent the power of the Mafia family. We can witness the transcendental nature of this parable as it rises to a universal level. No longer does the story exist on a mere realistic plane, depicting only the machinations of a criminal group operating from New York throughout the nation. *Prizzi's Honor* also lashes out at the hypocrisy that permeates our world. "Honor" has become a convenient code word that can be used by all who play the game: a perverse game that brings moral degeneration and destruction. It becomes a surrealistic painting of cultural absurdism—a nihilistic view that

A parody of romantic love develops in *Prizzi's Honor*, with the couple played by Kathleen Turner and Jack Nicholson.

produces the same painful, dark humor we find in *Dr. Strange-love*, *The Day of the Locust*, *Catch-22*, and *A Clockwork Orange*.

Some future social historian of the cinema may point to the eighties films *Reuben, Reuben* and *Prizzi's Honor* as works that continue an established tradition. It should be re-emphasized that the British filmmakers can be credited with an important breakthrough in the establishment of satirical works for a mass audience of cinemagoers. Even in the conservative fifties the British gave the world film versions of the eighteenth-century classic *The Beggar's Opera* and the twentieth-century dystopian novel *Animal Farm*. In the United States the 1954 animated short *The Unicorn in the Garden* provided a minor breakthrough in that decade. In the sixties the British production of *Tom Jones* and the American creation *Dr. Strangelove* provided a springboard for many adaptations of satirical literature into cinema. While the early eighties had a conservative trend that influenced the creation of a much lighter, less significant comedy film movement, *Reuben, Reuben* and *Prizzi's Honor* indicated that audiences still enjoyed satire and dark comedy. A rebirth of interest in these genres then evolved in the last half of the eighties. The so-called Baby Boomer generation, adults in their late thirties and early forties by this time, returned to the movie houses to see first-run features and rented video tapes of off-beat films which were not successful box-office hits. Furthermore, the efforts of individual cinema directors with unusual vision resulted in unique motion pictures—often with a surrealistic bent. Outstanding creations were David Lynch's *Blue Velvet* and Terry Gilliam's *Brazil*. Critical acclaim for these two films indicated that Lynch and Gilliam had scored with many journalistic evaluators in 1986, although, of course, some detractors found the works excessive and too obscure for their taste.

Two years earlier avant-garde filmmaker Lynch attempted a grandiose science fiction work, *Dune*. This movie sank into a cumbersome sand of imagery and incomprehensible plot lines and was understood well only by those who had read the novel on which the film was based. The average moviegoer also had more than a little difficulty with the strange surrealistic nuances of Lynch's *Blue Velvet*. However, Lynch's attack focused on the corruption and corrosion beneath the facade of a small city community. Images of what appears to be an idyllic life in a glowing summer sun are countered with images of the bizarre. Red roses by a white picket fence, a man standing on the running-board of an old firetruck waving at the camera, a white frame house built in the 1920s, children at a school crossing, an elderly man watering flowers on his lawn—all are images that rapidly switch to those that are tragic and ironic. The hose gets twisted and the man tries to free it, but he grabs the back of his neck in pain and collapses. As he is stretched out on the ground with the hose still clutched in his hand, a stream of water shoots into the air, attracting a dog to the spray. As the dog snaps playfully at the water, a toddler watches the play, not realizing what has happened. To the sound of what seems to be the clanking and chugging of underground machinery, the camera moves into the grass for a microscopic view of two grotesque insects in a life and death struggle. This symbolic prelude depicts a world where all is not as tranquil as it first seems. A brief scene follows, showing a young man visiting the stricken man in the hospital, obviously his father. As the young man wanders in a meadow that first appears to be one of bucolic beauty, the viewer witnesses the trash that has begun to spoil the land. Director Lynch, in a gesture of homage to Luis Buñuel, provides the inciting incident preceding the excursion into the corruption of the community. He has the protagonist discover a severed human ear crawling with ants—shades of Salvador Dali and Luis Buñuel's 1928 *The Andalusian Dog*, a surrealistic two-reeler. Fascinated by his find, the young man pursues the mystery of the severed ear and becomes embroiled in the undercover activities of a sadistic drug runner, his white slave mistress, and a pimp.

While many patrons of the movie houses of 1986 were thoroughly confused by such weird complications of *Blue Velvet*, it is possible that Lynch intended his film to be satirical and not taken as seriously as some obviously viewed the work. Juveniles of the fifties, Dennis Hopper and Dean Stockwell, who in the past often played exemplary characters, enacted with broad strokes comic, middle-aged degenerates to provide a key to the dark comedy of this satire. Hopper shows the drug dealer-abductor donning an oxygen mask and canister when he seduces a woman or kills someone who gets in his way. Stockwell swishes his way around his house of prostitution and obsequiously obeys the wishes of anyone who confronts him. How any perplexed viewer of the movie can take such portraits seriously can be explained only by the fact that most people who go to the movies are not acquainted with absurdist drama. As *Blue Velvet* became one of the most critically acclaimed movies of the year, it proved to be the vehicle for Dennis Hopper and Dean Stockwell to revive their careers which had essentially been in limbo.

In plot and complicated visual elements, Terry Gilliam's *Brazil* evolves as an equally captivating absurdist drama with many daydream surrealistic scenes. The film is not merely a rehash of material employed in George Orwell's *1984*. Two film adaptations of this novel, one in the fifties and another in the eighties, did not have even a smidgen of humor—the works were

A mother dominating her son, Sam Lowry (Jonathan Pryce), is portrayed by Katherine Helmond in this scene from *Brazil*.

almost unbearably grim. However, Gilliam has recast the tone into a parody of a futuristic police state. In this nightmare of things to come, Gilliam creates a satire as important as Lynch's handling of the corruption that exists beneath the surface of a small city in America. Gilliam's strange vision of a wacky, dark, urban world is overt—a vision that surpasses the nonsense generated by the Monty Python television and feature film works with which he was associated. Noted for his animated cartoon inserts in those Pythonic creations, Gilliam engulfs this world with umbilical electrical wiring and intestinal air ducts, figuratively and sometimes literally strangling big city apartments plus the inhabitants of this dystopia. Inefficiency reigns in a bureaucracy that originally was designed to make the metropolis more efficient. Departments generate sub-departments, creating a chain of command and endless duplication of forms, smothering the individual in a quagmire of frustration.

Updating Orwell's dark vision of the future, Gilliam innovatively creates a group of counterculture characters who are seldom-seen undercover rebels, members of an organization bent on short-circuiting a society buried in red tape. They cause disruption by terrorist activity: on one hand they bomb department stores, restaurants, and office buildings; on the other hand, they dispense Robin Hood services by providing electrical and plumbing help before the state can send technicians to repair cumbersome systems that are constantly breaking down. Dark comedy reigns in *Brazil* because a police force, often acting like a SWAT team, cannot catch the group that sabotages the government. In *1984* offenders are easily caught and brainwashed. Furthermore, the protagonist of *Brazil* indulges in fantastic daydreams of glory which create humor by overstatement. Sam Lowery imagines that he is a white knight in armor, with the wings of an angel. He can sweep into the clouds to meet his loved one, a woman whose profession in this dystopia is that of a truck driver. In his dreams she is transformed into a Botticelli beauty, floating in the heavens. A wimp in this oppressive future, Sam Lowery has won the affection of his true love through a dream that pits his alter-ego knight against a Samurai of King Kong proportions and, of course, he wins. Gilliam depicts the hapless hero escaping to a pleasant valley in the truck of his girlfriend. But the happy-ending resolution remains oblique and tenuous. Is this all merely a part of the dream, similar to the obscure resolutions of *Blue Velvet* and the 1987 *Raising Arizona*?

Surrealism becomes a vital part of the comedy in *Raising Arizona*. Daydreams of a ne'r-do-well, Herbert I. McConnough, form a pattern like that developed by Gilliam in *Brazil*. A compulsive robber of convenience stores, the blue-collar protagonist gets caught about as routinely as he robs. He conjures up pleasant dreams and nightmares. Abducting a baby for his wife because they aren't able to have children, he dreams one night of a pursuer hunting him down. Odd-ball humor evolves as his vision of a leather-clad motorcyclist takes on the dimensions of a hulk from hell—a grotesque giant of a man trying to collect a reward for the return of the baby. This bounty hunter, who can catch flies in midair between his thumb and finger, delights in blasting desert creatures with a sawed-off shotgun or a grenade. What appears to be a phantom becomes a reality. Herbert (or "Hi" as he is called) battles the road warrior with the tenacity of a Charlie Chaplin struggling in the early silent films with Eric Campbell, an actor well over two hundred pounds. These chase and fight antics produce a wealth of dark comedy but never achieve the status of satire. *Raising Arizona* also provides a fresh look at the comic struggles of a red-neck, nerd type, with both a lampoon of his aspirations in a world that has little use for him and his wish fulfillment dreams of future security with, at last, a covey of offspring and their children who respect him.

In the 1989 *Parents*, Randy Quaid as the father, Nick, believes he receives no respect from his ten-year-old son as he attempts to push him into manhood. While *Raising Arizona* drew a large audience during its theatrical release, and an even larger video rental audience, *Parents* confounded viewers who couldn't decide if the work was a horror film or a comedy. Not to be confused with *Parenthood*, released the same year, this film employed a strong motif of the son's nightmares tied to his suspicions about his parents' obsessive, strange culinary habits.

Director Bob Balaban and scriptwriter Christopher Hawthorne begin their tale with an innovative premise that could have developed into one of the best satires on fifties middle-class pretensions and corruption. There is figuratively and literally the corpse in the basement of this seemingly respectable, pleasant-mannered husband and wife who are suburban kin to Lynch's middle-class family in *Blue Velvet*. But in Lynch's fable the corruption exists outside the family—from the activities of the pimp and drug dealer in the city. In *Parents*, Nick and Lily (Mary Beth Hurt) passionately consume red meat and red wine, admonishing their runt of a son, Michael, for not eating what they love. Little wonder. Their offspring is not the normal fussy eater who prefers junk food to the variety of gourmet dishes of steak and organ meat prepared in various exotic sauces. Father Nick is a scientist for Toxico, a chemical firm that lives up to its name and even has a laboratory filled with corpses. Labeled on the door to this room is the identification "Division of Human Testing." Michael, played convincingly by sad-eyed Bryan

Madovsky, follows his father to this laboratory; and, since he sees his father cutting into the cavity of a cadaver, the boy assumes the corpse is the source for an evening meal. Speaking to Lily, Nick berates Michael, "Your son, the vegetarian." Then, with the sternness of a Puritan preacher of the past, he condemns the boy for not being like his father. Michael's worst nightmares flash in black-and-white images of his parents rolling in bed in some ghoulish sex act, with blood dripping from their vampire mouths. And, to the horror of this little fellow, almost in a state of anorexia, he discovers that the basement of the house has become a butcher shop to handle the parents' insatiable cannibalism.

Unfortunately, Balaban and Hawthorne cannot resolve their grotesque fable to produce the stunning satire that might have been. Once launched, their idea produces some excellent scenes—many of them with a subtlety seldom seen in American cinema—but invention lags in *Parents* and a brilliant notion fizzles into a conventional stalker movie climax, which is why the film often is thought to be merely a horror film. Michael and his school social worker (Sandy Dennis) discover a body in the basement. The ending shows the parents getting rid of the social worker by serving her for another epicurean dish and the father stalking the son after Michael rebels. These melodramatic twists do not support the satirical analogy that was designed to explore the corruption of the middle-class family.

Another dark comedy on death in 1989, *Heathers*, suffers the same weakness. Director Michael Lehmann and his writer, Daniel Waters, paint themselves into a corner as they lampoon murder, suicide, and insanity, comic themes using the aberrations of teenagers in a high school chain of being—that is, the social order that attempts to place groups into layers of subjugation. Three rich, beautiful girls, all named Heather, form a triad rule of Westerburg High. A hanger-on named Veronica tries to escape the domination of the three queen bees when she realizes the extent of their cruel humiliations of young women they consider their inferiors. A devil-like teenager, who goes by the name of J.D., helps Veronica from her plight by dispatching the bitch-snobs through ploys that disguise his murders as suicides; for good measure, he arranges the appearance of a double suicide of two football heroes who presumably cannot live any longer as homosexual lovers in a society that would not accept their alternate life-style. All of this intrigue and dark comedy could have made a social statement; however, the filmmakers capitulate to popular taste by revealing J.D. as merely a psychopath, not something from another world. Since Christian Slater as J.D. presents the viewer with a weak mimicry of Jack Nicolson's devil in the 1987 *The Witches of Eastwick*, more was expected, and a way of establishing something close to satire might have developed in the resolution. Furthermore, Veronica, played by Winona Ryder, who has been an accomplice to the crimes, has a change of heart and wishes to rid Westerburg High from a continued threat of J.D. As a result, the total work fades even in its attempt at dark comedy. *Heathers* cops out with an even weaker ending than *Parents*. J.D., after a struggle with Veronica, gets blown to atoms by the bomb with which he intended to destroy the high school, and Veronica strikes up a friendship with the least desirable young woman in the school—the heroine offers a night of eating popcorn and watching television.

The latter half of the eighties did have the absurdist film dramas that were employing the dream mode and surrealism; however, such works as *Blue Velvet*, *Brazil*, and *Parents* were rare if the evaluator considers the prominence of dark comedies that focused on picaresque characters. *Heathers* obviously fits this classification, as does *The Witches of Eastwick*—a film starring Cher, Michelle Pfeiffer, and Susan Sarandon as the witches, and Jack Nicholson as the devil, Daryl Van Horne. Adapted from John Updike's novel, the film is too obscure in social content to earn the high status of satire, but enough wit evolves from the adept handling of the novelist to produce one of the best film adaptations to hit the screens in the last part of the decade. At times the film exhibits the sophisticated sexual comedy of the Restoration dramas created in the late seventeenth century—dramas that revealed the wit of the women as equaling and sometimes surpassing that of the men in the battle of the sexes. The three witches eventually best the devil physically. With the seduction of each woman, he has given each supernatural powers. Combining their forces against a demon, they learn to hate because he treats them so shabbily, and they finally drive Horne from Eastwick. A clever film comedy, *The*

Witches of Eastwick has the irreverence of some of the best of
dark comedy, but significant social statements are buried. At
most, the film might be interpreted as a humorous analogy on
the increasing power of women over the traditional domination
of men.

The prominence of the picaresque character in film comedies
during the late eighties indicates a recurring interest among
filmmakers and audiences in dark comedy with vestiges of satire.
Most of these works, however, are not adaptations from novels,
plays, or short stories. Translations to the screen from the last
three decades, such as *The Horse's Mouth*, *Tom Jones*, and *The
World According to Garp*, reveal outstanding picaresque characters displaying significant social comment. While there are
now excellent movies with deviant portraits existing in, to name
a few, *Married to the Mob*, *Dirty Rotten Scoundrels*, and *A Fish
Called Wanda*, only slight commentary on our culture emerges
from these films. Part of the reason for the superiority of the
earlier works lies in the conception of the novelists, Joyce Cary,
Henry Fielding, and John Irving. Today there are important
attempts by screenwriters to produce original works, but their
efforts, at this time, seem pale when compared with previous
adaptations. While this may seem a subjective viewpoint on my
part, I believe a literary heritage or a strong literary movement
becomes necessary as a source for vital screen satire.

A source, a 1785 tale by Rudolf Raspe, *The Adventures of
Baron Munchausen*, provided this promise, as it fascinated director Terry Gilliam. A classic in a similar vein to *Gulliver's
Travels*, *Candide*, and *Gargantua* inspired the filmmaker to
adapt the fantastic stories of the picaresque braggart to the
screen. Baron Munchausen derived from a comic figure of
antiquity—first in Roman comedy, later in the *commedia
dell'arte*, and last of all as Falstaff in Shakespeare's plays. As a
weaver of incredible stories, the baron is an obvious rogue and
romantic whose feigned, unbelievable exploits become laughable. The eighteenth-century author Raspe employed this picaresque character to attack the pretensions of the intellectuals
of the so-called age of reason. Munchausen achieved his goal—
to impress by tall tales that defied all the rules of logic.

Director Gilliam indicated that he understood the target of
this classic satire by using a caption at the beginning of *The

Adventures of Baron Munchausen which first identified the time as the late eighteenth century; then, displayed a second title, "THE AGE OF REASON," followed immediately by shots of huge, ornate cannons belching smoke and cannon balls. After this, a war-ravaged city in Europe shows the effects of a conflict with Turkey. A seemingly cunning leader who profits from this war (played by Jonathan Pryce, who was the shy protagonist of *Brazil*) displays more emotion than logic as he directs the strategic movements of the European troops. With quirky reasoning that author Raspe satirized, he has a soldier who has killed many Turks in battle executed instead of declaring him a hero. This leader believes the soldier's effort was so superior that he set an example which would discourage other fighters who would realize they couldn't possibly equal the hero's feat.

With these touches Gilliam seems faithful to the intent of the original conception of Raspe. However, he does not seem to be able to maintain the focus of the first part of the film. Also, the drive and flair of *Brazil* do not materialize as the director gets bogged down with more style than substance, seemingly carried away with the grandeur of his vision in producing this fantasy. *The Adventures of Baron Munchausen* has visual splendors that equal and sometimes surpass the director's previous efforts, *Time Bandits* and *Brazil*. The baron's voyage to the moon in a balloon produces astonishing scenes that merge superior special effects with imaginative sets. Munchausen encounters the king and queen of the moon, played (with the help of matte shot) as giants by Robin Williams and Valentina Cortese. From the heavens, down comes the adventurer into an underworld where he encounters a jealous Vulcan (Oliver Reed) who tries to keep the baron from a romantic entanglement with Venus (Uma Thurman). A climactic battle with the Turks features an amazing superman assistant of the baron who hurls a harbor full of ships on the enemy. They're all very impressive episodes, to be sure, yet add up to little more than a feast for the eye and a fulfilled dream for the fantasy buff. Screenwriters Charles McKeown and Gilliam should have focused on developing the character of Munchausen, played by John Neville, in order to give him much stronger dialogue, especially his reflections on his perilous adventures coupled with his miraculous escapes. This concentration might have maintained more of the satirical intent of the original tales. Those evaluators who admired *Brazil* were probably expecting more from a filmmaker who could have given us a significant statement on a society of the past as it reflects on our age.

The decade of the eighties began with slight traces of dark and sophisticated humor in *Arthur, My Favorite Year*, and *Tootsie*, with some promise of a revival of the satirical tradition that established the late sixties and early seventies as a period with fertile creations. However, *Reuben, Reuben* and *Prizzi's Honor* revealed a trend toward the revival of a past tradition. *Brazil, Blue Velvet*, and *Full Metal Jacket* confirmed the rebirth when these films received wide acceptance, both by critical acclaim and by an older audience of the past returning to movie houses.

The literary tradition of satire and dark humor that emerged after World War II has suffered only a slight setback, with fewer novels and plays of the genre to provide strong sources for film adaptations. Nevertheless, some eighties films that were not adapted from the print medium achieved the level of satire. *Brazil, Blue Velvet*, and *Parents* emerged as original creations for the screen. And this is a hopeful sign. Since these works have the stamp of the independent filmmaker, the future for a vital screen satire looks bright. With an audience who appreciates film comedy with social comment, a more sophisticated comic cinema will usher in a new age for the medium, an age with the high quality of films created in the late sixties and early seventies—the golden period of dark humor and satire.

Index

Italicized page numbers refer to photographs.